To - our Colorado Mountain
      Family —

After all th many references to a
"My thical Hannah book" — here is th
final product — which we hope you
like. Our love as Ever —

      Dicie / DAD / RON
           Niehoff

> I do the very best I know how, the very best I can, and I mean to keep on doing so until the end. If the end brings me out all right, what is said against me won't amount to anything. If the end brings me out wrong, ten angels swearing I was right would make no difference. *A. Lincoln*

Photograph by William Mitcham,
Michigan State University.

John D. Wilson, President of Washington and Lee University, former Rhodes Scholar and second Director of the Honors College of Michigan State University, wrote Hannah in December 1983 with reference to their first meeting in 1949 and subsequent association and with reference to the Lincoln picture which Hannah has in the various offices which he occupies, including the present one.

Since that time, and especially in the past fifteen years, your character and values have almost constantly been on my mind . . . I don't think you can fully realize how much I treasure the association I was permitted to have with you over the years and how much I admire your steadfastness, your confidence and determination, your dignity and your courage.

I could recount dozens of episodes where a kind and wise word (now forgotten by you I am sure) meant much to me. *I still carry the Lincoln quotation you had on the wall behind your desk* and more importantly the reference you made to it.

# JOHN A. HANNAH

# JOHN A. HANNAH

*Versatile Administrator
and
Distinguished Public Servant*

RICHARD O. NIEHOFF

UNIVERSITY
PRESS OF
AMERICA

Lanham • New York • London

Co–published by arrangement
with Michigan State University

Library of Congress Cataloging-in-Publication Data

Niehoff, Richard O.
John A. Hannah : versatile administrator and distinguished public
    servant / Richard O. Niehoff.
        p.    cm.
"Co-published by arrangement with Michigan State University"–
    –T.p. verso.
    Bibliography: p.
    Includes index.
1. Hannah, John A., 1902–   . 2. Government executives– –United
States– –Biography.  3. Executives– –United States– –Biography.
                        I. Title.
        JK723.E9H276    1989      89–5334 CIP
                353'.00092'4– –dc19
                        [B]
            ISBN 0–8191–7343–6 (alk. paper)

All University Press of America books are produced on acid-free paper.
The paper used in this publication meets the minimum requirements of American
National Standard for Information Sciences—Permanence of Paper for Printed Library
Materials, ANSI Z39.48–1984.  ∞

To Sarah Shaw Hannah, who through more than fifty years of marriage to John Hannah, provided sustaining and flexible support for his many years as President of Michigan State University and for his other significant national and international public endeavors

# Contents

### MAJOR ACTIVITIES
### IN THE SERVICE OF THE UNITED STATES
### GOVERNMENT AND THE UNITED NATIONS

# Acknowledgments

The preparation of this book would not have been possible without indispensable help and support, notably:

• The encouragement and trust of John A. Hannah in requesting that I undertake the task, although not a trained historian or biographer. Hannah's only "directive" was to "stick with the facts."

• The superbly helpful and friendly assistance of Dr. Frederick Honhart, Director of the Michigan State University Archives and Historical Collections, and his colleagues who, without complaint, lugged box after box of archival material for my perusal. Similar assistance, albeit on a smaller scale, was provided by archivists at the Dwight Eisenhower and the Gerald Ford Presidential Libraries and the library staff of the Agency for International Development.

• The editorial skill, personal support, interest and encouragement of Dr. Harry L. Case, who examined draft after draft of manuscripts to clarify and improve my writing to make Hannah's accomplishments as a superb and versatile administrator as exciting as it genuinely is.

• The helpful comments of the anonymous reviewer assigned by the publisher of University Press of America, Inc. to examine a draft of this manuscript and also the helpful comments of friends Professors Carl Gross and Jerry Thornton.

• The expertise, patience and good humor of Catherine Moehring in transforming my dreadful handwriting into clear type.

• The financial support of the Kellogg Foundation which provided funds to Michigan State University to cover costs of travel, typing and other miscellaneous costs.

The encouragement and logistical support of Dr. Ralph H. Smuckler, Michigan State University's Dean of International Studies and Programs and his associates in the preparation of this book.

• The generous and thoughtful responses of a considerable number of often busy men who responded to my request for letters and telephone calls about their experiences with Hannah as close associates.

• The wifely and loving support and patience of Helen M. Niehoff, who cheerfully put aside other family plans to allow me to indulge in endless hours of research in various archival deposits and in drafting and redrafting this manuscript.

I, of course, make the conventional assertion of assuming full responsibility for the product.

Richard O. Niehoff
East Lansing, Michigan
*June, 1988*

# Preface

John A. Hannah is probably best known as the person who was primarily responsible for the evolution of the Michigan State College of Agriculture and Mechanic Arts (MSC) to Michigan State University (MSU)—the pioneer land-grant university and member of the prestigious Association of American Universities.* The purpose of this volume is to document and interpret the extensive experience of John Hannah in the service of the United States government, the United Nations, and the state of Michigan, national and international business, community, educational and governmental organizations. All of these activities occurred while Hannah served as President of MSU and after he retired from the Presidency.

But first some references to Hannah's origins and early history. These early personal interests and experiences are related to later professional applications and motivation in the conduct of other activities in which he engaged.

John A. Hannah was born on October 9, 1902 in Grand Rapids, Michigan. The following abbreviated *vita* of Hannah's family background, early and later formal education, interests and professional achievements is an unusual record of continuity and predictable consistency. There are no unexplained "detours" in his personal and professional life. His grandfather emigrated from Scotland, settled in Michigan and became involved in agriculture and floral cultivation. He was a market gardener owning extensive greenhouses and a floral company. His father was a successful farmer and active in school board affairs in the district. His maternal grandfather owned a big

---

*See Note number one in the Preface and subsequent notes for each chapter following.

farm. Altough of limited formal education, he was an authority on livestock and livestock diseases and was generally refered to as "Doc." His paternal grandmother and his mother were both educated school teachers. Hannah grew up with a sister and two brothers, both of whom graduated from MSC—one in Landscape Architecture and the other in Poultry Husbandry.

Hannah had his first years of elementary education in a rural school and the remainder in an elementary school in Grand Rapids. He graduated from high school at age 16 and then took two years of work at and graduated from the Grand Rapids Junior College. He was then admitted to the University of Michigan Law School. Hannah gives credit to his stimulating teachers in elementary, high school and junior college for cultivating a life-long interest in chemistry, botany, biology, history, physics and the English and German languages, subjects which became important to him in his career.

But perhaps the principal element in Hannah's early life, which was predictive of his later career, was his father's delegation to him, when he was six years old, of responsibility to care for the poultry flock. His responsibility for the poultry led him to experimentation with different breeds, studies of egg production, and thence into participation in local, regional and statewide poultry shows. He later became president of the State Poultry Association. Temporarily discouraged from further involvement in agriculture as a career by his grandfather, who saw little future in agriculture as a career, but good prospects in the practice of law, he enrolled in and spent one year at the University of Michigan Law School. Although he did not pursue his studies in law, he did, incidentally, develop a keen and life-long interest in intercollegiate sports as a result of the influence of his roommate, a member of the University of Michigan football team.

The temporary deflection from his interest in and already noteworthy achievements in the poultry field ended when he was persuaded by the then head of the Poultry Department of MSC to continue his studies in agriculture, particularly in poultry science. He also was promised a position as the Extension Agent in poultry, at a salary of $2500 a year, after completing work for a degree in agriculture. Hannah's demonstrated interest and competence in poultry; in what he had learned in basic supporting sciences in chemistry and related fields from his former teachers; and doubtless from his father who was interested and accomplished in the broader field of scientific agriculture, made it possible for him to pass all general background courses by examination, except technical courses in agriculture, and graduate with a Bachelor's degree in one year.

Hannah served successfully for the next ten years as the state-wide Extension Agent for poultry during which he became very well known throughout Michigan as a speaker, teacher, innovative motivator and friend of farmers and others.

He also saw the need for additional scientific research in genetics and other fields, in the production of eggs and meat and in the innovative early arrangements for removing chickens off the farms and placing them into factory-like operations. These technical and scientific developments were shared widely in international Congresses, sponsored by the World Poultry Science Association, held in Canada, Denmark, England, Germany, and in the United States. Involvement in these world congresses contributed to Hannah's international orientation and interest in global applications of scientific agriculture which he pursued for the rest of his professional life. Illustrative activities are documented in several of the following chapters. His reflections on the subject were expressed in his *A Memoir.**

> . . . As a result of my involvement in the world poultry Congresses and what happened in World War II, I came to believe that not much of lasting importance is likely to be settled on battlefields. The only hope for the human race, I am convinced, is to find a way for peoples of all colors, all races, and all religions to agree, not necessarily on politics or economic philosophies, but on how to get on with peaceful efforts at solving the most important human problems. . . . (page 24)

While President of the International Baby Chick Association, Hannah was appointed in 1932, on leave from MSU, to become the managing director of the Industry Hatching Breeder Code. The administration of the Code was one of the New Deal programs of the National Recovery Administration (NRA) under General Hugh Johnson with headquarters in Kansas City. The position involved travel throughout the United States to check on compliance with the requirements of the Code with ultimate responsibility for deciding whether hatchery breeder groups could remain in operation or not. After occupying this position for more than a year, he was offered the opportunity to join a large Chicago packing company at a salary three times that of his government position. He, however, returned to MSC. Hannah's reflec-

---

*See Note No. 2 in Preface notes for a complete bibliograpical reference to this volume.

tion on this offer was characteristic of his reaction to other similar offers in later years: "This required me to take a hard look at what I wanted to do with my life. If I wanted to make money this was a good opportunity. (But) I had become pretty well sold on the work of the Cooperative Extension Service." (*A Memoir* page 20)

Shortly thereafter, in 1934, he was invited to discuss with Dr. Shaw, who had become President of MSC,* to take the position of Secretary of the State Board of Agriculture. His qualifications for the position, as demonstrated by his general competence, energy, capacity to work effectively with Michigan farmers and others and to his dedication to Michigan agriculture and to the college, were well recognized by the Board which appointed him to the position in 1935.

Under President Shaw and the Board, Hannah demonstrated his versatile capacity to perform such responsible tasks as: securing increased appropriations from the State Legislature; working effectively with legislators of both political persuasions (a skill which he continued as President and later applied to his relationships with Federal legislators and committees); securing the cooperation of the Federal Works Progress Administration (WPA) in greatly expanding campus buildings and facilities for instruction, research and student housing; and in contributing more generally to the development of college-wide administrative and personnel policies and procedures. Hannah's outstanding performance as Secretary of the Board of Agriculture made him a natural candidate to succeed Dr. Shaw on the latter's retirement in 1941. The record of Hannah's services as President of the College, including the notable story of his successful effort to expand the College into a University of national standing has been recorded elsewhere (also note 1).

The preceding background information is provided to demonstrate the "seamless-web" of continuity which characterized Hannah's life and involvement in the administration of the University and in his off-campus activities. They also provide the framework for the chapters which comprise this volume. The material in the six chapters focus primarily on Hannah's qualities of versatile leadership, methods of work, relationships, and accomplishments in these varied activities.

In preparing this volume, major reliance has been placed on some 40–50 linear feet of archival records in the Hannah Collection in the

---

*Who later became his father-in-law when he married Dr. Shaw's daughter, Sarah May Shaw, in 1938. The couple have four children, Mary Elisabeth (Curzan), Robert Wilfred, Thomas Arthur and David Harold.

Michigan State University Archives and Historical Collections; in the comprehensive materials in the library of the Agency for International Development covering the period of Hannah's tenure as Administrator of the Agency; and materials in the Dwight D. Eisenhower and Gerald R. Ford Presidential Libraries. These materials were augmented by letters in response to the author's requests to some 20 persons closely associated with Hannah in his domestic and international activities.

This volume does not, of course, purport to be a comprehensive treatment of any of the programs and organizations in which Hannah played a leading role. Nor is it a case study in public administration in the technical sense. The relatively brief descriptions of the programs, administrative operations and relationships are intended to describe the milieu in which Hannah functioned and especially to highlight his contributions to the effective performance of these agencies. In essence it describes the *"anatomy"* *of decision making* in a number of highly important organizations!

John Hannah was not, in a scholarly sense, a student of administration and he did not author articles or textbooks on concepts and principles of administration. He was very able to understand, appreciate and practice the principles that others wrote about. In this sense he was materially assisted by Floyd W. Reeves* who served for several years as consultant to him on a broad range of personnel, organization and other policy aspects of administration in the early years of Hannah's presidency of the University. Two sources of information are cited to explain or illuminate principles which guided him in his distinguished performance as the long-time President of Michigan State University. One is his own responses to questions put to him by two of his close associates at the University which are recorded in his *A Memoir.*** The introduction to his comments follows:

> . . . First I am not sure that I ever prided myself as an administrator. I think the record indicates that such success as I had probably resulted in part at least from good fortune, hard work and perhaps some skill. I think that was true of my experience at Michigan State University. I am certain it was true in the twelve years I was Chairman of the United States Commission on Civil Rights. It was equally true of my term as Asst. Secretary of the Department of Defense for Manpower in the Pentagon

---

*Reeves was a Professor of Political Science and Administration at the University of Chicago for 14 years and an experienced administrator and advisor in the Federal government during the FDR era.

**Op. Cit.

were I had general supervision of five million men in the armed services and about three million more blue collar workers in the Defense Department. I believe it was also true of whatever success I had as Administrator of the United States Agency of International Development for four and one-half years; and equally true of such success as I had in planning the World Food Conference in Rome in November 1974 and since as Executive Director of the United Nations Food Council. However, I do not feel it appropriate for me to discuss my success or lack of it as an administrator. I would prefer to change the question to read: What are the general principles you followed in your administration of Michigan State University? (Pages 77 & 78)

The general principles which were enunciated in response to other questions on his administrative principles are paraphrased below:

• Belief in the importance and social value of the activity to be administered.

• The necessity for clear and acceptable objectives of the activity or organization.

• The selection, retention and promotion of able and dedicated personnel on a non-political basis.

• An active system and practice of internal communications for the purposes of morale of employees and for fostering of consensus in the decision-making process.

• A work method which emphasizes a factual and objective basis for selection of the most logical, pragmatic and defensible decisions from all possible options. In this connection he demonstrated the importance of being a good listener in the debates and discussion of alternatives of central importance in the process of democratic decision-making and of making full utilization of the ideas of all persons responsible for administration of consensual decisions.

• Relationships with colleagues and superiors based on mutual respect, candor and trust.

• The importance and welfare of people as the purpose of the activity.

What is left out in this partial listing of principles, because it would have been self-serving for Hannah to state them, are integrity, dedication, humility and leadership. These principles or attributes, and some to which reference has already been made, are verified and commented upon in greater detail by his associates, at the end of each chapter of the present volume. Students of administration and others interested in the organization and application of public policy by public, domestic and international agencies will find these comments of interest. The combination of these two sources of ideas about effective administration—Hannah's own and those of this colleagues—will go some distance to explain why and how John Hannah achieved his reputation as a versatile and consummate administrator.

My reflections on both of these sources of insight and on the record of his achievements, set forth in the following chapters, may further illuminate the application of the principles of administration which he espoused. It is quite clear that he thrived on diversity of backgrounds and points-of-view of persons most closely involved whether they be Presidents of the United States (eg. Eisenhower, Kennedy, Johnson, Ford or Nixon); Southern Governors (eg. John Battle or Doyle Carlton); articulate liberals and ideologues (eg. Father Hesburgh); or distinguished lawyers (eg. Robert Storey, George Johnson or Erwin N. Griswold); labor and business leaders. He also benefited from personal relationships with newspaper editors (eg. Eugene Patterson), political scientists (eg. Robert Rankin) and other highly qualified interesting, stimulating and companionable persons. He also numbered among his fellow university presidents and public servants such persons as James Conant, Milton Eisenhower, John Macy, Governors Nelson Rockefeller and G. Mennen Williams, John Gardner and numerous other persons.

Hannah was characterized by his colleagues as a good listener in committee or group settings, and an articulate and forceful spokesman on points or recommendations which derived from their discussions. He skillfully summarized their views and kept the discussion moving toward consensus or acceptable compromise. He was tolerant of the views of others with whom he may have disagreed personally. He strove for a meeting of minds or consensus where possible and for working compromises or recognized disagreements when necessary. If there were standards, provisions of law or Supreme Court decisions as in the case of civil rights, he persistently required adherence in discussing or making recommendations with reference to such provisions. To all other cases he looked to *facts*. He admired persons who could assemble and interpret facts and articulate choices, but he did not put his whole trust in the views of the experts. He often expressed the view that the problems of agriculture or education, for example, were too important to be left to the *experts* in these fields. Something more was needed to be added for comprehensive and practical solutions to these complex societal problems. But he was not tolerant of endless debate except where varied interpretations of the facts were present. He always did his homework, read the material of the agendas provided by the staff, and conscientiously reviewed and edited drafts or recomendations while they were being discussed and before being released to officials or to the public. He stood behind the recommendations, and the facts and reasoning which undergirded them, and ably defended them when necessary. His demeanor was calm in controversial situations and unflappable regarding criticism, a quality which he admired in Abraham Lincoln. He persistently and punctually kept the commitments he had made on behalf of the commissions which he chaired, most notably in the preparation of the 1959 report of the Civil Rights Commission, when the President and members of Congress would not have been unsympathetic to a delay.

Because of the critical importance of staff work in the successful operations of committees or commissions, he gave close attention to the qualifications of key staff personnel and then personally, and with the concurrence of his colleagues, delegated responsibility and recognized the good work of those selected. In no instance did politics or political preference apply to these appointments. He was fully successful in persuading the several Presidents under whom he served to minimize or to ignore political considerations even in their making Presidential appointments.

A basic, if not *the* basic component in Hannah's motivation was his conviction often expressed "that only people are important." He articulated this conviction, whether Negroes* or other minority groups were involved, or whether peasants or other low-income individuals or groups in the Third World were the focus of the activities. Concurrently, he maintained a conviction that universal education, properly adapted to the needs and conditions of people, was the best method of achieving higher personal and societal levels of welfare. He stoutly

---

*The terms Negro/Negroes/Negro Americans are very commonly used throughout the tenure of John Hannah as Chairman of the Civil Rights Commission (CRC) from 1957–1969. The term or terms were used in the archival records of the reports of the Commission to the President and the Congress; in speeches, press releases, testimony to Congressional committees; the numerous newspaper stories, editorials and in magazine articles; in letters to the Chairman from *C.B.S. News* and other sources; in minutes of the meetings of the CRC and other communications; in an article by Harris Wofford Jr., Special Assistant to President Kennedy; and by two members of the CRC, Dr. George Johnson and J. Ernest Wilkins. Accordingly, these terms, which appear as quotations from Commission reports or in the context of other Commission communications, are used by the author. In deference to readers who prefer the term "blacks," which is favored in current usage, it is used in all other references in the author's language.

believed in the necessity for an adequate military defense but expressed the belief "that not much will be won in military encounters in the foreseeable future."

Hannah got basic satisfactions in achieving higher levels of civil liberties and in achieving the goals of the several other agencies with which he was associated. He was highly skilled in resolving differences between the views of experts or associates who developed their views from widely different military, business or other backgrounds.

He was not ambitious for positions of potentially greater prestige, such as Deputy Secretary of Foreign Affairs, Secretary of the Air Force, Chairman of the Tennessee Valley Authority or other positions which he turned down in favor of continuing his association with the University. He was consistently modest about his achievements. Although a registered Republican and a close associate of Presidents Eisenhower and Ford and a sometime advisor to President Nixon, he was comfortable with, trusted by, and worked effectively with Democratic Presidents Kennedy and Johnson and with Congressmen on both sides of the aisle and associates of different political persuasions. In summary, he was basically apolitical. For most of his active life, his vision of the world was international in scope and concern.

Hannah is a tall, broad shouldered, personally impressive man with a strong and clear speaking voice and a friendly manner. He likes to associate with persons of accomplishments but takes little pleasure in prestigious social or ceremonial settings whether they are in the White House or military installations. He is basically an unpretentious person who loves to farm and be with his family. He has a great capacity to relax. His only dislike is for persons who get excessive satisfaction out of "talk-talk-talk."

## Chapter I

# Assistant Secretary for Defense for Manpower and Personnel[1]

Shortly after Dwight D. Eisenhower was elected President and while he was recruiting his top team of associates, he sent a hand-written note to Charles E. Wilson from his temporary quarters at the Brown Palace Hotel in Denver. Wilson had already been chosen as the Secretary of Defense. The note read: "When you get your new Personnel Asst. please ask him to see me at some convenient time. Tell him I'd like to talk to him about citizenship training in the Armed Forces." Signed DE.

Hannah, who had already been tentatively chosen by Wilson as the "Personnel Asst." wrote the President Elect on January 9, 1953, in his headquarters at the Commodore Hotel in New York, as follows:

Mr. Wilson has called my attention to your note to him of December 24 in which you suggested your desire to visit with his Personnel Assistant about citizenship training in the armed forces.

I shall be happy to visit with you at your convenience. It is encouraging to note your interest in this important subject.

It seems to me to be of considerable importance that we develop if possible long-term policies that may make it possible for the young men of the country and their parents to plan intelligently for fitting the required military service into their plans for education and the beginning of careers. In recent years, the public pronouncements have varied from month to month and given the impression of being arrived at on a whimsical basis. I shall be much interested in your views on this subject.

1

Another question which is frequently raised by the members of the Congress and the newspapers has to do with the efficiency and utilization of civilian and uniformed manpower in our defense organization. As a member of your team, I should appreciate the benefit of your thinking on the subject as well as any other that you think will be helpful to me.

But even before Hannah had the opportunity to indicate to the President-elect what he learned some of the principal tasks of the Assistant Secretary to be, General Eisenhower telegraphed the State Board of Agriculture (the policy board of Michigan State College) on December 31, 1952 as follows:

> Mr. Wilson and I have requested John A. Hannah to undertake the heavy responsibilities of Assistant Secretary of Defense for Manpower and Personnel. While I appreciate the importance of the commitment to you, I believe it would be most beneficial to the nation if you would grant him sabbatical leave for one year while he assists in the difficult tasks of organization which lie ahead. I shall be personally grateful to be able to count on having his support.

Hannah promptly wrote a follow-up memorandum to the State Board in which he informed them of the responsibilities of the position, as spelled out in the organization manual of the Defense Department, which included: (1) manpower requirements; (2) policies required for the administration and maintenance of adequate reserve forces; (3) responsibility for the information and education program; (4) and for responsibility for "representing the Department of Defense in all matters of manpower and personnel." Hannah noted that "at the present time approximately five million persons are included in the civilian personnel and armed services." He also wrote that he had not "sought the responsibility," but felt that a call of this kind was "akin to a call to military service in the defense of our country." He then spelled out for their consideration and approval the request of the President-elect within the following policy framework:

• That he continue as President of Michigan State College for the duration of the appointment of one calendar year.

• That during this period he would continue to spend some days each month on the campus, including attendance at regular Board meetings and such time as was required to prepare for those meetings and complete assignments resulting therefrom. He would also expect to spend every weekend with his family on campus and be available to transact college business and for conferences with staff personnel. He would also "make every effort" for hearings of legislative committees and appropriation hearings and other "matters of importance to the college."

• That during the period of the loan to the Defense Department his salary would conform to the usual sabbatical leave policy and be reduced to one-half of the regular rate.

• As a "safety valve" to the above provisions, Hannah proposed: "that after a reasonable number of months if in the opinion of the Board the operation of the college is being too seriously hampered by this arrangement, you reserve the right to suggest my return full time to the campus after a reasonable notice to the Secretary of Defense and the President."

Hannah predicted that this "unexpected development may well serve to make Michigan State College an even stronger institution" by bringing the college to the "attention of influential persons." But beyond that, "I hope to return to full-time duties better qualified to administer the affairs of the institution."

The Board approved the appointment within the conditions set forth by Hannah effective as of January 1, 1953. This was his first sabbatic leave after almost 30 years of service to the college. It was subsequently extended for another six months.

Before entering on duty, Hannah issued a press statement through the Presidential Press Secretary, in which he reiterated some of the same points made to the Board with the following additional points.

This assignment appears to be one of the most important responsibilities in the government service. At a time when all of our able-bodied young men are being called upon for an extended period of involuntary military service with the interruption of their careers or education, or both, and with the attendant family concern for their welfare, a particularly heavy responsibility rests with the government to make certain that effective use is made of all personnel, both civilian and in uniform.

In concurring with General Eisenhower's request to our Board that I be granted a year's sabbatic leave to allow me to assume these responsibilities, I have been encouraged to believe that I can be of useful service to all young men, and to their families, by helping to establish relatively stable manpower policies upon which they can depend in planning for the future. The uncertainties with respect to liability to military service which have plagued our young men in the past should be resolved if at all feasible.

I believe that military service can be made more meaningful to young men and women by giving more attention and emphasis to teaching them their roles as citizens both in uniform and when they have returned to civilian life. There are a few fundamental convictions that must be firmly held by a majority of our people if the advantages and opportunities of our American way of life are to endure.

In requesting an extension of Hannah's services, to the State Board, Secretary Wilson wrote:

> During the coming session of Congress we expect to be faced with many legislative problems in this area and feel that Dr. Hannah's great ability, together with the knowledge and experience he has gained during the past year, makes it vital that he continue to head this office during their presentation to Congress, since he has directed the formulation of the policies and legislation which will be under consideration.
>
> The President joins with me in requesting the Board to extend Dr. Hannah's leave of absence for an additional six months in order that he may see our present programs through the next session of Congress.

Hannah continued on the assignment on the same original basis until he returned to the campus full-time on August 1, 1954. He was succeeded by James M. Mitchell, an Acting Assistant Deputy Secretary. Mitchell had served as the Republican member of the U. S. Civil Service Commission under President Truman before becoming one of Hannah's deputies.

During his eighteen months in Washington, Hannah did get back to the campus on most weekends and for Board meetings, graduation convocations and other special student and faculty events, a few ''critical'' football games, and for other special events in which his participation was particularly important. He also arranged to have a special telephone hook-up to have almost instant access to the campus on his initiative or with one of his key colleagues to whom he had delegated broad responsibility for actions in his absence and to Board members who wished to consult with him. He also was visited in Washington by members of the Board and faculty to consult with him about University affairs. He also responded to a large number of letters on University matters.

Through contacts which he made in Washington on this assignment and others which followed, which are described in other chapters, Hannah's prediction that many government officials and others would come to know about Michigan State College, which became Michigan State University in 1955. One evidence of this prediction was that Hannah was able to persuade Presidents Harry Truman, Gerald R. Ford and Richard M. Nixon, and Adlai Stevenson, General MacArthur, Nelson Rockefeller and several others to deliver Commencement addresses and to meet with Board members, faculty and Michigan leaders and others while on campus.

The Board and faculty members were pleased that Hannah had been assigned to this first major governmental responsibility, on a leave of absence basis, which was followed by several others on a part-time basis.

There is no record of a political clearance* for Hannah although he was generally known as a Republican. His appointment, however, was applauded by a number of political leaders of both parties and by civic, industrial and labor leaders. Hannah had many earlier personal contacts with Charles E. Wilson, when he was President of the General Motors Corporation, and to a lesser extent with Dwight D. Eisenhower when he was President of Columbia University and with "Ike's brother, Milton Eisenhower, when both of them were involved in University affairs.

## Hannah's Work Method and Major Relationships

### With Staff of the Defense Department

Hannah's work method, apart from numerous meetings and lunches with Wilson alone or with sundry committee meetings of top Defense Department staff, focused on his weekly meetings with his ten top associates and daily conferences with his two Deputy Assistant Secretaries, James Mitchell referred to above, and Lieutenant General James Collins. From each of these officials he required written reports on major developments under their supervision with particular emphasis on developments involving two or more branches of the service. Matters which involved only matters under each associates' jurisdiction were dealt with in private conferences.

The principal functions of the ten officers under Hannah's supervision illustrate the broad scope of his responsibilities.

A. *Office of Manpower Requirements*
   1. Mobilization planning
   2. Control of civilian manpower programs

---

*James M. Mitchell reported in a note to the author that "when many government departments were making a large number of political appointments, the Defense Department very infrequently requested political clearance for appointment and (thus) strengthened the merit system of personnel administration within the department."

    3. Weekly reenlistment
    4. Army-Navy joint survey of Alaska
    5. Technical training
B. *Office of Manpower Supply*
    1. Manpower policy committee
    2. International manpower
    3. Training of scientists and engineers
    4. Selective recall of reservists
    5. Production allocation programs
C. *Office of Industrial Relations*
    1. Existing strikes
    2. Threatened strikes
D. *Office of Armed Forces Information & Education*
    1. Submission of six pamphlets
      a. "Know Your Communist Enemy"
      b. "Armed Forces and Your Life Plan"
      c. "Students and the Armed Services"
E. *Office of Civilian Personnel Matters*
    1. Overseas personnel study (under the direction of the White House staff)
    2. Shipments of household effects
    3. Delinquent income tax
    4. Civil Service Commission legislative program
F. *Office of Domestic Security Programs*
    1. Life Insurance Ass'n of America report on civil defense
    2. Explosive ordinance reconnaissance & disposal
    3. Thermal radiation attenuation clouds
    4. Reproduction of classified information by the Government Printing Office
G. *Domestic Security Programs*
    1. Evacuation policy
    2. Civil defense chemical defense training
    3. Military affiliate radio systems
    4. Effect of H-Bomb tests on proposed evacuation policy
    5. Revision of "How to be cleared for handling classified information"
H. *Office of Administrative Services*
    1. Administrative support for cabinet committee on "water resources" policy.
    2. Appropriations
    3. Budget for junior management program

I. *Reserve Forces Policy Board*
  1. Appropriations Act for fiscal year 1955
  2. Severance pay for reserve officer voluntary release from active duty
J. *Chaplain*

A large number of reports had to be carefully examined by Hannah each week for his staff meetings. In addition, he responded to a variety of communications from citizens and other government officials with reference to manpower questions, exceptions to regulations, and other problems.

## Relations With Secretary Wilson, President Eisenhower and the Press

Most of the important issues and problems reported to Hannah by his staff plus matters on which Secretary Wilson wanted Hannah's judgment and participation in the Secretary's staff meetings, were discussed in numerous private sessions, with the Secretary and on several occasions with President Eisenhower. In Hannah's 1953 appointment book, for example, there are some 45–50 notations of such meetings.

Following the standard set by Eisenhower[2], Secretary Wilson emphasized candor in his relationship with subordinates, as did Hannah.

In addition to work within the Department of Defense, Hannah also had numerous meetings with various dignitaries within and outside of the government and with such persons as Jean Blair of the *New York Times,* Stuart Alsop of *The Washington Post* and others.

Hannah also made several important speeches to civic and educational groups and conducted several press conferences on defense and related subjects.

## Major Accomplishments

### Racial Integration of the Armed Forces

Racial integration of the armed forces was a long and stormy story. Lee Nichols, who chronicled the major incidents, personalities, political issues, internal stresses in the branches of the armed forces and stages in the evolution of policies and practices, wrote at the conclusion of his thorough study in 1953 that

> It will take future historians, with access to still unavailable records, personal letters etc. to evaluate precisely the many diverse factors that have made possible the successful military revolution of the past ten years.[3]

Nichols further commented in his study of the problem in the following words:

> It is also a story of men of courage and foresight who were able to see that military efficiency and democratic ideals could go hand in hand; men like Franklin D. Roosevelt, who pushed and prodded the armed forces into allowing greater opportunities for Negroes during World War II, James V. Forrestal . . . ; Stuart Symington . . . ; Christopher Sargent . . . ; Harry S. Truman, a stubborn man from Missouri who insisted on taking literally the Bible and the Constitution when they spoke of equality and brotherhood; of many others inside and outside the military services who led, or inspired or helped, or went willingly along, with the new tide of racial change.[4]

To implement these convictions, President Truman issued an Executive Order on July 26, 1948 which stated that henceforth there should be "equality of treatment and opportunity for all persons in the armed forces without regard to race, color or national origin . . ." Picking up the threads of this complex story at a later date, Nicols wrote that just before his inauguration on March 20, 1953, General Eisenhower (with reference to funding schools for children of military personnel) stated "that he did not see how any American could legally, logically, or morally justify discrimination in the use of Federal funds."[5]

A still later development which brought Hannah into the stream of major influence on interpretation of the armed forces were the recommendations of the 1963 report of the United States Civil Rights Commission (see pages 92–93 Chapter 3). The White House reported at about the same time that the Army was making a survey on the question of getting state and local governments to end segregation in schools which they operated. The Defense Department's school policy . . . appeared by the fall of 1953 to be "crystallizing in this pattern." All schools for children of military personnel located on military bases . . . would be unsegregated within the next year or two. Hannah named the 1955 fall term as the "target date for ending the last segregation in post-dependent schools." Later he moved this target up to June 1954.

On the larger front, Hannah, in February 1954 in a radio address, sounded a clarion call for total integration in the armed forces as a matter of principle.

> The obligation to defend our country and our beliefs are borne equally by all of our citizens without regard to race or color or religion . . . We believe in the essential dignity of every human being, and that, within certain limits necessary to maintain an orderly society, each individual should have an opportunity to determine the course and pattern of his existence . . . It should be a real gratification to all thinking Americans to know that our Armed Forces are leading the way in demonstrating both at home and abroad that America provides opportunities for all of her people . . . In spite of all predictions to the contrary I have yet to find a field commander in any service that has anything but commendation for complete racial integration. . . . We are demonstrating in action as well as words that we really believe in social justice, economic justice and political justice for all people of all races and colors.[6]

### Integration Report

At the end of his term of service as Assistant Secretary, Hannah had prepared for release an "Integration Report." Starting with a report of the statement of principles just mentioned, this report summarized major accomplishments as follows:

*Schools*

The directive stating that "the operations of all school facilities located on military installations shall be conducted without segregation on the basis of race or color . . . . as soon as practicable but no later than September 1, 1955, preceded by four months the Supreme Court decision against segregation in public education. (Brown vs. Board of Education)

*Air Force Technical Training*

Negro airmen were given the choice of attending schools in states requiring segregation or to schools which "accept both white and Negro airmen."

*Navy Recruit Training*

Provided an equal opportunity for Negro airmen to choose their branch of service on the basis of "orientation, testing and training," instead of limiting them to the traditional job of stewards.

*Army Orders*

The Department of the Army issued regulations on April 23, 1954 which "directed the omission of racial designation in orders covering the reassignment of members between Army Reserve units." This regulation facilitated the participation of Negro personnel in Army Reserve Units on the same basis as those then obtained for personnel on active duty.

*Facilities and Civilian Employees*

The Navy (followed by the Army and Air Force) directed the "complete elimination of all barriers to the free use of previously segregated facilities on Government owned shore stations."

*Defense Contracts*

The Secretary of Defense issued a directive on June 11, 1954 with follow-up educational programs, to facilitate procurement of personnel involved in defense contracts to abide with "the spirit, intent and requirements of the President's policy."

*Armed Forces*

With only minor and transitory conditions, "there are no longer any all Negro units in the services."

*Proportions*

Statistics were provided which demonstrated the extent to which the proportion of Negroes increased (not drastically but significantly) in categories of Army, Navy, Air Force and Marine officers and men.

**Other Developments included:**

• "Evaluation of battle-tested results to date indicates a marked increase in overall combat effectiveness through integration."

• "Economics in manpower, material and money as resulted from the elimination of racially duplicated facilities and operations."

• "There have been no 'untoward incidents' in spite of the rapid changes."

Other problems, which remained for solution, included:

• Resolving complex problems involving ROTC, National Guard, and other civilian components which are beyond military control.

• Eliminating barriers which stand in the way of utilizing women employees to their full potential.

• Treatment of Negroes in uniform in domestic U.S. environment to feel as much at home as they do overseas. Similar improvements in community relations involving Negroes were also cited in housing, education and recreation.

## Reserve Officers Training Program (ROTC)

One of the knottiest problems which confronted Hannah when he became Assistant Secretary of Defense, was the problems of training officer personnel for the military services. This problem was part of a much larger one whch was related to establishing new policies and procedures for the nation's total reserve system. President Eisenhower on August 1, 1953, had appointed a "National Security Training Commission" which reported their findings on December 14, 1953.* The Commission recommended that a revised program be established not later than January 1, 1955 to "build a trained non-veteran (citizen) reserve for defense of the country." The report and subsequent recommendations by the president for passage of legislation for a "National Reserve Plan," was strongly supported by military officers but was, apparently, subject to protracted congressional debate as commented on by Hannah in a letter to Carter Burgess, his successor as an Assistant Secretary of Defense, when he wrote on Feb. 15, 1955:

> As I wander about in a very limited sphere, I have an opportunity now and then to put in a plug for the reserve program and continue to be impressed with the unanimity of approval when it is understood. I am sure that this is another example of the fact that the country is often ahead of the Congress and the people in Washington.

It is beyond the scope of this chapter to follow up on the destinies of this legislation which was debated long after Hannah had returned to the Presidency of Michigan State University. His attention on the more limited problem of training reserve officers was focused primarily on what universities could contribute, particularly Land Grant Colleges and Universities.

These institutions were established by Congress at the request of President Abraham Lincoln, in 1862, for the training of students in agriculture, mechanic arts (engineering) and "military tactics." Hannah, enthusiastically, promoted ROTC programs at Michigan State University and more generally as an active member and past president of the Land Grant Association and also as Assistant Secretary of Defense. His strong viewpoint in support of the role of academic institutions to be the principal source of training for officers was somewhat modified as he became better informed of the role of the Military, Naval and Air Force Academies. He frankly expressed his change of viewpoint when he testified before the Congress on H.R.

---

*Report of the Commission to the President—Dwight D. Eisenhower Library.

5337 of the 83rd Congress which was examining the need for establishing the Air Force Academy. His views:

It is the view of some able and sincere educators that the educational needs of the services could be met adequately by institutions under civilian control. They point out that many of our finest military leaders have come from our civilian colleges and universities. They argue that graduates of civilian institutions bring into the services a highly desirable variety of background, training and experience and often a high degree of desirable specialization. I came to my present duties in the Department of Defense with that point of view. I have studied the so-called Stearns report, and I remained convinced that undergraduate training of career officers could best be given in civilian colleges and universities, with the Academies restricted to post-graduate training in various military specialties. My subsequent experiences in close association with large numbers of graduates of West Point and Annapolis and visits to the two Academies have led me to a complete change of viewpoint and I am now strongly convinced of the wisdom of establishing an Air Force Academy, believing it to be necessary from the standpoint of national defense, and wholly desirable from an educational point of view.

A few years later in July 1957, when colleges and universities were confronted with students who were in a somewhat rebellious mood regarding compulsory ROTC training, Hannah wrote to Secretary Wilson in a Dear "C.E." letter, with copies to all members of the Association of Land Grant Colleges and Universities.

The land-grant colleges and universities, with the single exception of the University of Minnesota, have continued to require two years of basic ROTC training of all able-bodied male students and have offered the advanced courses on an optional basis. The advanced courses lead to commissioning as a second lieutenant in the Army or the Air Force

In recent years there have been so many changes in ROTC programs and attitudes that several of the universities have become irritated and seriously question the real attitude of the Defense Department toward ROTC

I am reminded, however, that before World War I and again before World War II the only continuing program for production of Army officers, which then included the Air Force, was the ROTC program. In 1941 during the buildup of our Army when we had the first 120,000 officers in the Army, approximately 95,000 of them were products of the ROTC. It is not impossible that the nation at some future date may again find itself as dependent upon ROTC-produced officers as we were in the early days of World War II.

Recently Texas A & M and several other land-grant colleges have either eliminated compulsory ROTC or indicated that they are about to do so. As a result of this action, the American Association of Land-Grant Colleges and State Universities addressed a letter to the Defense Department asking the attitude of the Defense Department toward compulsory ROTC.

It appears to me that those responsible for drafting the reply had no real appreciation of the probable outcome of an expression that compulsory ROTC meant little to the Defense Department and that this was really a matter for each institution to decide for itself.

It is my hope that someone thoroughly familiar with the Army ROTC and the role that it has played in the past and the role that it may be called upon to play in the future be urged to look into this matter before more of our universities cancel the compulsory ROTC requirement.

Two years later, June 1, 1959, however, the "Armed Forces Policy Council" issued an "advice of action" statement indicating that the "Department of Defense favors elective basis ROTC leaving the actual determination to the institutional authorities. There is adequate justification (however) for additional support from the Federal government to institutions having ROTC units."

Additional support for ROTC instructional facilities to universities providing such facilities were not provided, however, on the basis primarily of an opinion of the Director of the Bureau of the Budget in the Executive office of the White House.

Somewhat later, March 1967, Hannah, again taking up the cause of the ROTC, wrote Robert S. McNamara, Secretary of Defense (with copies to officials of the Association of Land Grant Colleges and Universities):

> The land-grant universities as a basic part of their charter required compulsory ROTC until a few years ago when the Pentagon decided that compulsory ROTC was no longer important in its planning, and subsequent to that most of the land-grant universities have shifted to a voluntary Senior ROTC unit . . . .
>
> At the request of the Pentagon, university administrators have encouraged a vigorous program designed to interest students in ROTC programs and in earning second lieutenant commissions along with their bachelors' degrees.
>
> We are now shocked to find that an arbitrary decision has been made in the Pentagon to cut back the quota for students to be enrolled in the junior year ROTC programs effective next fall.
>
> In my view, this basic decision was wrong and not in the best interest of either the Army or of the country. Its implementation is worse . . . .
>
> The purpose of this letter is two-fold. First, to request that you look

into this entire matter and re-examine the advisability of curtailing production of Army officers through Senior ROTC units; second, to re-
examine the quota system as it has been established.

This sequence of events represented a genuine frustration to Hannah
in his efforts to support the ROTC as an integral part of manpower
training for officers in the Department of Defense.

In anticipation of his leaving the Pentagon, Hannah wrote to Secretary Wilson on June 21, 1954, mentioning a few items to which he
would give his attention before and after his departure. Included in the
brief list, which demonstrated his sensitivity to human problems, were
the following:

> To complete a few "little pieces of business" such as (1) to take a trip to
> Germany at the request of our chaplains "to settle the problems there
> with reference to existing restrictions on marriage by members of our
> armed forces that greatly distress our chaplains and others . . . .," (2) to
> clear up some undesirable situations in Japan and elsewhere in the Far
> East that have been persistently reported by reputable persons, (3) to
> visit Air Bases in French Morocco, particularly "where we have numer-
> ous complaints from our men and their families emphasizing our failure
> to provide reasonable satisfactory conditions for enlisted men . . . ."
>
> To return if necessary to ". . . get our Reserve program approved by
> the National Security Council and as far down the road as possible." And
> to return to undertake other assignments if they did *not* require prolonged
> absences from Michigan State College.

He also commended his civilian deputy, James M. Mitchell, for his
work and recommended him as his successor and asked that the
Secretary forward his personal letter of resignation to the President
"at a time you choose as most propitious."

In retiring from the position of Assistant Secretary of Defense,
Hannah commented on his work and experiences in the Pentagon in a
personal letter to President Eisenhower.

> I am deeply grateful to you for your very generous statements in accepting
> my resignation. I leave with real regret, largely because of my respect
> and admiration for you and your objectives and with the feeling that I am
> departing before very much has really been accomplished in the Man-
> power and Personnel area of the Defense Department. I am certain,
> however, that the climate left to my successor in so far as relationships
> with the Department, and with the Services, and with other agencies of
> the government is vastly improved, and that there is now in this operation
> the nucleus of an organization that can and, with reasonable leadership,
> will become truly effective in attaining your goal of effective use of all of

our human resources, military and civilian; and an adequate plan for any all-out emergency.

As I return to Michigan State College, I want you to know that in the event of an all-out emergency, I am ready to serve you in any capacity.

Hannah expressed similar thoughts to his friend and administrative superior, the Secretary of Defense.

The President responded to Hannah's resignation in warm and understanding words as to Hannah's requirement to return to the University.

It is with deep regret that I received your letter of resignation as Assistant Secretary of Defense. With the security problems still facing this government, we can ill afford to lose men with your foresight, integrity and judgment.

During the past year and one-half, your constant endeavors toward better utilization of defense manpower have amounted to a major contribution to the national security. I am keenly appreciative also of your efforts in developing the role of our Reserve Forces and in improving the welfare and morale of servicemen everywhere.

Had you not already served beyond the period originally agreed, I would feel compelled to ask that you remain as Assistant Secretary of Defense for a longer term. However, I appreciate the necessity for you to return to Michigan State College at this time, and am accepting your resignation to be effective July 31, 1954 with the understanding that you will continue to serve as chairman of the United States Section of the Permanent Joint Board on Defense of Canada and the United States.

## Other Hannah Activities in Association With the Department of Defense

### Training Academies of the Army, Navy and Air Force

Hannah's position as Assistant Secretary of Defense for Manpower and Personnel included oversight of the curriculum, teaching personnel and training programs for officers of the Army, Navy and Air Force in their respective academies. He discharged these responsibilities, in part, as a civilian member of Boards of Visitors of these Academies.*

The character of his work with the Academies is perhaps best

---

*Before the Air Force Academy was dedicated in 1955 in Colorado, training for officers of the Air Force was conducted by the "Air University" located at the Air Force base at Montgomery, Alabama.

illustrated by his special involvement in the creation of the Air Force
Academy. In terms of available records, his involvement began on
January 15, 1954, when he testified before the House of Representa-
tives Armed Services Committee. Excerpts from his testimony follow:

> Defense consists of a combination of men, material and money. It takes
> men to use the material effectively, to maintain it, design it and manage
> it. It takes men to spend the money wisely and to conserve it. In the last
> analysis a limiting factor in the Defense Department like in most other
> human activities is the quality of its manpower. The continuing quality
> and effectiveness of the Air Force will be largely dependent upon the
> quality of its professional leadership . . . .
>
> Last spring President Eisenhower turned over to me the annual reports
> of the Boards of Visitors. I appear before you today with a firm conviction
> that the existing academies deserve more attention than they have re-
> ceived in recent years . . .
>
> The Defense Department is a huge operation involving the expenditure
> of vast sums of money. When tens of billions are being spent to assure
> our survival it is easy to become so involved in considerations of atomic
> vs. standard weapons, guided missiles, radar screens, remote detection
> centers, carriers vs. land bases, and on and on and forget that as we plan
> for the future there is no more important consideration than the wisest
> programs for training our future military leaders—Army, Navy, and
> Air.

After praising the loyalty and dedication to service and standards of
integrity and personal ethics of the graduates of West Point and
Annapolis and, although he highly evaluated the ROTC civilian programs for officer-candidates trained in universities, he concluded that
the creation of an Air Force University was essential to round out a
full-fledged long-range program for officers of the Air Force.
With reference to recruitment of the faculty, Hannah continued:

> It should be possible to attract to the faculty of such an Academy the
> nation's foremost authorities on aviation, who would be both an inspira-
> tion to their fellow teachers and their students, and a vital force in the
> advancement of research and development.

Hannah then served as a member of the Board of Visitors of the Air
Force Academy, appointed by the President, for three years from
1956–1959. Other members of the Board appointed at the same time
included, Dr. Arthur H. Compton, former Chancellor of Washington
University; Major General James McCormack Jr. (USAF Retired),
Vice President of the Massachusetts Institute of Technology and for-

mer Director of the Military Applications Division in the United States Atomic Energy Commission; Edward P. Curtis, Vice President Eastman Kokak Company; and Victor Emanuel, Chairman of the Board for the AVCO Corporation.

Some of the kinds of problems and issues which were brought to Hannah's attention for his advice and counsel are illustrated in the following by Lt. General H. R. Harmon, Superintendent of the Academy. An issue arose apparently as to the number of the teaching staff which were estimated in the so-called "manning table" at the time of the opening of the Academy. The costs of the staff was related to the total construction and equipping of the Academy which was limited to a Congressional limit of $125,000,000. An estimated overrun of $37,000,000 by the architects had to be dealt with. The Secretary of the Air Force, Mr. Talbott, urged the Superintendent to consult with Hannah on the problem, specifically as to the proposed facility is: (1) "sound or unsound educationally" and (2) "justifiable or extravagant from the point of view of the taxpayer."

After studying the problem and relevant papers brought to Hannah's attention by Colonel A. E. Bordeau, Hannah made the following response to these important points, among others, to the Superintendent. (1) There needs to be a differentiation between the construction costs (runways etc.) and the necessary supporting facilities (library etc.); (2) as to the size of the teaching staff and other employees, he commented: "As to the standards we use in civilian universities they are high but it would be presumptuous for any civilian to indicate that the teaching schedule or teaching program or faculty organization pattern . . . should conform to civilian standards. . . . An increase in the teaching sections from 12 to 20 would save a few personnel but the dollar savings would not be significant when measured against the overall costs . . . or loss to the country in having qualified personnel;" (3) with reference to possible and practical cost savings, Hannah recommended: (a) that the first priority be given to construction of the necessary classrooms and other teaching facilities, (b) that an equally high priority be given to adequate dormitories, recreational facilities, chapels, and lounges etc. for the cadets, (c) that comparable priority be given to quarters for the Commandant and academic personnel, (d) that some savings (approximately 10%) could be made by requiring that all officer personnel and department heads do some teaching. No reductions, however, should be made for instructors in foreign languages.

Hannah concluded by predicting that "Congress will provide what-

ever facilities are required in these categories without feeling that there
has been a violation of the original cost commitments."

The successor Superintendent of the Academy continued to seek
Hannah's judgment on the ". . . records of our key faculty members
and give us an opinion on their apparent quality."

In connection with the possible location of the Air Force Academy,
at Battle Creek, Michigan, Hannah requested that the Michigan site be
considered but made no more effort beyond this gesture.

**National War College**

Hannah was also a member of the Board of Consultants of the
National War College from 1957–1960. In addition to military person-
nel, some of whom had retired, civilian members included (during
Hannah's tenure) Bernard Brodie of the Rand Corporation; Robert
Murphy, Deputy Under-Secretary of the State Department; John J.
McCloy, Chairman of the Board of the Chase National Bank; Robert
M. Cutter, President Old Colony Trust Company; Loy W. Henderson,
Deputy Under Secretary of State; and other civic and business leaders.
In addition to attending meetings which did not interfere with his
duties as President of MSU, he was asked for his advice on the
selection of academic members of the faculty and to review and
comment on major plans such as the tentative outline for the 1957–58
program of lectures and courses by faculty and outside consultants on
such topics as: Conflict and Power, process of Formulating U.S.
National Security Policy, The Communist Threat, Free World Allies
and Associates of the United States, The Uncommitted Countries of
Africa and Asia, Field Appraisal Studies of the National Security
Policy and similar topics.

Hannah was also a member of the Aerospace Education Foundation
and the Air Force Association.

These significant opportunities provided Hannah to associate with
national military and civilian leaders concerned with broad policy
problems connected with the national defense and for him to contribute
his vast knowledge deriving from his experience with educational
institutions and personnel. His activities were regarded as contributing
to the prestige of Michigan State University and of himself for further
services to the United States Government.

Hannah's "style" of participating and chairing various sessions in
connection with committee work of these organizations (as was typical
of other organizations) is illustrated by a letter from one of his

academic colleagues on the War College Committee in which he wrote: "Please allow me to express my gratitude for the excellent session. We appreciated the way in which you led us along to the framing of our final report without the endless delays and quibbling which had marked the closing sessions in 1955 and 1956."

### Approval for Attendance of Canadian and British Officers for Training at the U.S. National War College

One of the complex policy positions which Hannah advocated while Assistant Secretary of Defense, which he continued to espouse while Chairman of the U.S. Section of the Permanent United States/Canadian Joint Board on Defense (PJBD), was the admission of Canadian and British officers in the National War College. This issue came to Hannah's attention in October 1954 when the Secretary of the U.S. Section (PJBD) provided Hannah with a memorandum which indicated that "beginning about 1946, three Canadian and three British officers were admitted to the National War College each year, while the United States sent officers to the Canadian Defense College at Kingston and to the Imperial Defense College at London." In 1950, however, the U.S. Joint Chiefs of Staff (JCS) decided that the British and Canadians could no longer be invited "owing to their fear that, because of our NATO commitments, we would have to invite students from all other NATO countries." This position persisted even though the State Department "has said that it would accept the burden of refusing any requests from other countries."

The JCS continued to struggle with this dilemma in the subsequent four years even though the Commandant of the National War College informed the Chairman of the JCS that the Board of Consultants (on which Hannah served as a member) expressed the hope that "some way could be found to admit students from Canada and Great Britain without creating undue problems with other nations."

The situation continued to embarrass the Canadian members of the PJBD and was a topic on the agenda of the Board. Hannah continued to understand and support the Canadian position.

Colonel David Crocker (who had become Executive Secretary of the USA Section of the PJBD) wrote Hannah on 5 December 1958, however, that the JCS continued to find that "there was no acceptable way to admit students from *Canada* to the National War College," partly because it would be "diplomatically unwise" to accept only Canadian officers in light that both Canadian and officers from Great

Britain had both been invited in earlier years. Furthermore, the JCS persisted in the position that opening the doors to both Canadian and British officers would result in the need to invite officers from other Allied countries.

In April 1959, Frank M. Coffin, Congressman from Maine, urged General Nathan F. Twining, Chairman of the JCS, to reconsider the position of the JCS with particular reference to the admission of Canadians "in view of our closely integrated continental defense effort." Hannah was informed of Congressman Coffin's further correspondence with General Twining who had asked Hannah's advice as to whether it would be worthwhile "to probe further." Hannah (as President of Michigan State University) responded to the Congressman's request for advice in an uncharacteristically frank letter to him dated June 15, 1959, as follows: "In view of the adamant position of the chiefs of staff, there is probably not much more you can do, but I still do not agree with their position."

No further records on this issue were available to the author but it is believed that Hannah did not give up his position. Further discussions with the PJBD and further efforts by interested Congressmen and possibly others convinced the predecessor to Secretary Robert Mc-Namara to send a memorandum (unsigned) to the British Ministry of Defense as follows:

> Last September Sir Richard Powell discussed with me the possibility of admitting British officers to the National War College. At that time I informed Sir Richard that I would look into this matter upon my return to Washington.
>
> On the basis of a subsequent examination, I am most gratified to report that we are prepared to admit one officer each from the Army, Navy and Air Force of the United Kingdom in the regular course of instruction at the National War College, beginning August 1960. We propose to offer the Canadian Government comparable arrangements. The foregoing decision will not be extended to any other countires. Accordingly, I am sure you will appreciate our desire to minimize publicity on this decision.

Hannah's sustained interest and concern, advocacy and action in resolving this issue finally paid off!

## Member Defense Department Advisory Committee on Professional and Technical Compensation

In 1956 (approximately two years after Hannah resigned from the Defense Department), Hannah undertook an assignment as a member of the Advisory Committee on "Professional and Technical Compensation." Ralph J. Cordiner, President of the General Electric Company, served as Chairman of the Committee which included several high-ranking military and civilian personnel.

The major focus of the Committee was on the special problems of compensation and related costs involved in recruiting, assigning, and retaining highly trained technical personnel for the increasingly complex tasks of the Defense Department. This primary focus of the Committee was examined in the working relationships of these highly skilled personnel to other personnel in the whole defense department. Cognizance was thus taken of the far-reaching technological changes which were affecting both civilian and military personnel at all levels, and the enormous and increasing costs involved in maintaining an effective defense establishment. Hannah's previous experience as Assistant Secretary of Defense and as a University president interested in problems of this character were highly relevant and useful to the Cordiner Committee.

The task was made more difficult by the traditional compensation scales which were heavily weighted on the basis of longevity of service rather than the difficulties of the operations. The Committee recommended more rational compensation plans and manpower management programs which were also designed to achieve a number of other goals such as: (1) better use of high-cost items of equipment; (2) increased combat readiness; (3) reduction of costly accidents which killed many employees and destroyed expensive equipment. These objectives were examined by each of the armed services and verified by the Committee as real and achievable.

The additional costs of all recommendations were estimated to be offset by savings of as much as five billion dollars in the cost of national defense over a five year period.

Furthermore, the committee's major recommendations were believed to provide specific long-term solutions to the basic manpower problems of the armed services such as:

• Excessive turnover and loss of key military personnel, particularly among officers and high level technicians.
• Low incentives for outstanding performance.
• Excessive amounts of personnel, equipment, and money tied up in training at the expense of combat readiness.
• Lowered morale in times of peace.
• Imbalance of skills, with too high a proportion of easy-to-learn skills and shortage of more difficult leadership and technical skills.

The final report in addition to dealing with these problems included recommendations for providing more adequate housing and greater educational opportunities for armed service personnel.

The Staff Director, in a letter to the Chairman, which advised him of the testimony of key military personnel who testified before the Senate Appropriations Committee, stated that ". . . All Service Secretaries and all Service Chiefs have stated that they are in agreement with the Committee's recommendation(s).

Hannah's contribution to the work of the committee was recognized by the Secretary of Defense as follows:

> I believe that the work of the Defense Advisory Committee on Professional and Technical Compensation will long be remembered with gratitude by the men and women of the Armed Forces. It was this Committee, and the outstanding job which it did in studying and analyzing the personnel problems of the services, which led the way to the greatly improved program now being placed in effect. I think that you, and your asociates on the Committee, are to be congratulated and highly commended.
>
> Obviously, the new Pay Bill will not solve all our problems, but I believe that it, together with other significant personnel actions we are taking based on the recommendations of the Advisory Committee, will result in a positive and far reaching strengthening of our defense capabilities.

And by the Secretary of the Navy who wrote to Hannah as follows:

> The Cordiner Committee Report is a tribute to the leadership and positive action as a member. By its content, particularly in the manner it is aimed to meet changing concepts in present and foreseeable weapons systems, it reflects your important and timely assistance in this endeavor. . . .
>
> Men like yourself, in superior positions in the field of education who continue to take time from your busy schedules to advise and guide us in matters such as this show exemplary selflessness and patriotism.

### Excerpts from Comments on Several Aspects of Hannah's Leadership in the Department of Defense

*From the Assistant Secretary of the Army—*
*Hugh M. Milton II (MSUAHC)*

> It is impossible for me to say how much I shall miss you. You are such a student of human nature that you know well how I have come to rely

upon your sound advice and direction in the multitudinous and complex problems in the personnel field of the Department of the Army. Without you to rely upon, I feel that it would have been beyond my ability to cope with the problems of the past few months. My admiration for you grew with each contact, and the affable manner in which you listened to my problems shall remain a cherished memory.

*From General Herbert Butler Powell* (Retired) (Letter to the author dated Sept. 21, 1985)

After the previous administration Dr. Hannah was a breath of fresh air. He listened to the problems of all of the services carefully and was helpful in the solutions. He inspired confidence by his fair, calm and sincere approach.

The manpower problems during this period stemmed largely from President Eisenhower's strategic concept of relying on deterrence and reducing conventional forces, especially ground forces while depending on allied land forces on the Soviet periphery. This concept was to reduce the budget, especially defense spending . . . While watching the present political activity to reduce defense spending it makes me want to say, "This is where I came in." Dr. Hannah was caught in the middle of this situation. On one hand there was not only a limitation of manpower, but pressure to reduce it. On the other hand was the necessity to support conventional forces in Europe, Korea and a dozen other countries. He managed this situation, in my opinion, with great skill, keeping enough resources to keep our strategic position going without hopelessly opposing Ike's position.

*From General James F. Collins* (Retired) (Letter to the author dated 23 July 1985)

As you probably know, Dr. Hannah was not enthusiastic about going to the Pentagon to be Assistant Secretary of Defense for Manpower . . . It was President Eisenhower who urged him to go for a special reason or purpose. General Marshall a year or so earlier almost attained a Universal Military Training Plan for the youth of the country but it was lost in the House vote. He, like President Eisenhower, thought we needed better training of the youth in the country.

Dr. Hannah with his background at Michigan State went right to work. He had managed and built Michigan State for about 12 years. He was doing many of the things in Michigan that he would be doing in Washington such as legislative matters, press, state personnel etc. which came in handy. He soon knew the matters of manpower and the other areas he was to supervise such as Reserve Forces Committees, National Guard committees and also a committee of chaplains.

The military and civilian relationship with Dr. Hannah was fine. These people soon learned that he was fair and that he quickly learned the "nut" of the particular problem being discussed and went quickly to a decision.

There are few Asst. Secretaries who can compare with the capable manner he worked. Asst. Secretaries are usually there for a short period, many are there for prestige, others for advancement. Few are the dedicated who are doing their part for the government. John Hannah was one of the latter and I was fortunate to work with him.

*From James M. Mitchell,* Deputy Secretary (MSUAHC)

Your breadth of understanding and calm courage have made it a real privilege to work with you during the past year and a half. I have learned a great deal from you about the qualities of leadership.

*From Lynette Trimble*—a Secretary (MSUAHC)

Working for you, Sir, was one of the most pleasant experiences I have ever had. It was personally very satisfying to be associated with a person who is genuinely respected and one who is sincerely concerned with and capable of solving the big problems in the world.

In summary, Hannah's experience as Assistant Secretary of Defense for Manpower and Personnel was both personally satisfying and professionally successful.

## Chapter II

# American Chairman of the Permanent Joint United States– Canadian Defense Board (PJBD)[1]

John Hannah was appointed as the United States Chairman of the PJBD by President Eisenhower in 1954, shortly after completing his full-time service as Assistant Secretary of Defense (Manpower and Personnel) and returning to the presidency of Michigan State College. He was recommended to President Eisenhower by Charles E. Wilson, Secretary of Defense and by John Foster Dulles, Secretary of State. His appointment was approved by President Eisenhower with the title of Assistant to the Secretary of Defense, a title which Hannah has suggested in a letter to Secretary Wilson dated September 23, 1954. Hannah wrote:

I have given some thought to the work of the Permanent Joint Board on Defense, Canada–U.S., after I leave my post as Assistant Secretary of Defense (M&P) and return to the presidency of Michigan State College. I submit the following suggestions for your consideration.

I feel that it would be definitely helpful to me in working with the Military Services if you would give me a continuing appointment as an assistant to the Secretary of Defense on a consultant basis. Such an arrangement would give me some status and stature with the Air Force, Navy, and Army that I will not otherwise have. It would permit me to have a desk in the office of PJBD in the Pentagon, which may be rarely used, but would provide a base of operations when here. It would permit me to travel to necessary meetings of the PJBD or on other necessary and desirable trips to and from Board meetings or on other occasions in connection with that we hope will be the important work of this Board, at the expense of the Defense Department, without having to have prior approval by some employee of the Defense Department assigned to the PJBD.

Secretary Wilson agreed to Hannah's suggestion and added:

None of us here in the Department of Defense want to lose the advice and counsel which you can give us—and we all consider you on a leave-of-absence back to Michigan State College.

Hannah served in this capacity for 10 years, until 1964.

*Origin and Purpose of the PJBD.* The PJBD was launched on August 18, 1940 by a joint statement of President Roosevelt and Mackenzie King, Prime Minister of Canada, known as the "Ogdensburg Agreement.[11] The text of the agreement follows:

The Prime Minister and the President have discussed the mutual problems of defense in relation to the safety of Canada and the United States.

It has been agreed that a Permanent Joint Board on Defense shall be set up at once by the two countries.

This Permanent Joint Board on Defense shall commence immediate studies relating to sea, land, and air problems including personnel and material.

It will consider in the broad sense the defense of the north half of the Western Hemisphere.

The Permanent Joint Board on Defense will consist of four or five members from each country, most of them from the Services. It will meet shortly.

This formal agreement reflected the cordial and trusting relationship between the United States and Canada which had existed for most of the history of the two countries, dramatized by the longest undefended border existing between any two countries. The new threat from Hitler's Germany to the security of the two countries created the need to establish a joint defense system.

*Responsibilities of the Chairman.* The first formal definition of the duties of the United States Chairman was expressed in a memorandum by Maj. Gen. Guy V. Henry, Acting Chairman of the United States section of the PJBD, issued 20 November 1953. The PJBD was described as a "Presidential agency which operated in an advisory capacity with no executive authority.'' The Chairman, as a Presidential appointee, was responsible for:

• Advising the President on matters pertaining to those Canada–United States defense matters which have been referred to the Board.
• Acting as a spokesman for the United States Government at combined meetings of the Board.
• Determining the United States position on Canada–United States defense matters referred to the Board.
• Acting as presiding officer at meetings of the Board when the Board meets on United States territory.
• Conducting meetings of the United States section of the Board, involving the determination of the agenda and the frequency of the meetings.

The work of the PJBD which developed involved many complex and novel technical matters, including designing and installing an early warning electronic surveillance system in Northern Canada. Hannah's role was diplomatic and managerial.

## Hannah's Request for Appraisal of the PJBD

After serving three years as Chairman of the United States Section of the PJBD on the occasion of Wilson's resignation as Secretary of Defense, Hannah wrote Secretary Wilson an analytical and characteristically frank "Dear C.E." letter on August 14, 1957. The context and tone of this letter characterized his objective style as an administrator and was also characteristic of his excellent relationship with Secretary Wilson.

> In view of this situation (Wilson's resignation), it seemed pertinent to suggest that you and Mr. Dulles may want to take a hard look at the Permanent Joint Board on Defense and decide whether it is likely to fill a useful role in the future. If there are doubts as to its usefulness, this would be a propituous time to close it out. The new Canadian government has no traditional attachment to the Board, and I think that General McNaughton, the Canadian Chairman, is contemplating retiring from the Board in the not too distant future. I am willing to continue on if the President wishes me to or I will be happy to step aside.

He went on to assure Secretary Wilson that the letter was not a polite gesture but a serious suggestion that the future role of the Board be critically appraised.

Our government has far too many agencies, commissions, and boards that continue long after their usefulness has disappeared using dollars and energies that could be better expended elsewhere.

Furthermore, Hannah wrote that although the time was propitious for a review by both governments, his suggestion did not rest on any "personal doubt" which he had as to the Board's usefulness.

Hannah continued that he had enjoyed the opportunity to serve as the United States Chairman, and then provided some details on developments, described below, which he believed had made some useful contributions to better relationships between our two countries.

As of now, the relationship between the military services of the two countries is excellent. The newly announced integration of the Continental Air Defense will require and assure continuing correlation of the Air arms of both countries. The land segment of the electronic warning lines are in operation. There seems to be on our side a real appreciation of the importance of continuing cooperation between the two governments at every level and in all areas of mutual interest.

This positive appraisal was shared by General A. G. L. McNaughton, Chairman of the Canadian Section of the Joint Board, who wrote to Hannah expressing his views and those of the Canadian government.

In response to Hannah's suggestion, the newly appointed Secretary of Defense, Neil McElroy, sent a "Dear John" letter to Hannah mentioning that Secretary Wilson had sent a copy of Hannah's letter to Secretary of State Dulles. He added:

While I am not completely familiar with the operations of the Permanent Joint Board, I find that the opinion of the State Department is shared by the Defense Department and I am of the opinion that it is a most useful agency and one that should not be materially modified nor abolished at this time.

Knowing of your great experience in dealing with these problems, I personally hope that you can continue to serve as the Chairman of the U.S. Section of this Board. I would like to know the other members of the Board better, both from the United States and from Canada, and would welcome the opportunity to have a visit with them at an early date. The next time it is convenient for you to come to Washington, I hope that we can have a good visit together on this matter.

The first response of the State Department to Hannah's request for a searching reappraisal of the future of the PJBD, transmitted to Hannah by the State Department member of the PJBD on Sept. 25, 1957 was clearly positive. In addition, it added considerable more detail on the organization and operational procedures of the Joint Board. A second briefer, but no less positive appraisal, was sent by Acting Secretary Christian A. Herter to Neil H. McElroy, on Oct. 9, 1957. Excerpts of the Herter response follow:

> Practically all of the important joint defense projects undertaken by the two governments since 1940 were originally discussed by the Board and may have resulted from the Board's recommendations.
>
> In its seventeen years of existence, the Board has come to enjoy exceptional prestige in Canada and is regarded by Canadians as a symbol of their special relationship with the United States.
>
> The Department of State is convinced that this strong attachment for the Board persists within the Canadian Government today. Any suggestion by the United States to abolish the Board would in all likelihood come as a shock to their national pride, particularly in the absence of a prior dissolution of other bilateral United States boards . . .
>
> As for the Board's future usefulness, the Department of State sees no reason why it sould not continue to play a useful role in furthering the joint defense efforts of both countries . . . Being composed of both military and political representatives of both countries, the Board has the special advantage of being able to bring together in one forum the military and political viewpoints of both countries where they can be discussed openly and frankly in an atmosphere of informality and friendliness. No doubt many recent successfully concluded defense projects would have come to fruition with much greater difficulty, had it not been for earlier discussions at Board meetings which smoothed the way for subsequent negotiations at the diplomatic level. With a country as politically sensitive as Canada in matters affecting its sovereignty, there should continue to be room for the Board to perform valuable service in considering problems having political overtones which will inevitably arise in connection with joint defense measures.

Following this exchange, Hannah was requested to continue to serve as Chairman for three more years.

Three years later, in anticipation of another major change in leadership of the government, Hannah wrote to President-Elect John F. Kennedy on Nov. 17, 1960, with copies to Robert McNamara, Secretary of Defense-designate, and to Dean Rusk, Kennedy's choice for Secretary of State. Excerpts of this letter follow:

> I have a full appreciation of the magnitude of the responsibilities that now rest with you, and of the complexity of the decisions before you. I do not wish to add to your burden and would have preferred an opportunity to visit with you in person. . . . However, I believe the following matters should be called to you attention immediately.

Seven years ago I was designated by President Eisenhower as the United States Chairman of the Permanent Joint Board on Defense, Canada–United States. This Board was created in 1940 by President Roosevelt and Prime Minister King to coordinate the defenses of the two nations. In the intervening twenty years there have been four United States chairmen: Mayor LaGuardia, Dean Acheson, General Henry and the writer. This Board continues to serve a useful purpose, although somewhat superseded by the joint meetings of Ministers and United States Cabinet members in recent years . . .

As a result of my experience, I would suggest that the United States Chairman should not only be acceptable to the Secretary of State and the Secretary of Defense, but also enjoy their full confidence so that when necessary he can speak with some assurance that he is speaking for our government. In the past, because of President Eisenhower's interest in this field, I have reported directly to him, although as a matter of fact I have not bothered him very often.

I herewith submit my resignation to take effect at your pleasure. It would be my recommendation that the new chairmen spend some time with the State Department member of the Board with the Defense Department members, familiarizing himself with the work of the Board prior to the first meetings of the Board (scheduled to be held on January 24, 1961) in which he is to participate as United States chairman. . . .

The Permanent Joint Board on Defense is a very small part of the great complex organization that you are about to preside over. The purpose of this note is to determine whether or not you would like me to proceed as the United States chairman of this group through the January meeting.

The real purpose of this letter is to make clear to you that I shall not be offended if you wish to name a new chairman prior to the scheduled January meeting.

President Kennedy chose not to accept Hannah's proffered resignation and requested him in a letter of April 4, 1961 to continue to serve, which he did until September 12, 1963, when he was replaced by H. Freeman Matthews. President Kennedy wrote to Hannah on Oct. 12, 1963:

A little more than two years ago, during a conversation we had at the White House, you mentioned to me the heavy demands of your various public activities, and your responsibilities as President of Michigan State University. You referred to your service as Chairman of the United States Section of the Permanent Joint Board on Defense (United States–Canada), stating that you would be pleased to continue in this capacity for a limited period. I said I would bear in mind the necessity of your eventual replacement as Chairman.

I have now decided to appoint the Honorable H. Freeman Matthews as Chairman of the United States Section.

I fully appreciate the distinguished contribution you have made to our national security as Chairman of the United States Section, and I wish to take this opportunity to express my gratitude for your efforts in the important field of United States–Canadian relations.

## Organization, Membership and Operating Procedures of the PJBD During Hannah's Tenure as Chairman

The Herter summary of the State Department's response to Hannah's request for a reappraisal of the PJBD provides the essential facts about the organization, membership and operating procedures which were in effect during Hannah's tenure. It also provided some clues as to the somewhat informal, but highly important, policy and administrative environment in which Hannah worked. No specific instructions had been issued by President Roosevelt and Prime Minister Mackenzie King when they decided to establish the PJBD. Further development was left to the executive authorities of the two countries. This tradition was continued. Highlights of the report follow:

*Organization.*—The Joint board "with complete equality of its two components and two coequal chairman" served as a policy board.

• Members of the three military services and diplomatic departments of the two countries participated.

• Each component (or section) had its own secretary drawn from their diplomatic departments.

*Voting Procedure and Records.*—Voting, in the conventional sense, under the organizational arrangements indicated above, was impractical.

• No open disagreements were recorded. The disparate views of the two sections were noted "with as much detail as necessary, while hope for early progress was often expressed." This practice led some people to call it "the note and hope Board."
• Board meetings were scheduled at approximately three monthly intervals, often involving inspection of each others defense installations.
• Agenda were mutually agreed upon before each meeting.
• At least twenty-six meetings were held during Hannah's tenure chiefly on weekends.

• "Journal records" (not verbatim accounts) were written by the two secretaries which must be jointly approved before submission to the Board for final approval at subsequent meetings. This procedure for record keeping had the advantage of leaving the door open for later compromise, after the first words had been spoken and positions taken. The records of the subsequent discussions became the final Journal entries.

*Advisory Functions of the Board.* Because the Board was limited to a purely advisory role, "the only thing that could emanate from it was called a recommendation." The Board issued 33 of these unanimously approved recommendations during the second World War, some of them fairly complex and obviously the result of long and arduous meetings. After the recommendations are reviewed by the relevant "filters," they were issued "simultaneously by the two Sections through their respective diplomatic departments to the heads of two governments for final approval. Acceptance by both governments of a Board recommendation simply means that they have decided to act in parallel fashion . . . But there is no contractual obligation to do so. Either country may witdraw its approval of a recommendation at any time."

*Follow-up Activities on Advisory Recommendations of the Board.* Even though the Board is an advisory body, "actually however it has a great deal to do, indirectly with the execution of policy. The importance of the positions of the members of their access to their superiors, plus the thoroughness of their review, makes it possible to affect action." Dr. Hannah (for example) reported to the President and had access to leading figures in the defense establishment which was also true of General McNaughton who was similar access to Canadian officials. Furthermore, on the American side, Hannah had an Executive Secretariat set up in the Pentagon to follow through from meeting to meeting. The State Department values the association of their representatives with military members. The result of the formal and informal collaboration have since 1940 brought the armed services of the two countries progressively closer together both in activities and outlook, most particularly in the field of air defense. Some of the inspiration toward this cooperation has come, of course, from the Board itself. Whatever the cause, the unanimity of outlook is now so satisfactory that the air forces of the two countries have been able to develop understandings without benefit of the Board's blessing and have found an increasing number of matters capable of settlement without assistance of the Board's advice.

## Conclusions of the Herter Review

From the State Department's viewpoint, the answer to the question (of the Board's usefulness) is not hard to find. All we need do is to recall that the Board provides a worthy forum for the expression of opinions molded both in the Department and the Embassy in Ottawa. Some extremely delicate subjects have been broached successfully during Board meetings largely because of its widely representative nature . . .

Furthermore, it is almost axiomatic that intelligent people cannot convene every so often for three or four days of unbroken association in a variety of activities without coming to know each other quite well. Consequently, the Board has developed firm bonds between highly placed officials on both sides. These are the bonds of confidence and mutual respect which, however intangible, nevertheless leaven the activities of the other joint military groups, which were aired by the Board and which now emulate its spirit. Dissolution of the Board would be somewhat like removing the keystone of an arch, insofar as these other military groups are concerned. Owing to its prestige in military matters, the Board in all likelihood would provide a useful focal point during any future national emergency of a prolonged nature affecting both countries.

## Communications Regarding the Work of the PJBD

Because of the complex technical work, organizational relations both within and between the joint armed forces and the sometimes delicate diplomatic relationships between the United States and Canadian governments, candid, timely, and sometimes highly confidential written communications were necessary between the principal parties to the joint enterprise. The principal of these were: (1) between the Chairman and the President; (2) between the several Secretaries of Defense and Hannah; (3) between Hannah and other top military officials; and (4) to and from USA members of the PJBD and staff assistants.

Some highlights of such written communications follow:

### Between Hannah and President Eisenhower

*May 7, 1954.* The "launching" letter from Eisenhower to Hannah occurred when Hannah was still the Assistant Secretary of Defense.

He wrote: "As you know, I attach great importance to the maintenance of strong, mutually beneficial relationships between Canada
and the United States . . . I would like to have you report to me in
person at least every three months or more often if you consider it
necessary."

*July 18, 1958.* Between May 1954 and June 1958 Hannah had doubtless had several oral sessions with the President but on June 18, 1958
in a "Dear John" letter (signed D.E.), he indicated he would be
"delighted to see you again" and was sure that an appointment
could be made during the next month. Because the President was
due to visit Canada shortly, he specifically indicated that he wanted
to be brought up to date on the work of the PJBD.

*August 29, 1960.* Hannah referred to meetings "some months ago
when we were discussing various matters in your office, one of the
items discussed was on our civil defense program. I indicated at that
time that this matter was receiving the attention of the Permanent
Joint Board on Defense–Canada and United States. Attached is a
copy of an extract from the minutes of the last meeting of the PJBD.
The purpose of this letter is to suggest the possibility that you may
want the National Security Council to take a hard and critical look
at our present organization for civil defense. It is my personal view
that what we have is totally inadequate. . . ."

*September 12, 1960.* The President in another "Dear John" letter,
signed D.E., expressed interest in Hannah's suggestion that the ". . .
National Security Council take a look at our present organization
for civil defense" and continued to fill Hannah in on what was being
developed and by whom on the subject. He suggested that Hannah
see Arthur Flemming (a White House assistant for organizational
matters) when he next came to Washington.

**Between Hannah and President Kennedy** (in addition to letter of Nov.
17, 1960 previously referred to)

*Nov. 17, 1960.* As before indicated, Hannah addressed a letter to
Senator John F. Kennedy before he took office as President inform-
ing the President-Elect of several important facts about the organization and program of the PJBD. He offered his resignation "to take
effect at your pleasure."

He continued to indicate that his principal duty was as President
of Michigan State University which was itself a "heavy responsibility." And also that he had "learned much from my various roles
assigned to me by President Truman and President Eisenhower."

*May 23, 1963.* Hannah wrote President Kennedy for "guidance or counsel that you would like to offer in connection with the next meeting of the PJBD" to be held in Canada wich Hannah believed was very important because "the climate for encouraging approval of long-range objectives that have been in mind for the past several years is much more possible now than it was prior to the change of government in Canada." He then wrote that:

> I have always viewed my role as the United States Chairman as one of serving as a catalytic agent to encourage the attainment of objectives that have been agreed upon by the Department of Defense and the Department of State. There have been times in the past when PJBD has made significant contributions toward smoothing out roads that might otherwise have been rough to travel. It is my desire to do whatever I can to attain the objectives you have in mind, and I will welcome any guidance or suggestions.

Because President Kennedy was not to be in office when Hannah was scheduled to come to Washington to testify to a Senate Committee on Civil Rights legislation, he asked Hannah to meet with members of the State Department on the substance and objectives of "Ecquiwalt meetings."

After President Kennedy's assassination in November, 1963, Hannah continued to serve as Chairman at President Johnson's request.

### Selected Communications with Secretary Wilson*

*April 30, 1954.* After attending the first meeting of the PJBD, Hannah sent a memorandum to Secretary Wilson to clarify arrangements for reporting on the work of the Joint Committee.

> Historically the Board was created by a joint agreement between the President of the United States and the Prime Minister of Canada. During the early years of the Board under the U.S. Chairmanship of Mayor LaGuardia, he reported periodically in person to President Roosevelt. His successor, General Henry, discontinued the practice.

———

*Hannah had both a warm personal and professional relationship with Secretary Wilson. Some aspects of this relationship are described elsewhere, particularly in Appendix F which provides his reflections on several key aspects of administration based on his experiences as Assistant Secretary of Defense for Manpower and Personnel.

I am fully aware of the tremendous burdens carried by our President. I think, however, the matter is of sufficient importance to justify a brief report following each quarterly meeting delivered in person to the President, the Secretary of Defense and the Secretary of State

Possibly you will be willing to raise this question with the President and I shall, of course, follow your recommendations.

*November 4, 1954.* This letter suggests some of the progress being made and some of the "diplomatic" aspects of the relationship between the United States and Canada in getting on with the job.

It has been my consistent understanding resulting from our various conversations and a conference with President Eisenhower that the construction of the Distant Early Warning line was urgent and of the highest priority. At the meeting of the Permanent Joint Board for Defense in British Columbia in July, we succeeded in convincing the Canadian members that this project from the United States point of view was urgent. They returned to Ottawa, and as a result of the impetus of our meeting, the Canadian government agreed in principle to the construction of the DEW line. . .

If we get prompt Canadian government approval and if we can get all of the red tape in our own Defense Department operations unwound so that we can use with full effectiveness the 1955 construction season, at best the DEW line will not be operational until sometime in 1957 . . .

The purpose of this letter is to urge that you take whatever steps you deem appropriate to notify the Canadian government that it is the desire of the United States that they give early formal approval to the necessary diplomatic arrangements to permit us to begin immediately.

It is my understanding that some of our people are not too happy with the insistence of the Canadians that electronic equipment that is available in Canada be given equal or preferential treatment for installation in the portion of the line located on Canadian terrority. However, this is not the immediate issue.

*September 27, 1955.* Hannah took the occasion to expand on their telephone conversation regarding progress being made on the joint project in a "Dear C.E." letter.

I want to confirm the statement that I made to you over the telephone with reference to the progress being made in connection with the DEW line. We returned Friday evening from an inspection trip to the western end of the line in Canada and Alaska. Two weeks earlier, as guests of the Canadians, we had inspected the eastern segment of the mid-Canada line from west of Hudson Bay to Knob Lake and Port Hope.

The progress that has been made in the ten months since the DEW project was authorized is almost unbelievable. It makes one proud to be an American and impresses one with the potential of our country to do a job when it makes up its mind to do it.

The fact that approximately 250,000 tons of material are now delivered on sites all across the north end of this continent well within the Arctic circle is a colosssal accomplishment. Some of this freight had to be air lifted. Much of it was sea carried by the Navy, and some of it will have to be hauled laterally by cat trains on the snow and ice this winter . . .

The real purpose of this letter is to emphasize how strongly I feel that no budget balancing operation should be permitted to interfere with or delay the completion of the DEW project or the SAGE project. I am sure that it is poor defense to delay them and I think it is poor politics.

## Examples of other Communications Between Hannah, Other Officials of the Defense Department and the United States Staff Members of the PJBD

Some 20–25 communications involved exchanges of letters with Secretaries Donald A. Quarles, Robert McNamara, Thomas Gates Jr., and Paul Nitze, and with Robert T. Stevens, Secretary of the Army. One to Secretary Stevens demonstrates Hannah's concern for a colleague in trouble and his own philosophy of how to handle such problems.

To Robert Stevens, Secretary of the Army, who was being maligned by Senator McCarthy, he wrote:

I am afraid that you have been so close to the McCarthy controversy and have been talked to, and stared at, and talked and written about by so many that it has become all out of the proper perspective in your thinking. I urge you to take the next three or four weeks and get away from the Pentagon, the Army, newspaper reporters etc. The open spaces of Montana, the sun, the stars and time to contemplate the difference between the unimportant and the fundamentals will, I am sure, convince you that the irritating criticisms of people that have to fill newspaper space or radio time for a living are very unimportant. They are quickly forgotten, and mean nothing to your friends in the first place.

It bothers me to see you so keyed up and perturbed. It just isn't that important . . .

I have a basic philosophy that helps me. I prefer to be liked but when I am criticized as everyone in public life sometimes is, I take another look and if I decide that I am right, I go right on down the road, and do not

fret about it. Six months from now this will all be an interesting topic to
visit about and nothing more.

To James Douglas, Acting Secretary of the Air Force, regarding the
best way to help the Royal Canadian Air Force's (RCAF) job get done
on the project was through the PJBD, thus filling a temporary policy
"vacuum" in the Canadian government.

> I think that items of this kind can be considerably expedited if handled
> through the PJBD rather than service to service contacts alone. The
> RCAF, without the firm support of McNaughton, (Hannah's co-chairman
> on the Canadian side), the DD (Defense Department) and the Department
> of External Affairs has difficulty in getting early government approval.
> The new Canadian government finds itself between the devil and the deep
> blue sea with reference to United States cooperation.

Several other problems arose in the course of Hannah's chairmanship between the PJBD and other sections of the Defense Department
ranging from rather trivial problems to appointments of military personnel, to positions on the PJBD staff, and to a more important and
complex organization and reporting problem of relationships between
the PJBD, the Joint Defense Cabinet Committee and the International
Security office of the Defense Department. These problems were
characteristically called to Hannah's attention by key staffers of the
PJBD. Hannah's responses to some of these problems follow.

With reference to the shifting appointments (by rotation or otherwise) of office personnel to handle "office routines," Hannah wrote
on Sept. 2, 1959, to Major General Thomas C. Darcy.

> With reference to the seniority of the colonels in the central office, this
> matter of serial number seniority has always seemed silly to me. When I
> first came into the PJBD picture in 1954, Colonel Grayling, an Army
> colonel, was responsible for the office. I assumed that when Colonel
> Crocker (presumably a younger colonel) replaced Colonel Ward that he
> too would be responsible for the office routines. It seems not unreasona-
> ble that since the Air Force member of the Board (Major General Darcy)
> has always been regarded by me as the senior military member, regardless
> of the serial numbers held by the various military representatives, it was
> sensible to have the person responsible for the office routines represent
> one of the other services. From my point of view, Colonel Crocker has
> rendered excellent service.

On the more consequential matter of the functions of the PJBD in
relation to the joint Cabinet Committee of the United States and
Canada (comprising the ministers of State, Finance and Defense of

both countries and the International Security Section of the U.S. Dept. of Defense), created protracted debate and exchange of letters and memorandum which concerned Hannah very much. President Eisenhower, with prompting from Hannah, resolved the question in a "Dear Neil" letter on July 1958 (signed "D.E.") as follows:

> Possibly I told you about the discussion with the Canadian Prime Minister respecting the formation of the Joint Cabinet Committee conprising the Ministers of State, Finance and Defense from both countries. Speaking generally, its purpose will be to make sure that both governments have a coordinated viewpoint toward our joint efforts to produce an adequate security for our two countries, and to serve in a supervisory position with respect to the Permanent Joint Board for Defense. The functions of the Permanent Joint Board for Defense of the two nations will in no way be impaired. I should think that when the Joint Committee holds a meeting, it would have before it both Canadian and United States representatives of the PJBD.
>
> It is still necessary that none of the services within the Defense Department attempt to shortcut the PJBD in bringing joint defense problems to the attention of political officials. We must be very careful in this particular regard; their appropriate contact is the PJBD.

Major General Darcy in a comprehensive memo addressed to the military advisor—International Security (ISA)—on "Terms of Reference" (the language of which was agreed to by Dr. Hannah), referred to President Eisenhower's 1958 letter and to a later conference in 1960 between Hannah and the President in which David W. Kendall (a Presidential Assistant) was requested by the President to *"remind all concerned that the appropriate contact in bringing joint defense problems to the attention of political officials is the Permanent Joint Board of Defense, Canada–United States."* (Italics added)

### United States–Canadian Policy Issues and Hannah's Role in Resolving Them

As previously indicated, relationships between the two countries, as reflected in the formal agenda items of the PJBD and the informal discussions between members of the Board and staff, involved highly complex technological issues and more subtle diplomatic issues. Hannah was highly involved in these matters, background information for which was provided by the United States staff and from diplomatic dispatches from the United States Ambassador to Canada, news dispatches from Canada and other relevant information. There was much to read, digest and comment upon.

The PJBD provided a built-in forum for ventilation of issues involving defense between Canada and the U.S.; but defense questions frequently impinged upon other policy areas. Hannah sensed the delicacy and nuances of the relationship. Issues briefly recorded and documented in the Hannah archival collection at Michigan State University include such items as: (1) differences between the two countries in dealing with Cuba, Canada having maintained diplomatic and commercial relations with Cuba; (2) differences in trade policies with China, particularly in wheat sales; (3) diversion of Canadian lake water to Chicago; (4) admission of Canadian officers to the National War College; (5) storage of defensive nuclear weapons in Canada; and (6) ratification of the Columbia River Treaty. The tone of Hannah's handling the often touchy relationships is illustrated in the following excerpts of a letter to Donald A. Quarles, Deputy Secretary of Defense, with copies to General McNaughton, Chairman of the Canadian Section of the PJBD and to General Thomas C. Darcy, Air Force member of the American Section.

> As a result of discussions held at this meeting with General McNaughton and others, I am more convinced than ever of the importance of reaching an early agreement with Canada covering the utilization of her industrial resources in the production of items required for defense of our two countries.
>
> The decisions expected of Canada involving the interruption of the program for the development and manufacture of manned aircraft and the interruption of the development and manufacture of complete guided missiles poses some very real economic and political problems for Canada.
>
> I feel that the time has come for a truly objective appraisal of our joint interests by representatives of both countries. There must be a realization that the best interests of the United States are served by utilizing the Canadian potential for production of weapons and other military requirements. I fear that too many of those on our side are inclined to enter negotiations of this kind with a fixed mental commitment that all complicated weapons and equipments must be made within the United States by United States manufacturers.
>
> The purpose of this letter is to urge upon you your full support in encouraging an early settlement of this problem.

As a follow-up on Hannah's letter to Secretary Quarles, Hannah was informed of an important policy memorandum prepared by Secretary Quarles for Secretary Herter, of the State Department, which summarized his conference with Ambassador Heeney and Minister Ritchey of Canada. At this conference certain topics of current high interest in Canada, particularly those related to defense production and production sharing, matters of equitable sharing, possibility of "preferential treatment" and other matters of mutual concern with the effect of various policies on each country were discussed. The memorandum ended on a cordial diplomatic note as follows: ". . . that we in the U.S. were most appreciative of the cooperation we have had from Canada in defense matters and most anxious to find solutions of our common problems which would be acceptable to Canada and practicable from our standpoint."

## Comments on Hannah's Chairmanship on His Retirement From the PJBD

### By Canadians

• *From General L. D. Wilgress, Canadian Chairman following General A. G. L. MacNaughton.*

It was with feelings of the deepest regret that I learned this week of your pending retirement from the position of Chairman of the United States Section of the Canada-United States Permanent Joint Board on Defense, a position which you have filled with distinction for the past ten years. I am sure that these feelings will be shared by all the other members of the Canadian Section of the Board, as well as by the members of the Canadian Government who have been keeping in close touch with the Board's activities.

During the long period you served on the Board, you always showed an understanding for and sympathy with the problems created for Canada through the close cooperation in defense mattes that have developed between our two countries and I would be failing in my duty if I did not extend to you our thanks and appreciation for this friendly attitude towards Canada.*

You will be able to relinquish your connection with the Board in full knowledge that you have made a major positive contribution to defense cooperation between Canada and the United States and to the overall standing of the Board. For this also, I wish to express my heartfelt thanks and appreciation.

---

*Hannah qualified under Professor T. V. Smith's definition of a diplomat who could "compromise the issues without compromising himself."

• *From Frank Miller, Air Chief Marshal (Chairman, Chiefs of Staff)*

Rather belatedly I am writing to tender the thanks of the Chiefs of Staff of the Canadian Forces and myself for your many years of outstanding service in your capacity as Co-Chairman of the Permanent Joint Board on Defense. In all our associations with the Board and yourself, the Canadian Services always felt they had in you an understanding friend and authoritative spokesman in the interests of our common defense. Some of the times during your tenure on the Board were not easy ones in which to maintain good and understanding relationships, but we now, I feel, have emerged into a climate of better understanding and I am sure that your contribution in avoiding further deterioration was a major factor during these past times. May I also say on a personal basis how much I enjoyed my association with you on the Board at the time when I served on it some years ago. I am sure that we will all miss your friendship and your wise counsel.

• *From Lester Pearson, Prime Minister of Canada*

It is with very real regret that I have learned of your resignation as Chairman of the United States Section of the Permanent Joint Board on Defense.

I well recall, from my days as Secretary of State for External Affairs, your valuable work as United States Chairman. As a Canadian, I appreciate highly the great contribution you have made, during your long tenure of that important post, to the effective collaboration between our two countries in the complex and important field of the defense of the continent we share.

## By United States Officials

• *From Admiral H. T. Johnson*

Before relinquishing my association with the Board entirely, I would like to make an observation or two of my own. I have been much impressed by the guidance that you have provided to the U.S. Section of the Board. The manner in which you have conducted yourself, the facility with which you reached the heart of an issue, your understanding of the position of our great ally, the patience you displayed on the few petty and sometimes continuing problems, the lucidity with your expounded U.S. views, and your continued readiness to suggest feasible, just solutions, to problems have all inspired by admiration . . .

I have found my association with the Canadians and with the other members and associates of the Board refreshing, educational and useful. The close association and frank exchange of opinions at the regular Board meetings led to the resolution of issues and effective action. I have never returned from a meeting without some valuable information and the satisfaction of accomplishing something on some naval issues. I am certain that the other Service representatives must quite often find that the Board is valuable to the military services quite beyond that which is necessarily a function of the Board and that which appears on the Agenda.

• *From Thomas C. Darcy, Major General, U.S. Air Force*

I want to express to you my admiration and gratitude for the effective and most understanding manner in which you have filled the role of Chairman of the U.S. Section during the period of my association with that body. I never cease to marvel at your ready grasp of all details of the many projects and at your extraordinary ability to express yourself logically and convincingly on all occasions. I have often wished that you were heading up the U.S. Delegation to our Mexican and Brazilian Commissions!

• *From Colonel David Crocker, Executive Assistant to Hannah*

Dr. Hannah, in summary, was like a patient father with the squabbles of his Major General/Rear Admiral children. A calm word, a wise decision was all that was generally needed to settle disputes. Some of this was due to Dr. Hannah's position as a Presidential appointee. Much of this was attributable to his keen intellect, rapid assimilation and analysis of any problem and truly magnificent leadership.

He inspired equal respect on the Canadian side and nurtured, through his example, similar respect by the entire U.S. side for the Canadian section. He and his Canadian counterparts ran an extremely happy ship.

• *From President Lyndon B. Johnson*

It has always been a real pleasure dealing with you during your tenure in the Pentagon. I regret your decision to leave public service at this time but can understand your desire to return to Michigan State College.

# Epilogue

The work of the PJBD was of great importance to the military security of North America and to the extension of cordial and cooperative relationships between Canada and the United States. There were many long and strenuous meetings of the Board at which important decisions were made and complex issues resolved; numerous technical papers had to be read and digested; and some tiring and enervating inspection trips were made. But one air trip taken on April 11, 1954, over the frigid regions of Canada in a Canadian DC plane to Churchill–

Resolute, Canada, was a notable exception. On this trip Hannah was accompanied by the Canadian Minister of National Defense, the United States Ambassador to Canada, General McNaughton and several other military and diplomatic notables. The lines of a reporter for the *CBC Times* caught up the humor and thrill of the experience in the following report:

> Welcome to Resolute Bay Hotel
> Reasonable rates
> In the heart of Canada's North Land
> Surrounded by miles and miles of nothing but
>     miles and miles
> The service is poor
> The climate is hell
> But you've got to stay here
> There is no other hotel
> Finest bar in civilization
> The town of Resolute pronounced Desolate
> Choice housing sites near bus and car lines
> Used dog sleds and polar bear skins for hire
>
> I have caught the sense
> Of life with high auroras and the flow
> Of wide majestic spaces;
> Of light abundant; and of keen impassioned faces;
> Transfigured underneath its vivid glow.

Hannah glows when he chats about this experience!

## Chapter III

# Civil Rights Commission (CRC) 1957–1969[1]

John Hannah was appointed Chairman of the Civil Rights Commission in January 1957 by President Eisenhower. He was appointed after Justice Reed had resigned as the initial nominee for the chairmanship to avoid possible conflict of interest in hearing cases involving alleged racial discrimination which may have come before the United States Supreme Court. President Eisenhower was well acquainted with Hannah's ability to work successfully in varied educational and governmental organizations, two of which he had appointed him to head shortly before his Chairmanship of the CRC. Hannah continued to serve as Chairman until Sept. 17, 1969 under Presidents Kennedy, Johnson and Nixon.

The legal bases for the Commission's work were the Civil Rights Act of 1957, enacted by Congress as Public Law 85-315, and more broadly the decisions of the Supreme Court regarding discriminatory practices. In pursuit of these mandatory requirements, the role of the Commission was basically fact finding and reporting such facts to the President for administrative action and for recommending remedial legislation by the Congress. The Commission thus reported both to the President and the Congress. It began operations at a time of great social unrest and conflict over the facts of discriminatory practices and ways to deal with them for domestic tranquillity and justice and for our international reputation as an enlightened democracy. The initial duration of the

45

Civil Rights Act was for two years and was supported from the President's Emergency Fund until Congress made the first appropriation of $750,000.

*Confirmation Hearings.* Hannah in testifying, on February 24, 1958, before the Judiciary Committee of the Senate, described the dimensions of the job to be done by the Commission and the motivation of Commission members in undertaking the task.

> No member of the Commission sought membership on it. I believe that my experience and attitude is typical of the reaction of each of us. When finally approached I could think of a very considerable number of reasons why I should not undertake this assignment. Upon reflection, however, it appeared clear to me that few if any problems of civil rights and compatible relationships between all the races and creeds which constitute America. We feel that this problem is important, both from the standpoint of domestic tranquillity and because of the profound effect it has with our relationships with the people of the rest of the world.

After making clear that the Commission was not charged "to deal with all facets of the problems which have developed or might develop with reference to the economic, social, religious, or other possible forms of discrimination," Hannah enumerated the specific duties of the Commission, as set forth in Section 104 of the Civil Rights Act, to:

*Investigate* the deprivations of the rights of citizens of the United States to *vote* by reason of their color, race, religion, or national origin.

*Study* and collect information relating to legal developments which constitute a *denial* of equal protection of the law under the constitution.

*Appraise* the laws and policies of the Federal government with respect to equal protection of the laws under the Constitution.

*Make* interim reports and a final report to the President and the Congress no later than two years from the date of the enactment of the law.

Hannah expressed the hope that the Commission would have the benefit of the Senators' judgment, guidance and help "to make a useful contribution to our country. It is willing to . . . do our best of which it is capable, and now submits itself to you for your consideration."

Although Senators Ervin and Eastland expressed concern that the

Federal government would be drastically revising the traditional relationship between the Federal Government and the States in the area of civil rights, all members of the Commission were confirmed in March, 1958.

*The Commissioners.* The Civil Rights Act required that the President appoint three members of a Republican persuasion or affiliation and three members having a Democratic persuasion or affiliation. The first group included the following:

*John A. Hannah,* Republican, although a registered Republican and sometimes active as an advisor to Republican Governors, Congressmen and Presidents (and on one occasion was urged to run for the Governorship of Michigan), was fully capable of functioning in a nonpartisan manner. He was well known to President Eisenhower for his achievements as President of Michigan State University and for the two major Federal organizations to which President Eisenhower had appointed him. He was 49 years of age at the time of his initial appointment.

*Robert Gerald Storey,* Democrat, was appointed as Vice Chairman. He brought a distinguised career as a lawyer who served as President of the Southwest Legal Foundation, and Dean of Southern Methodist University Law School. In the public service area he had been, among other important activities, a member of the Hoover Commission and executive trial counsel for the United States in Nuremberg trials of major Axis war criminals.

*John S. Battle,* Democrat, was a former member of the Virginia General Assembly and former Governor of the state of Virginia and a partner in a thriving law firm in Charlottesville, Virginia. He was an articulate spokesman for Southern culture and traditions. He resigned in 1959 in the belief "that he could no longer serve usefully since he was at odds with the majority of the Commissioners."

*Doyle Elam Carlton,* Democrat, was a former governor of Florida and also an able spokesman for the culture and traditions of the South. He was an ardent associate of the doctrine of "States Rights" and a minimum of Federal intrusion in these rights. He resigned in 1959 to return to his private law practice.

*Reverend Theodore M. Hesburgh* C.S.C. (Father Ted as he came to be called), was personally closest to Hannah as a consequence of their long association as presidents of major academic institutions (Michigan State and Notre Dame Universities) and because of their serving together in various academic and civic committees. Father Ted had an established record of support for and participation in liberal, civic and ethical causes and was highly motivated to effect changes in the area of civil rights. Throughout their joint tenure on the Commission Hannah and Hesburgh shared convictions, strategies and practical measures to further the work of the Commission. Hesburgh considered himself a political independent, although from the viewpoint of the statutory formula for an equal representation of Democrats and Republicans, he was considered a Republican. At the age of 42 years, he was the youngest Commissioner.

*J. Ernest Wilkins,* Republican, was the first Negro member of the Commission. He was considered a "moderate" on civil rights issues but certainly not an "Uncle Tom." He saw his role as a spokesman for his race but was not militant in his manner. He came to the Commission from a major position in the Department of Labor but his tenure was brief due to his death in January 1959.

*George Marion Johnson,* Republican, succeeded J. Ernest Wilkins after serving as Director of the Office of Laws, Plans and Research for the Civil Rights Commission. He came to the Commission from the position of professor and Dean of the Howard Law School. He had earlier served as Assistant Executive Secretary of the President's Committee on Fair Employment Practices. He became a close associate of Chairman Hannah. He resigned from the Commission to join Michigan State University as Professor of Education and key member of the faculty of the University of Nigeria which was established with the assistance of Michigan State University. He was a dignified and scholarly advocate of civil rights.

The above list constituted the first group of Commissioners under Hannah's leadership. Other Commissioners with distinguished records who were appointed to succeed the first group (Hannah and Hesburgh remaining) changed the composition of the Commission to a more homogeneous body and less given to regional or partisan advocacy but not less interested in advancement of civil rights. These Commissioners included:

*Spottswood Robinson III,* like Johnson, whom he replaced on the Commission in 1961, was also a former Dean of the Howard University Law School. His appointment was criticized as a successor to Johnson by Senator Eastland and other Southern Senators, but confirmed on a split vote of the Judiciary Committee. He served as a Commissioner for two years and resigned to take an appointment as a Federal judge.

*Robert Rankin* came to the Commission from Duke University, where he was a professor of political science. He had earlier served as an advisor to the Commission in the preparation of the 1959 Report of the Commission. Although a Southerner and a Democrat he was much more moderate in the espousal of civil rights than John Battle and Doyle Carlton. He was criticized in the confirmation hearings by Senators Ellender and Eastland for being too much influenced by Chairman Hannah. Nevertheless, he was confirmed on a split vote of the Judiciary Committee. He resigned in 1962.

*Erwin N. Griswold* was a distinguished lawyer and former Dean of the Harvard Law School who served as a Commissioner from 1961–1967 before becoming Solicitor General of the United States in the Department of Justice. Among other contributions to the work of the Commission he stoutly defended Commission actions on contested hearings in Alabama and Mississippi.

*Eugene Patterson* was the first newsman to become a Commissioner, in 1964, from a distinguished career as the Executive Editor of the Atlanta Journal and Constitution, Editor of the Atlantic Constitution, and Managing Editor of the Washington Post before returning to the southland as President and Editor of the St. Petersburg Times. He won a Pulitzer Prize for his editorials and served as President of the American Society of Newspaper Editors.

*Frankie M. Freeman* was the first woman to serve as a Commissioner, joining in the latter years of Hannah's chairmanship. She was trained as a lawyer at Howard University and Hampton Institute. She worked in several agencies of the Federal government before serving as Associate General Counsel of the St. Louis Housing and Land Clearance Authority. She was active in housing, redevelopment, League of Women Votes, National Council of Negro Women and other civic organizations before and after becoming a Commissioner.

Throughout the tenure of Hannah's chairmanship, the Commission had gained sufficient stature under his leadership, and with the cooperation of three Presidents and the Judiciary Committee of the Senate, to attract persons with distinguished backgrounds and belief in the work of the Commission to serve essentially without compensation.

## Interpersonal Relations and Early Operations of the Commission: Congressional and Commission Hearings[2]

As can be seen from the above, except for previous association of John Hannah and Father Hesburgh, the first Commissioners were essentially strangers to each other, coming to their tasks from widely different backgrounds and orientations to civil rights issues. These divergences were conspicuously apparent from the testimony given in the first meeting of the Judiciary Committee of the Senate which was responsible for passing on their appointments.

Hannah was thus confronted, from the first day, with the challenge to weld the Commission into an effective working body to administer the policies and programs for civil rights set forth in the Act, instead of a "debating society" on the issues. He testified to the Judiciary Committee that an attempt would be made to reach consensus on basic issues but failing that, he assured the committee that the viewpoints of those who differed from the majority would be fully reflected in the reports to the President and the Congress.

Some of the questions raised by the Senators and the responses of the Commissioners follow. For example, John Battle, in responding to Senator Ervin's question "Did anyone ask your views before accepting this appointment," said that a Presidential assistant who interviewed him said that "the President was anxious to have a commission reflecting various views from various sections of the country and he felt that it might be helpful if there was some member of the Commission who had . . . the strong Southern views which I entertain." In response to a series of questions by Senator Ervin to Governor Carlton which were focused on the legal possibility of extending the protections of the 14th Amendment of the Constitution to "mob" action (as in the Little Rock confrontation of Negroes* wanting to enroll in an all white school), Carlton responded ". . . Certainly not." In contrast, to the same line of questioning of Ernest Wilkins, Wilkins responded as a lawyer ". . . Of course, I would have to have all the facts before I hand down a decision in any kind of case. . . ." As the dialogue progressed on the fear that Senator Ervin had ". . . of complete subordination of the activities of the state to the Federal government,"Wilkins responded, "I think I would say, in the civil rights field, I suppose you would find as many opinions as you find individuals."

With reference to Senator Ervin's question of Father Hesburgh's views of and beliefs about racial integration, he responded ". . . I think I would say that I believe that the Constitution says, that all people are created with equal rights under the Constitution and the law."

Senator Ervin, after Hannah had summarized the duties of the Commission, as set forth in Section 104 of the Act, said to Hannah: "I

---

*See Page xx of the Preface for an explanation of the use of Negro/Negroes/Negro Americans in this chapter.

am concerned with State and Federal relations very much and I think it is exceedingly important for you to do what you can to preserve the proper relations and to say further as I have said before, I think you all have about the most tremendous responsibility I have ever seen imposed on the shoulders of six men.'' To this challenge Hannah responded modestly but firmly. "We recognize the seriousness of the responsibility, and there is a sincere desire on the part of each member of the Commission to do the best we can to discharge this responsibility and be good for the country.'' Hannah was also asked to respond to the following five searching questions:

(1) "Does the Commission have the authority to investigate Little Rock occurrences?"
(2) "How many staff would you need?"
(3) Question regarding relationship with the Justice Department.
(4) "Are you subject to instructions from some high authority now as a member of the Commission, or as the Chairman?"
(5)"Will the Commission use itself as an investigating body for the benefit of the Justice Department under certain circumstances?" (Since the Justice Department lacks the subpoena power of great investigatory importance and the Commission has such power).

To which Hannah responded:

(1)"This is not our field.''
(2) "The quantity and quality (of staff) would wait until we have a Staff Director confirmed and on the job.''
(3) "It is my understanding that we were to operate completely separated from the Justice Department. It is our feeling that we have no interlocking responsibility at all.''
(4) "No sir.''
(5) "Not being quite as quick, possibly, as I should have been, I called Mr. Rogers, the Attorney General, to ask if he had any suggestions and his quick response was that it would be a serious mistake if there was any relationship between the Attorney General's office and the Commission. Assured that he probably was right, I didn't go any further.'' . . . "It is my feeling that we should use the subpoena power to gain the information to carry out our responsibilities but not be used to gain information for any other agency of the government.''

The basis for Hannah's reflection of the views of the whole Commission on the broad framework of responsibility derived from frank discussions which the Commission had in meetings before the confirmation hearings.

Subsequent meetings of the Senate Judiciary Committee on the confirmation of the other Commissioners, Johnson, Robinson, Rankin, Griswold, Patterson and Freeman brought out other aspects of policy and pesonal viewpoints of prospective Commissioners, but all of them were less important in setting the broad framework of policy and relationship than were the hearings on the first group of Commissioners.

All of the Commissioners, appointed by the several Presidents while Hannah was Chairman, were confirmed by the Senate.

### Internal Management of the Civil Rights Commission

Hannah as Chairman of the Commission was treated as the head of a Federal agency, reporting directly to the President. In leading and managing the Commission, Hannah recognized the necessity of having a highly competent, racially unbiased staff, especially for the following considerations:

• The part time nature of his, and the other Commissioners' appointments which meant that the burden of the work would consequently have to be done by the staff with a minimum of detailed supervision. Delegation to the staff for the bulk of the operations would leave the Commission to be concerned primarily with top-policy matters, key relationships with the President, members of Congress, the press and with concerned outside bodies and for the collective responsibility for final review of staff reports and draft recommendations to the President and the Congress. The Chairman would be primarily concerned with orchestrating the whole discussion and decision making process.

• Because the essential work of the Commission involved an understanding of the legal provisions of the civil rights laws, but not enforcement thereof, professional liaison with the Department of Justice and with members of Congress, most of whom were lawyers, was required. The Staff Director and key members of the staff would accordingly need to be highly trained as lawyers. This situation was also recognized in the enabling act making the Staff Director an appointee of the President, with the consent of the Senate, at a salary of $22,500.

• Because the Commission was an advisory body to the President and the Congress, the extent to which their advisory assistance was unanimous, or nearly so, substantially lessened the danger that partisan responses would be made to the recommendations of the Commission. This required a large measure of concern with the *facts* on the part of the staff in preparing draft reports and recommendations for Commission review. Since the six members of the Commission were associated with both major political parties and from the North and the South doubly underlined the necessity for factual treatment of the data produced in the surveys, testimony at hearings and other sources of information which constituted the substance supporting the Commission's recommendations. As Chairman, Hannah had the critical position of guiding the policies for the processes of data collection, interpretation and review to achieve the maximum possible unanimity. Sloppy staff work would have made it impossible to achieve this goal, and Hannah's job nearly impossible to perform. Accordingly Hannah, in leading the Commission's deliberations, with reference to the nomination of the several Staff Directors to the President and in separate personal discussions with the several Presidents under whom he worked, maintained the position that the Staff Director was to be a merit appointment, free from partisan political considerations. Furthermore, he dignified the occupants of the Staff Director position by involving them directly in meetings in the White House, attendance at all Commission meetings, preparing detailed testimony for Congressional hearings on the budget, and other important actions. The Commission approved Hannah's recommendation that the Staff Director be delegated responsibility to recruit and nominate all other major staff positions and to personally appoint all other positions. As a matter of policy, all appointments to the staff were on a merit basis and all Staff Directors, after the first, were promoted from within the organization.

Informational flow to the members of the Commission and staff from outside sources, and from within the Commission was important for the coordination of the Commission's operations and for keeping Commissioners and staff aware of what was happening on civil rights issues throughout the country as revealed in the media and elsewhere.

Of major importance, for informational purposes, was circulation of draft copies of Commission reports and recommendations. The review of these reports, which were required by statute, and of numerous other reports, constituted the bulk of Commission discussions and work load. A review of these reports indicated that Hannah examined draft reports with great care, as the other Commissioners were urged

to do. He eliminated unnecessary provocative phrases, thus letting the
facts speak for themselves.

Hannah presided over almost all of the more than a hundred meetings of the Commission, most of which were held on Saturdays and
weekends, unless he was required to be at critical University functions
or out of the country on University business. Most Commission
meetings were held in Washington but meetings were also held at about
ten other key locations.

The Chairman and each of the Commissioners were paid $50.00 for
each day they attended meetings and hearings (rate raised to $75.00)
plus $12.00 per diem living and travel expenses. The records of days
worked and total compensation received was made a matter of record
in the appropriation hearings of the House of Representatives. It is
quite apparent the financial remuneration to the Commissioners was of
little or no incentive. Furthermore, distinguished members of the State
Advisory Committees volunteered their services and oten did not even
request travel or living expenses.

The Board of Trustees of Michigan State Univesity approved his
being away from the University as necessary to act as Chairman of the
Commission and expressed pride, as did Governor Williams,* in his
important contribution to the national welfare. He maintained close
touch with Trustees and other University officials, to whom he delegated considerable responsibility. He also attended or presided at all
important University events which required his participation.


### Preparation for the First Report of the Commission (1959)

Almost ten months elapsed before the time the Commissiones were
appointed and confirmed and the time they were required to make a
report on facts regarding the status of civil rights and on recommendations to the President and the Congress for improvement in civil
rights. Naturally some of this time was spent in getting established as
a new and controvesial federal agency. More importantly, considerable
time was taken in getting thoroughly acquainted with each other and
with their duties and obligations as set forth in the Civil Rights Act of
1957. They also spent time to define and to secure consensus on
objective fact-finding procedures which they would follow in the conduct of their work. The Commissioners and their legal assistants (each

---

*Interview with Governor G. Mennen Williams

one had an assistant of his own choice) also spent considerable time in establishing, selecting and recruiting the members of State Advisory Committees made up of leading citizens from varying professional, racial and community service backgrounds. All members of such committees had to be approved by the whole Commission to assure objectivity and representativeness of all interested groups. Furthermore, through depth analyses and discussions, the Commission had to determine priorities for their efforts. Voting rights, education and housing were selected as priority targets.

But the most significant factor in the delay of getting started on their first priority was in getting bona-fida sworn affidavits of denials of voting rights. These were necessary before the Commission could send out members of the staff to make field investigations to verify such complaints. Harris Wofford, who served as legal assistant to Commissioner Hesburgh, describes the somewhat humorous but tense situation as follows:

> One morning in August, we laughed when an envelope came from a "Professor Bashful." Even when we found that the document inside alleged denials of the right to vote and that it was notarized, we still suspected someone was putting us on. Emmet J. Bashful's affidavit was too good to be true. But when a telephone check found that yes, there was a Professor Bashful, we jumped with delight. Within a week, after assembling all the information we could, we presented Professor Bashful's complaint to the Commission. It was a broad charge, alleging "that through threats of bodily harm and losing of jobs, and other means, Negro residents of Gadsden County, Florida, are being deprived of the right to vote." Some of the Commissioners were understandably troubled that the professor did not claim that he himself was being denied the right to vote. Nevertheless, even though it was not quite the kind of complaint Congress had in mind, the Commission decided by a unanimous vote to conduct an immediate field investigation. News of the Commission's action surprised and encouraged Negro leadership, and soon other complaints, in better order, started coming from Alabama, and then from Louisiana and Mississippi.
>
> At first it was difficult for Commission investigators (almost all of them white) even to locate the negro complainants. Professor Bashful was neither intimidated nor bashful, but others who had tried to register and been turned down were suspicious of unknown white men, and would often give no information. Investigators had to explain their purpose and prove their identification before doors would open. A smile finally started spreading over the face of an old Alabama Negro woman, who had been rocking silently on her porch while the Commission agent tried to con-

vince her he was there to help. With wide eyes, she finally said, "You mean the Big Government has come? The Big Government has really come all the way down here to help us! The Big Government is finally going to do something to let me vote?" It was the first time in sixty years, she said, that the federal government had shown any interest in the colored people of Alabama.

The impact of the Commission's prompt response—of its investigators appearing on the site, respectfully interviewing complainants, diligently seeking other witnesses, and persistently questioning local registrars and asking for their records—was profound.

. . . Encouraged by the Commission's action and urged on by Martin King in Montgomery, more and more Negroes in the Black Belt counties of Alabama and other Southern states began submitting detailed sworn allegations that indicated a widespread pattern of restricting registration to whites. In the next months complaints came in from twenty-nine counties in eight states. In fifteen of these counties, including five in Alabama, Negroes constituted a majority of the population but only a relatively small number (or none) were registered.[3]

Thus the state was set for a series of hearings on voting rights, education and housing, which provided hard data for the preparation of the first report of the Commission. The first of such hearings was in Montgomery, Alabama.

Even before the hearing was called to order, however, a civil rights problem arose with reference to accommodations for Commissioner Wilkins and black members of the staff. Father "Ted" Hesburgh, who had come to Montgomery a few days early, reported the situation and how Hannah solved the problem.

Characteristically, John wrote all of the large hotels there requesting reservations and indicating that we had both a black on the Commission and blacks on our staff. He had word back from all the hotels that they couldn't possibly accommodate a mixed group and John said, "not to worry," we'll just stay at the Montgomery Air University since both he and I were well acquainted with the General in charge there. He made the request of the General and we received a letter back from him saying that we couldn't stay at the BOQ (Bachelors Officer's Quarters) because the Major in charge of public relations had assured him that no one in that area would possibly understand a mixed group staying in the BOQ . . .

Again quite calmly, John said "not to worry, I'll just take the request to the Secretary of the Air Force," who was a friend of his. The Secretary of the Air Force replied that he had to follow the judgment of the base commander. Again John was relaxed and said, "don't worry, I'll go to Charlie Wilson," (Engine Charlie, as he was known, former president of

General Motors) who was a good friend of John's and mine too. Again the Secretary of Defense, Mr. Wilson, wrote John saying that because of the judgment of the base commander and the Secretary of the Air Force, he didn't feel he should reverse their decision. I guess they thought we'd have to stay in tents on the main town square.

At that point, John really got angry. He called up President Eisenhower directly and said, "Mr. President, you gave us a very tough job to do and when we begin to do it, we can't find a place to live. Perhaps that's typical of the problem we're facing . . ." When he described the situation and the previous correspondence to the President, Ike had one of his typical flairs of temper. President Eisenhower was not a flaming liberal, or an outspoken advocate of civil rights, but he knew basic injustice when he saw it. The upshot was that we were able to stay at the BOQ simply because we had an executive order from the President of the United States. That is perhaps the best indication of the state of civil rights in the south of the year 1958.[4]

John Hannah opened the hearings in his customary calm manner, to set the tone of the hearing, before a packed house of emotion-charged citizens and officials in the Federal court house in Montgomery. Commissioners Battle, Carlton, Wilkins, Hesburg and Storey were present. In his opening remarks Hannah informed the audience of the legal obligations of the Civil Rights Commission to investigate "allegations in writing or under affirmation that certain citizens are deprived of their rights to vote . . . by reason of their color, race, religion, or national origin." *Prosecutions, indictments* or other forms of law *enforcement,* however, were beyond the power of the Commission.* He further said that (1) the emphasis of the Commission and its staff is on objectivity, and as the Commission views it, objectivity presupposes getting *all* of the facts; (2) the Commission does not consider itself a *protagonist* for one view or another; (3) the Commission was established in the hope that through dispassionate evaluation and appraisal of the facts that some sort of *reason* and *light* could be brought to bear upon *problems of national importance* which have been frequently and passionately *debated* but *seldom* soberly assessed; (4) the Commission was keenly aware of the forward strides which had been taken throughout the South in recent years in admitting Negroes to exercise of the voting franchise; (5) the location of the hearing in Alabama was not to "*single* out the *state of Alabama* for criticism or censure" but the largest number of *valid voting complaints* had come

---

* All italicized matter was underlined in the original Hannah notes to indicate the importance which he attached to the points.

from Alabama. He then introduced Storey, as the Vice-Chairman of the Commission, a distinguished attorney, and former Dean of the Law School of the Southern Methodist University in Dallas, Texas, to preside at the hearing. The unanimous choice of Storey, a lawyer and Southerner, was clearly a strategical choice of the Commission to avoid a confrontational atmosphere.

Storey reaffirmed Hannah's emphasis on ascertaining the facts about an "issue that is vital to every American citizen" by a non-partisan body appointed by the President of the United States. He then went on to personalize the difficult assignment, which neither he or the other Commissioners sought to undertake, in these poignant words:

> This is a difficult assignment, at least for me, because it is raising fundamental questions about the political processes of my own region. My father was born and educated in Alabama. I have close relatives and good friends in this state. My grandfathers were Confederate soldiers, so there are many thoughts and memories going through my mind as we meet in Montgomery, the cradle of the Confederacy. But history moves on, we are one nation now. Hence, this bi-partisan Commission composed of two Presidents of great universities and four lawyers have a solemn duty to perform. We are sworn to uphold the Constitution of the United States. Our sole purpose is to find the facts. . . . As the President said when the Commission was created, these problems of civil rights can only be solved by understanding and reason. Similarly, the Democratic leader of the Senate, Lyndon Johnson of my state, indicated that the Commission can gather facts instead of charges; it can sift out the truth from the fancies; and it can return the recommendations which will be of assistance to reasonable men. It is in this spirit that we are here.

Storey then detailed the procedures under which the hearings would be conducted: (1) "constitutional rights of the witnesses will be protected . . ;" (2) witnesses . . . "may be accompanied by their own counsel" but not in any sense "an adversary proceeding;" (3) complaining parties who have submitted sworn statements will be called first; followed by appropriate public official; (4) all testimony will be under oath; (5) "a transcript of the testimony of all witnesses will be made," and made available for inspection. He then called upon the first of witnesses who had been deprived of "their right to vote and to have that vote counted by reason of their color, race, religion or national origin."

In spite of the calm and objective spirit which Hannah attempted to create and the orderly procedures set forth by Storey, the hearing became quite disorderly and confrontational, especially in the afternoon when judges and registrars either refused to testify or pled the Fifth Amendment (self-incrimination) possibilities as members of the Commission probed their responses to allegations of citizens who had been refused the right to vote, some of whom were from the county in which Tuskegee Institute was located, and had Ph.D. degrees or other professional credentials. Some Alabama county officials professed ignorance of the laws under which they were operating and were not able or willing to provide registration figures. Two registrars not only withheld voting records but indicated that they had been impounded that very morning by the State Circuit Court. The Commission then queried several probate judges, one of whom admitted that of the fourteen thousand Negroes in one county, not a single one was registered. The refusal of the Alabama officials to cooperate with the Commission's effort to get the facts set off a volley of criticism from even Southern newspapers, which, although not entirely favorable to the creation of the Civil Rights Commission, were highly critical of the cover-up behavior of Alabama officials. Hannah intervened in the hearings to announce that the Commission had decided to turn over the complete hearings to the Attorney General for such action as he deemed appropriate to help the Commission receive the records necessary to perform its duties under the law. Although the Attorney General took action on the Commission's request, the Alabama legislature passed a bill which authorized the destruction of all rejected voting applications. The controversy was continued in Louisiana which will be described in the next section. The whole show of defiance infuriated President Eisenhower who described the actions as "reprehensible."

But the bombshell, as a Montgomery newspaper reported in an editorial on Dec. 9, 1958, came at the end of the afternoon session when Commissioner Battle, a former governor of Virginia, read a highly personal and emotional statement:

> Mr. Chairman and ladies and gentlemen, like Dean Storey, I have come to the state of my ancestors. My father was proud to be an Alabamian. My grandfather, Cullen A. Battle, was my constant companion during my boyhood days and, in the War between the States, the commanding officer of a brigade of Alabama troops which was honored by a resolution of the Confederate Congress, thanking the Alabama officers and Alabama men for their services to the Confederacy.
>
> My grandfather was subsequently denied his seat in Congress, to which the people of Alabama had elected him, because he had served the Confederate cause.

So I come to the people of Alabama as a friend—I think I may be permitted to say—returning to the house of my father, and none of you white citizens and officials of Alabama believe more strongly than I do in the segregation of the races as the right and proper way of life in the South. It is, in my judgment, the only way in which racial integrity can be preserved and thus prove beneficial to both races.

It is from this background, ladies and gentlemen, that I am constrained to say, in all friendliness, that I fear the officials of Alabama and certain of its counties have made an error in doing that which appears to be an attempt to cover up their actions in relation to the exercise of the ballot by some people who may be entitled thereto.

The majority of the members of the next Congress will not be sympathetic to the South, and punitive legislation may be passed, and this hearing may be used in advocacy of that legislation, which will react adversely to us in Virginia and to you in Alabama.

Of course, it is not up to me, nor would I presume to suggest how any counsel or any official should govern himself; but we are adjourning this hearing until tomorrow morning, and may I say to you, as one who is tremendously interested in the southern cause: Will you kindly reevaluate the situation and see if there is not some way you, in fairness to your convictions, to the officials, may cooperate a little bit more fully with this Commission and not have it said by our enemies in Congress that the people of Alabama were not willing to explain their conduct when requested to do so.

The deliberations of the Commission, some legislative actions, and public reactions, as reflected in newspaper editorials which followed the Alabama hearing, influenced the Commissioners in preparing their first (1959) report to the President and the Congress. The other hearings are described in the following.

*Hearings on Education and Housing.* Before conducting hearings on discriminatory practices in education and housing the Commission gave careful consideration to how best to deal with these two areas which were critical to the preparation of their first report. They concluded, as a matter of policy, that the hearings format was highly useful. Not only did this policy broaden the areas in which segregation was practiced but it took the "monkey off the backs" of the south (for voting rights) and demonstrated vividly that other sections of the country had probems in civil rights which the Commission had to address. More specifically, whereas "Dixie" was very vulnerable on voting rights, the areas of segregated education and housing pretty much involved the whole country, particularly the large cities. Furthermore, as the factual evidence of segregation was documented, a close connection, or relationship, developed between education and housing, as was more fully developed later when the Commission delved more deeply into the relationship of employment opportunities and the administration of justice to aspects of civil rights. The policy adopted by the Commission to include education and housing in the first 1959 report had the further value of demonstrating to the President, the Congress, and the general public that the country was faced with a bigger and more general problem than may have been known, but not seriously recognized except by vigilant civil rights activists and especially concerned citizens.

The Nashville, Tennessee hearing, held on March 5 and 6, 1959, focused on the policies and practices of 700 school districts in 13 states which had already taken some steps to integrate. The discussions were based on well documented cases, in 17 cities, towns and rural communities in Kansas, Washington, Maryland, Delaware, Tennessee and Oklahoma. These cases were drawn from 8692 school systems, less than 1000 of which, in 1959, were desegregated. School officials, Board members, principals and superintendents participated in the hearings focused on problems and constructive methods of accelerating the "deliberate speed" for integration of schools mandated by the Supreme Court. The Commission was very pleased with the cooperation which they received in this and other hearings on education and in the subsequent results, which were incorporated in the 1959 report.

In New York, Chicago and Atlanta, the Commission sponsored hearings on housing in February, April, and May of 1959. These were comprehensive in scope and depth of factual analyses of problems of segregation, particularly in the urban ghettos of these cities. Father Hesburgh took special responsibility for chairing these hearings on behalf of the Commission. Participants included state and city officials, officers of many quasi-public organizations, representatives from the Urban League and NAACP, real estate boards, banks and savings and loan associations. This mix of the principal governmental, business, civil rights and other civic organizations brought out all of the critical problems and some of the relatively few constructive measures which were being taken to alleviate some of the worst problems.

The experience of Atlanta in providing good housing for Negroes who could afford to escape slums and ghettos especially attracted Hannah's attention. He started a dialogue with a Mr. Williamson, President of the Negro Real Estate Board, who did not see, as Hannah did, that the Atlanta experiment was a constructive step in resolving the housing problem for Negroes who could afford to escape the restrictions of the ghetto. Vice President Storey took up the argument with Williamson, which got so heated that "Hannah intervened to pour a little oil on these troubled waters." The questioning was leading down a road which the Commission did not want to travel; discrimination in housing was an important issue . . . but, in Hannah's view, what was described as existing in Atlanta's represented "a better situation than prevailed in many northern cities." Hannah's comments had the effect of avoiding further confrontation and the hearing continued on a calmer note.

These hearings on housing and the field investigations conducted by the staff provided material for the 1959 report and to a degree stimulated President Kennedy to issue, in 1962, a limited executive order barring discrimination in federally assisted housing.

*Shreveport Hearing on Voting Rights.* The Louisiana hearing in Shreveport on July 13, 1959, provided a new factor in restrictions on voting rights which was uncovered in a document of instructions to registrars, police jurors and citizen councils which read: "We are in a life and death struggle with the Communists and the NAACP to preserve the liberties of our people." This overt denial of rights, rather than the more abstract factor of apathy, became the principal focus of Commission concern and provided another incident in which Hannah demonstrated his capacity for leadership and determination to get on with the job in spite of unforeseen hurdles. Hesburgh describes the situation as follows as he arrived in Shreveport the day before the hearings were to begin:

> As I checked into the BOQ at the SAC (Strategic Air Command) air base there, I was given a summons by the Federal Marshall. It was an injunction from the local judge, Ben Dawkins, enjoining us from holding a hearing in Shreveport, because he declared that the Commission was unconstitutional and, therefore, had no rights to hold a hearing . . . Again John brought order out of chaos. He immediately arranged to have Judge Dawkins' opinion and judgment tried in Federal Court. I believe it was one of the quickest trials that went all the way through the system to the Supreme Court. The three judge court subsequently held in our favor, I believe the judgment being two to one, and then the Supreme Court unanimously upheld the constitutionality of our Commission . . . John Hannah will be in legal history since his name is one of the names appearing on the title of that case (Hannah vs. Lauche). In a way, Judge

Dawkins did as a favor because now there could be no doubt about the fact that we were doing what the Congress had asked us to do.*

In addition to its own investigations and hearings, the Commissioners were aware of the "yeast" that was working in the area of civil rights before they took office. These included the sit-ins, freedom marches, the march on Washington and the confrontations in Selma and Watts. Closer to the date when the Commission was established was the Little Rock incident when Governor Faubus of Arkansas challenged the Eisenhower administration over the enforcement of a court ruling that called for integration of the all white high school in Little Rock. This incident not only challenged the power of the central government to enforce school desegregation but it shook the conscience of the country and our prestige in the world. It also finally established the policy of the Commission not to be engaged in enforcement activities.

*Other Information Available to the Commission.* In addition to sources of information available to the Commissioners from reports on field investigations made by the staff, frequent reports of complaints were also received and classified by states according to types of complaints, voting rights, administration of justice etc. Informal conferences, letters, news stories and editorials from a score or more of representative newspapers from all over the country were clipped, classified and circulated to the Commissioners. The Montgomery hearings precipitated numerous accounts and editorials focused on issues which surfaced in the hearings, especially Governor Battle's dramatic soul-searching testimony over refusal of the Alabama officials to make registration records available to the Commission. Some noted, however, the unanimous decision of the Commission to call upon the U.S. Attorney General to resolve the issue even though the Governor elect of Alabama, Mr. Patterson, and other officials had vociferously challenged the Commission's action. The *Birmingham Herald,* on the other hand, gave considerable space to Hannah's opening statement. The *New York times* and the *Detroit News,* among other northern papers, also reported the news.

All of the information available to the Commissioners set the stage for the July 11–15, 1959 meeting of the Commission, arranged by Father Hesburgh at the Notre Dame University Land-O-Lakes resort facility in Wisconsin, when the final decisions on draft recommendations were finally reviewed before publication. These draft recommendations had been gone over very carefully at earlier meetings of the

---

*Hesburgh, see Note 4, page 248.

Commission, with vigorous debate on the substance as well as the language of some of them. There might have been more dissension and confusion over the texts, in Father Hesburgh's judgment, presumably shared by his colleagues on the Commission, if it hadn't been for Hannah's especially close review of the language used by the staff in the several drafts. Hesburgh's words:

> Our staff was very enthusiastic and tended to write in a rather florid fashion using many adjectives and verbs. John would take the red pencil to all of those extravagant words and I can still hear him saying to the staff, "You don't have to say that the situation is outrageously unjust. It's enough to say that it's unjust and back it up with the facts. Outrageously just leaves us open to argument. We want to lay out the facts clearly and to draw conclusions from them and then the recommended legislation will be rather obvious. We ought to do this without getting ourselves in a big argument about the meaning of outrageous." This was just another indication of his good common sense, his sense of fairness, and to get the job done when it seemed impossible.[5]

### The 1959 Report:* With Liberty and Justice for all[6]

The 1959 report of the Commission was submitted formally to the President and the Congress on September 9, 1959 and signed by all members of the Commission. The report was officially submitted to the Congress exactly two years after the establishment of the Commission as promised by Hannah even though several months had elapsed since their nomination by the President on November 7, 1957. The meeting of this extremely exacting statutory deadline was a tribute to the dedicated commissioners and the staff and to Hannah's leadership. An informal session of the Commission with President Eisenhower was held in September 1959 to alert him to the character of the forthcoming recommendations. After a relaxed presentation, Hesburgh quoted him as saying, "I never expected you gentlemen to agree to anything and here you've come up with (a) practically unanimous report and a very tough one too."

Apparently some time was spent in fishing and socialization before

---

*Because of the critical importance of this first report of the Commission in establishing its reputation for objective reporting of the facts about discriminatory practices in voting, housing and education, and the temperate, but firm, recommendations to the President and the Congress for remedial measures, a more complete digest of the 1959 report is included than of subsequent reports.

a final long-night meeting of the Commission laid the report to rest, with nearly unanimous agreement on the principal recommendations. Hesburgh recalls that there were 12 recommendations, 11 of which were passed unanimously. But one on education was objected to by the former governor of Virginia for being "too sociological." Hesburgh went on to say that: "I recall at breakfast the next morning the southerners looked at each other and said, 'we were had last night,' but the Governor of Virginia said, 'Yes, we were had, but we agreed and will be gentlemen about it.' Perhaps it is one of the best testimonies to John Hannah's leadership. . . ."

The text of the transmittal letter included these relatively modest words of evaluation: "We believe that this report, along with the separately printed record of hearings held by the Commission, will provide information of permanent value to the executive and legislative branches of the government. . . ."

The introductory comments reiterated the basis for which the Commission was created, at the request of President Eisenhower for a "full-scale public study," the first since Congress passed its first bill on civil rights since 1875. Supporting statements by the Attorney General, Herbert Brownell Jr., the House Judiciary Committee and the majority leader of the Senate, Lyndon Johnson, were included. The investigatory and advisory functions of the Commission were spelled out with the clear mandate that it "was not to be a Commission for the enforcement of civil rights." It was granted authority, however, to issue subpoenas and seek enforcement thereof in connection with its fact finding investigations but enforcement powers would remain in the Department of Justice.

Recognition was given for the reports of the State Advisory Committees on the conditions of civil rights in their respective states, and to other sources of background information of value to the Commission's deliberations.

With reference to the degree of consensus reached by the Commissioners on each of the complex and thorny issues before it, the following passage in the report is of interest on this point:

> In asking men of different backgrounds and of different regions of the country to serve as Commissioners, the President could not have expected unanimity. Very substantial agreement has been reached on most of the fundamental facts and problems. The disagreement is about how best to remedy the denials of the right to vote and the equal protection of the laws under the Constitution which the Commission has found to exist. The differences are not surprising. Problems of racial injustice have been

present in varying forms since the birth of the nation. . . . But no way has yet been found, although many measures have been tried. . . . The Civil War and Reconstruction did not accomplish the task.

So it is still necessary for men to reason together about these questions and to continue to search for the answers. This the Commission has tried to do. Because reasonable men differ on the best remedial measures, it was agreed that the Commissioners should express their disagreements whenever deemed important, either in footnotes or in supplementary statements.

Recommendations on voting, education and housing were made by unanimous or majority Commission action. These are followed by "proposals which are recommendations made by fewer than a majority of the Commission, and these in turn are followed by "separate statements" or "supplementary statements" of disagreement, of explanation or of additional views, signed by one or more Commissioners. Individual general statements appear at the end of the Report[7]

The section on *"Constitutional Background of Civil Rights"* began with a lucid, philosophical, and historically-based recital of pertinent material to answer the first question which was asked by the Commission itself: "What are civil rights in the United States?" References were made to the so-called Civil Rights Amendments which were added to the Constitution after 1865 and the Bill of Rights of 1791 which required the Commission to review more than the opinions of the Supreme Court. The framers of the Declaration of Independence of 1776, which first enunciated the "principle that all men are created equal," believed that the principles of the Declaration were established by the "Laws of Nature and of Nature's God." These principles further asserted that all men are endowed by the creator with certain unalienable rights and that among them were "life, liberty and the pursuit of happiness;" that to secure these rights "governments are instituted among men, deriving their just powers from the consent of the governed. . . ." The gap between the great American promises of equal opportunity and equal justice under the law and the inadequate fulfillment of these promises, created a continuing problem of how to narrow the gap. The conflict of opinions which ensued focused on this problem and tended to provide those who would expand the areas of civil liberties from those who would limit such areas. This conflict, in effect, is what the 1958 Commission on Civil Rights was caught up in. The *Federalist Papers* were cited as a principal source of documentation of these debates. The civil rights provisions of the Magna Carta (13th Century) in which King John promisied that "cities, boroughs, and towns were not only promised their liberties but that no one will sell, deny or delay rights or justices," were mentioned.

The Commission cited the fact that the Founding Fathers provided, in addition to the guarantee by the United States, that every state in the Union would have a Republican form of government which would prescribe the manner of elections of Senators and Representatives, and that Congress may at any time make or alter such regulations. The Bill of Rights set forth certain rights, but only in terms of limiting the powers of the Federal government. Thus the states were continually free to limit voting rights of Negroes, women, and others. This provision seriously distressed Jefferson but he approved it on the ground "that half a loaf is better than no bread." Bringing the record up to the time of the Civil War, the Commission noted that only "once has the American constitutional process failed" in the Dred Scott decision which stated that "Negroes were not people of the United States." The emancipation of the slaves created a new body of citizens whose rights were still to be defined and realized.

Continuing the background factors which guided the Commission's framework for their task, the Commission summarized the 13th, 14th and 15th Amendments to the Constitution as follows:

> The Thirteenth Amendment abolished slavery, the Fourteenth Amendment made the freed Negroes citizens of the United States and the states wherein they reside and promised them the equal protection of the laws, and the Fifteenth Amendment provided that the right to vote shall not be denied or abridged on account of race, color or previous conditions of servitude.[8]

But these monumental amendments, left unadministered, left "some four million human beings . . . who had known nothing but slavery, who had almost no education or training for citizenship, suddenly turned into the mainstream of America life as free men and women." Congress passed civil rights laws in 1866, 1870 and 1875 which they assumed would put some teeth in the 14th and 15th Amendments but the Supreme Court held the provisions in the 1875 Civil Rights Act to be unconstitutional. As a final high water mark of judicial restrictions of the 14th Amendment, the Court articulated the doctrine of "separate but equal," which stood as judicial gospel until Brown vs. Board of Education in 1954. Furthermore, Jim Crow laws and customs proliferated even after Reconstruction had essentially ended, with legal support of the Supreme Court's sanction for segregation. The South interpreted this constitutional framework for civil rights by maintaining segregated schools and northern cities to which Negroes migrated to find better paying jobs, created slums or ghettos.

In summary of the agonizing appraisal of the history of U.S. efforts to deal with the civil rights problem which occupied the attention of the Commission in guiding them to proceed to administer the law, they concluded that:

> Denial of those rights and principles necessarily involves the nation as a whole. For the idea of government by the consent of the governed is the essence of this Republic, then for the sake of the American experience in self-government, and not just for the vindication of the claims of certain persons or groups, the right to vote and the equal protection of the laws must be secured and protected throughout the land. Above all, it is the Republic that requires a free and self-respecting electorate, at least a Republic conceived in liberty and dedicated to the proposition that all men are created equal.[9]

The Commission's final words added an international dimension to its motivation to improve our disappointing record on expanding civil rights—a factor to which Hannah gave great importance from the very beginning of the Commission's work.

> We are in a world where colored people constitute a majority of the human race, where many new free governments are being formed, where self government is being tested, where the basic human dignity of the individual person is being denied by totalitarian systems, it is more than ever essential that American principles and historic purposes be understood. These standards, these ideas and ideals, are what America is all about.[10]

Vice Chairman Storey, for himself and his fellow Commissioners from the South, Battle and Carlton, wrote a statement of "exception" to the Commission's analysis of the historical record on civil rights arguing that:

> At the time the Constitution was drafted, the discussion of development of the suffrage . . . was not made part of our fundamental law and that there is no provision requiring "equal protection of the laws" anywhere in the original Constitution, nor in the further Amendments, which safeguard certain rights of the individual against encroachment by the Federal government alone.[11]

But the Commission decided that it was their job, under the Civil Rights Act of 1957, to get and present the actual facts of current voting and other restrictions of civil rights and to formulate recommendations to eliminate these restrictions. Although Storey and his colleagues found the Commission recommendations hard to accept, they also found it very difficult to ignore the factual evidence of denial of civil rights which the investigations and the hearings in which they participated clearly showed.

The Supreme Court began to modify these restrictive state laws and practices in the early years of the twentieth century by striking down laws which required segregation in interstate buses and commerce; in the practice of "grandfather" clauses under which Negroes were deprived of their right to vote; and more generally to hold that "separate educational facilities are inherently unequal." Although these cases created much debate, the final authority of the Supreme Court to interpret the Constitution, and the Amendments thereto, was not questioned. The Commission took hope in the Supreme Court which demonstrated its flexibility to adjust to changes in interpretation of Constitutional provisions. This generalization was central in the Commission's thinking because they saw that the solution to the then current civil rights issues with which they were struggling lay in the constitutional framework backed up by a documentation of the facts and the acceptance of the facts by the public, through an educational process of persuasion. This was personally comfortable for Hannah and basically to his fellow Commissioners, even granting that some fundamental changes had to be made in the thinking of the members from the South. These members were probably helped in making the adjustments by their legal training, their honesty, and open-mindedness to their overwhelming evidence of denial of voting and other rights brought out by the field investigations of the staff and the sworn testimony of the hearings. The Commission's eloquent, diplomatic, lofty, and persuasive words:

> Finally the Commission is full of hope because as Lincoln said, "intelligence, patriotism, Christianity, and a firm reliance on Him, who has never yet forsaken this favored land, are still competent to adjust in the best way all our present difficulty." The "mystic chords of memory" remind us that dissent, even to the great propositions established in the Constitution, is in the American tradition, and that the white people of the South have behind them the tradition of Jefferson, Madison and Jackson and the other great southerners who drafted or fought for this country's original declaration of human equality and bill of rights. The Commission shares Lincoln's faith that the whole American people will be "again touched by the better angels of our nature."[12]

*Voting Rights.* The Commission saw the right to vote as the cornerstone of the Republic and the key to all other civil rights. It was joined in this conviction by the then Attorney General, Herbert Brownell Jr., and Senators Lyndon Johnson (Texas), Leverett Saltonstall (Massachusetts) and Paul Douglas (Illinois). But their case had to be documented with a review of the history and current facts about voting restrictions in the several states. These may be briefly summarized as follows.

At the time of the Revolution, of approximately two million free citizens, no more than 120,000 could meet the voting requirements of the original thirteen states. The vote was denied to citizens who were adjudged to be mentally impaired, guilty of certain crimes, not of good moral character of lacking in the ability to read the Constitution or the laws. Negroes, not being citizens, of course, had no right to vote. As new states were admitted to the Union, different qualifications for voting came to be expressed. Under the Emanipation Proclamation and the 13th, 14th and 15th Amendments, four million Negro slaves became citizens with the constitutional right to vote, but only one of the Confederate states extended suffrage to Negroes. Fear kept many Negroes from the polls and southern states amended their constitutions to include poll tax, literacy tests and "grandfather" clauses to exclude Negroes from voting. Moreover, the Democratic Party barred Negroes from membership in the party, thus creating an all white primary.

Despite these restrictive measures, registrations in the South had reached about 1.2 million in 1956. But these registrations represented only about 25% of the Negroes. The records of Northern and Western states showed only minor restrictions, largely of Indians, Puerto Ricans and persons of Mongolian descent. But the more detailed records of counties showed great variation, which in some instances could be explained by apathy.

The Commission sought to get at the root causes of voter apathy and specific denials of the right to vote through full investigation of voting complaints as highlighted in the critical hearings in Alabama in 1958 and in Louisiana where a new fear factor of actions by alleged Communists and the NAACP restricted the exercise of voting rights of Negroes.

The recommendations on voting rights which follow were thus backed up by findings of the investigations, hearings, advisory committee reports and from other verified sources.

No. 1—In order to solve the problem of the general deficiency of reliable information pertaining to voting and non-voting, the Commission recommended:

> That the Bureau of the Census be authorized and directed to undertake, in connection with the census of 1960 . . . a nationwide and territorial

compilation of registration and voting statistics which shall include a count of individuals by race, color and national origin who are registered, and a determination of the extent to which such individuals have voted since the prior decennial census.[13]

No.2—Because of the lack of uniform provisions for the retention and public inspection of all records pertaining to registration and voting, the Commission recommended:

That the Congress require that all State and Territorial registration and voting records shall be public records and must be preserved for a period of 5 years, during which time they shall be subject to public inspection, provided that all care be taken to preserve the secrecy of the ballot.[14]

No. 3—To remedy deliberate inaction of boards of registrars, or through various devices and subterfuges, to fail to register qualified electors for reason of race or color, the commission recommended an amendment to the Civil Rights Act of 1957 which would make such actions, or inactions, illegal.

No. 4—To remedy confusion as to the power of the Commission to compel local authorities to produce registration records directly and not to rely on the power and cumbersome procedure of the Attorney General to order "a contumacious witness to comply with a Commission subpoena," the Commission recommended:

That in cases of contumacy or refusal to obey a subpoena . . . for the attendance and testimony of witnesses on the production of written or other matters, the Commission should be enpowered to apply to the appropriate U.S. district court for an order enforcing such subpoena.[15]

No. 5—Because of the Commission's findings of sworn complaints of denials to vote by reason of color or race in seven states and because of open resistance of some registration officials to testify or provide information, or even to be unavailable because of timely resignations, or otherwise to impede justice, the Commission recommended:

That upon receipt by the President of the United States of sworn affidavits by nine or more individuals . . . alleging that the applicants have unsuccessfully attempted to register . . . because of color, religion or national origin, the President shall refer such affidavits to the Commission on Civil Rights, if extended.*[16]

The Commission would then be required to investigate and validate such allegations and report its findings to the President, who would

---

*The Commission was scheduled to end after two years.

designate a Federal officer or employee in the area to act as a temporary registrar designate who:

> shall administer the state qualification laws and issue to all individuals
> found qualified registration certificates which shall entitle them to vote
> for any candidate for the Federal offices of President (and other named
> candidates) . . . Jurisdiction shall be retained until such time as the
> President determines that the presence of the appointed registrar is no
> longer necessary.[17]

Commissioner Battle concurred in the objective that all properly
qualified American citizens have the right to vote but dissented from
the recommendation that a Federal registrar be named. His objection
was based on the incursion of the Federal government in the "election
process so jealously guarded and carefully reserved by the States by
the founding Fathers," a general position which he took in the Senate
hearings on his nomination to be a member of the Commission.

Chairman Hannah and Commissioners Hesburgh and Johnson, possibly in a desire to simplify voting procedures, fostered no doubt by all
the complications, evasions of responsibility and outright defiance of
the law which they witnessed in securing an extension of civil rights to
Negroes and other disadvantaged groups to vote, joined in a proposal
to secure a 23rd Constitutional Amendment to establish universal
suffrage. They expressed their conviction in the following words:

> We believe that the time has come for the United States to take the last
> of its many steps toward free and universal suffrage. The ratification of
> this amendment would be a reaffirmation of our faith in the principles
> upon which this nation was founded. It would reassure lovers of freedom
> throughout the world in which hundreds of millions of people, most of
> them colored, are becoming free and are hesitating between alternative
> paths of national development.[18]

It is not surprising that this proposal would not be concurred in by
Vice Chairman Storey and Commissioners Carlton and Battle. They
affirmed that they "supported and voted for all (other) recommendations of the Commission to strengthen the laws and improve the
administration of registration and voting procedures. However, we
cannot join our distinguished colleagues in the recommendation of the
proposed constitutional amendment."

*Public Education.* The Commission's approach to the thorny problems
of racial segregation in public educational institutions was less firmly
based than in the area of voting rights. In keeping with the fixed

principle of looking for answers, first with the decisions of the courts, especially the Supreme Court, the Commission first examined what the Supreme Court decided and what it did not decide or order. There was no question that the 1954 court decision condemned racial discrimination and the earlier doctrine of "separate but equal," but the process of achieving integration was seen to be a process of readjustment. Accordingly, the first line of attack was to ascertain what the courts had decided and what actions school authorities had taken to comply with the challenge, or circumvent these decisions. The proposed amendment to the state constitution of Louisiana, for example, to provide separate schools for white and Negro children, *not because of race*, had been struck down by the Fifth U.S. Circuit Court of Appeals. Other tactics were tried by other states to justify their policies of operating segregated schools. Admitting that differences in interpretation of court rulings were "subtle and profound," the Commission nevertheless indicated that it was a plain fact:

> that in public education, in voting and public housing, Negro Americans are not seeking any novel or special privileges for themselves. They are not trying to compel the nation's Federal, State or local governments to do anything for them which these governments are not already doing for other Americans. They ask only that these governments *not* do things that deny to Negroes the rights with the Constitution promises to all Americans.[19]

The Commission then went on to summarize its findings of the experience of school systems in various states in achieving integration in their schools, citing principally the evidence of results achieved and problems encountered. But little progress had been made in the South, based in part on differences in ratios of white and Negro children and in psychological fears of both whites and Negroes as to what would happen if more rapid integration was attempted. These fears included the possibility of lowered academic standards, strained social relations between whites and Negroes and the competance of Negro teachers. The Commission was satisfied that the factual evidence of schools which had experimented with and achieved high degrees of integration, under 6-3-3 year court approved plans did not support the fears indicated. Furthermore, they admitted that the requirements of the courts for "deliberate speed" were imprecise and needed more court decisions to clarify compliance or non-compliance with the law.

The Commission then turned to policies and practices of the Federal government with reference to making large grants, principally to higher education, and to the variable results achieved in states with differeing patterns of segregation and integration. Inasmuch as more than one billion dollars of Federal funds were disbursed in 1957 to institutions of higher education, the Commission addressed itself to its Congressional assignment to "appraise the laws and policies of the Federal government with respect to equal protection of the laws under the Constituion."

Chairman Hannah and Commissioners Hesburgh and Johnson, taking cognizance of the large grants being made to colleges and universities "without regard to the fundamental principle of equal protection and equal treatment," joined in a recommendation that Federal funds be withheld from such institutions, public and private, which refuse "on racial grounds to admit students otherwise qualified for admission." Commissioner Johnson went further, in a separate statement, to apply the same recommendation to all elementary and secondary schools which receive Federal grants. He elaborated on this position in a closing statement at the end of the complete report.

Vice Chairman Storey and the other southern commissioners made a separate statement on the restriction of Federal funds to institutions of higher education on grounds that legal measures, on the basis of the 14th Amendment, be applied rather than economic measures, to achieve integration. Furthermore, they held that the application of the restriction to private educational institutions at all levels was "beyond the scope of the Commission's duties."

The Commission finally stressed the philosophical basis of the court decisions which rested on a conception of human nature which lay deeply in the "world revolution of colonial and subject people . . ." based in the deepest innate needs and urges of their natures "to impel every human being, black, yellow no less than white, toward life, liberty and the pursuit of happiness." But recognizing that:

> honest men may honestly differ, as Americans have in the school segregation controversy, about whose rights are paramount in any given conflict. To resolve such differences peaceably is the purpose of the law; the alternative is anarchy. It was such a resolution that the Supreme Court made in 1954.[20]

*Housing.* The Commission found through investigation, hearings in New York, Chicago and Atlanta, reports of their Advisory Committees, and data from other sources that problems of discrimination in housing, by reason of color, race, religion or national origin, was even more complex than in the areas of education and voting, and that discriminatory conditions existed, to some extent, in all parts of the country. What was at issue they said was:

> not the imposition of any residential pattern of racial integration. Rather it is the right of every American to equal opportunity for decent housing. There may be many Americans who prefer to live in neighborhoods with people of their own race, color or national origin . . . But if some Americans because (of legal or other restrictions) have no choice but to grow up and live in conditions of squalor and rigidly confined areas, then all America suffers . . .
>
> If through the actions of city, state or Federal governments some Americans are denied freedom of choice and equality of opportunity in housing, the constitutional rule of equal protection and equal justice under law is being violated.[21]

In examining the facts of housing situations as the basis for their recommendations, the commission took cognizance of the existence of a housing crisis; of the large percentage of non-white families living in dilapidated dwellings without plumbing, nearly three times the proportion of white families living under such conditions; of residential patterns which fostered discrimination; of city and state laws which permitted discriminatory patterns; of Federal laws, policies and practices of the Federal Housing Administration, Veterans Administration, Housing and Home Finance Agency and other agencies which did not use their power to foster integration but in some cases had the opposite effect; and of business and private programs and policies, real estate boards, etc., all of which collectively contributed to a denial of basic civil rights. Furthermore:

> It is the public policy of the United States, declared by the Congress and the President, and in accord with the purpose of the Constitution, that every American family shall have equal opportunity to secure a decent home in a decent neighborhood.[22]

The Commission recommended:

1. That appropriate bi-racial committees or commission on housing be established in every city and state with a substantial non-white population . . .

(Commissioners Johnson and Hesburgh added, in a separate statement, that real estate boards also admit qualified Negroes to membership).

2. That the President issue an executive order:

directed to all Federal agencies to shape their policies and practices to make the maximum contribution to the achievement of the objective of equal opportunity in housing. . . .[23]

3. Keeping in mind the large, even potentially larger, influence which Federal agencies could have on fostering, if not requiring, elimination of discriminatory policies in housing, that the Federal Housing and Veterans Administrations:

strengthen their present agreements with state and cities having laws against discrimination . . . to require builders which are subject to these laws and which have the benefit of mortgage insurance and loan guarantee programs, made availale by these agencies, and to agree in writing to abide by such laws.[24]

4. Noting the need for an expanded public housing program and to avoid further concentration of housing in present centers of racial concentration, that the Public Housing Administration take:

affirmative action to encourage the selection of sites by local housing authorities on open lands in good areas and to encourage the construction of smaller projects in residential neighborhoods rather than large "high-rise" apartments which tend to set a special group apart in a community of its own.[25]

5. Observing the large number of city and private programs of slum clearance and urban redevelopment which are aided by Federal funds made available by the Urban Renewal Administration, that this agency of the government take positive steps to assure that in the preparation of overall community programs for these purposes that "minority groups are in fact included among the citizens whose participation is required."

It is clear from the above recommendations that the Commission, although acknowledging the importance that the many private and civic organizations which had fostered and promoted better and less discriminatory housing for minority groups, put its major trust in the fuller and more positive use of Federal powers and agencies to make their contribution to achieve an improvement in housing for disadvantaged citizens.

Vice Chairman Storey and the other two Democratic Commissioners added a "Supplementary Statement on Housing" which favored the general view that equal justice was required for all races, in the field of housing or elsewhere. This did not mean:

that the Government owes everyone a house regardless of his ambition, industry, or will to provide for himself. When generosity takes away self-reliance or the determination of one to improve his own lot, it ceases to be a blessing. We should help but not pamper. Some parts of the foregoing report are argumentative, with suggestions keyed to integration, rather than housing . . . which is our prime objective. The repeated expression "freedom of choice," "open housing," "open market" and "scatteration" suggest a fixed program of mixing the races anywhere and everywhere regardless of the wishes of either race and particular problems involved.[26]

Commissioners Hesburgh and Johnson, without Hannah's concurrence, added another "supplementary statement" which advocated that special attention and financial assistance should be given to needs of persons' homes which were destroyed because of federally aided programs of urban renewal and highways to conform to an act of Congress which "requires that decent, safe, and sanitary dwellings be available at rents and prices within the financial means of displaced persons." They also pointed out the need for involvement of minority-group participation in planning Federally financed urban renewal and slum clearance programs and also for the increased availability of low-cost housing for non-white Americans as well as other low-income families.

*The Problem as a Whole.* In a reflective statement, the Commissioners unanimously commented on the interrelationships of civil rights in voting, education and housing as the "organic nature of the problem as a whole." With reference to voting, the Commission concluded that "to a large extent this is a racial problem." The only denials to vote, with a signle exception, which had come to their attention were by reason of race or color. Discrimination in education and housing were of a somewhat different nature but practiced more generally against non-whites. The civil rights of 18 million Negro American citizens in all three areas were the principal focus of the Commission's approximately first two years of effort. But the "fundamental interrelationship between the subject of voting, education and housing makes it impossible for the problem to be solved by the improvement of any one factor alone." For if the right to vote is secured but equal opportunity is not made available in education and housing, that right is diminished by apathy and ignorance. Likewise, if compulsory discrimination is ended in public education but children continue to live in slums . . . its "conditions for good education and good citizenship will still not be

obtained." Also, if decent housing is made available to non-whites but
"their education and habits of citizenship are not raised, new neighborhoods will degenerate into slums." Furthermore, the Commission
did not overlook the "fundamental cause of prejudice (which) is hidden
in the minds and hearts of men" which will not be cured entirely by
concentrating constantly on discrimination. But it may "be cured, or
reduced, or at least forgotten if sights can be raised to new and
challenging targets," in better education for the "unfolding 20th century;" for more equal housing and for the right to vote on "issues on
which people want to vote." In the largest dimension of the problem:

> what is involved is the warning against the division of society into Two
> Cities. The Constitution of the United States, which was ordained to
> establish one society with equal justice under law, stands against such a
> division. America, which already has come closer to equality or oppor-
> tunity than any other country, must succeed where others have
> failed.[27]

But the almost 200 pages of the 1959 report and the dissents and
separate statements of several of the Commissioners referred to above
did not offer enough space or latitude to express all of the major ideas
which evolved within the Commission over almost two years of discussion, study and reflections on staff and advisory studies and hearings.

Accordingly, a final opportunity for those Commissioners who
wished to make "general statements" of their viewpoints and convictions was provided at the end of the 1959 report. Commissioner Battle
used the opportunity to express his strong disagreement "with the
nature and tenor of the report." In his judgment, the report was "not
an impartial statement such as I believe to have been the intent of the
Congress, but rather, in large part, an argument in advocacy of
preconceived ideas in the field of race relations." Hannah's reaction
to Battle's dissent, as quoted in *Time Magazine* for Sept. 24, 1959, was
a low key response, which characterized his leadership, by reminding
the readers of *Time* that racial discrimination was a problem "that is
native to neither North or South. It is rather a dilemma that concerns
all Americans." Perhaps the tone and substance of this reaction of
Hannah to Battle's dissent, and probably many more of a similar
nature by Hannah and the other Commissioners, led Battle to express
his views "without in any way impugning the motives of any member
of the Commission, for each of whom I have the highest regard."
Nevertheless, he resigned from the Commission at the end of two
years. Hannah continued to keep in touch with him and to visit him in
his home.

Hesburgh expanded his views in a well reasoned statement of his deepest beliefs about the sacredness of human beings, the majesty of the Constitution and the "American dream," and the potential of all persons given the opportunity to vote, to be educated, decently housed and provided with the opportunity to gainful employment to become good, respected and well motivated citizens. Contrarywise, if these opportunities are denied to non-white citizens, the problems for them and society become "eternally insoluble." He also dispelled the myth of "white superiority" as being "philosophically, theologically and scientifically" absurd. He closed with an expansion of his beliefs on specific recommendations with which he joined Hannah and Johnson on the desirability of a constitutional amendment to give all qualified voters the right to vote in all elections, the passage of which would make it possible for America to "proclaim to all the world that we have full faith in the democratic process, without equivocation, chicanery, or subterfuge."

George Johnson expanded his thinking in the context of present constitutional and other legal guarantees of civil rights. He argued for additional legislation to empower the Attorney General to "correct flagrant abuses of the rights of some American citizens," principally Negroes and other minority groups. But he saw possible solutions not only in the legal arena but in the Federal government taking leadership:

> To bring together leaders of both races, who in good faith could explore ways and means to reduce tensions, create better understanding, increase respect for law and order, and organize the resources of the nation in a concerted effort to eradicate within the foreseeable future inequalities based on race, color, or national origin.[28]

The publication of the 1959 report of the Commission essentially broke open the log jam of national unrest and massive denials of civil liberties, particularly in the area of voting but modestly in the ares of education and housing, and to set the stage for further developments in these and other aspects of civil rights which were to be the challenge of the Civil Rights Commission as its life was periodically extended and as it gained stature with the President, the Congress and the American people. John Hannah was a central, if not the central, leader in mobilizing the forces which led to these advancements by his recognized cool, but firm, competent, dedicated and dispassionate leadership. A different chairman, with less skill and experience in leadership, would probably have aggravated the already serious tensions within the Commission and the public at large.

Hannah demonstrated his ability to weld a group, essentially of strangers, into a working team to remove, or diminish, barriers to civil rights which had plagued this nation from its founding. This is not to assert that he accomplished this result single-handedly, but through his leadership and the close collaboration, especially of Commissioners Hesburgh, Johnson and Storey, and the sense of Commissioners Battle and Carlton's fairness, flexibility and respect for the provisions of the Constitution and the civil rights laws, his job was made much easier. Hannah and all the other Commissioners were also aided in that task by the competence of the staff and the support of the President, legislators and the public. But Hannah's leadership was the key to putting all the components together in an effective coalition.

## The 1961 Report[29]

The 1961 report differed considerably from the 1959 report in several respects, for a number of reasons. First and foremost was the difference in the composition of the membership of the Commission. Governors John Battle and Doyle Carlton had resigned from the Commission and were replaced by Dean Erwin Griswold of the Harvard Law School and Robert Rankin, Professor of Political Science at Duke university. Spottswood Robinson, a distinguished Negro lawyer, replaced George Johnson. While all of the new Commissioners were strong advocates of civil rights, they were more moderate in their views than were their predecessors. Also, the Commission by 1961 had established a reputation with the President, the Congress, and the public as a non-partisan, objective, factually oriented body. A third factor was the momentum which the staff research, public hearings, conferences and advisory committee reports had provided the Commission for better documenting denials of voting and other civil rights. Furthermore, a fourth consideration as the fact that the Commission was better organized, staffed with more experienced lawyers and that relationships with the White House, the Congress and other organizations had been more sharply defined. Also, the establishment of a civil rights task force in the White House, headed by Harris Wofford, had made communications with the White House more efficient. The net effect of these considerations was an increasing number of unanimous recommendations of the Commission and in the volume of factual evidence which supported their recommendations.

The 1961 report was published in five separate volumes devoted to voting, education, housing, employment and justice. The latter two subjects had not been covered in the 1959 report.

*Voting*. The report on voting rights opened with a summary of progress made in civil rights since the Commission published its first report, citing: (1) Congressional passage of the second Civil Rights Act in 1960; (2) court decisions of the Federal government to secure the "constitutional rights of its citizens against invasion by the states;" and other actions of the President and decisions of the Supreme Court which changed the environment in which voting and other civil rights were being discussed and appropriate remedial actions taken.

Problems were mentioned which were still unsolved such as the fact that "in some 100 counties in eight southern states there is reason to believe that Negro citizens are prevented, by outright discrimination or by fear of physical violence or economic reprisal, from exercising the right to vote." Also such problems as "unlawful violence by the police is not a regional but a national shame;" unconstitutional inequality in public education in many cities "throughout the nation;" discriminatory employment practices particularly against Negroes; racial segregation in some branches of the Armed Services; unavailability of adequate housing because of race, religion, or ancestry; and that some practices of the Federal Government give "indirect support to discriminatory practices in education, training programs, access to public facilities and housing."

The bulk of the 380 pages of the report provided factual data on the status of the right to vote; non-voting in 13 states, most of them Southern; gerry mandering and malapportionment; and civil rights in "Blue Belt Counties."

On the basis of the evidence cited on abrogation of voting rights, the Commission made the following major recommendations for action by the President and the Congress to:

• Establish, by Congressional legislation, that completion of the 6th grade of formal education is a qualification for voting, instead of literacy tests or other "understanding" or "educational" tests.

• Prohibit, by Congressional action, any action or initiative which deprives or threatens citizens in their attempt to exercise their franchise to register, vote and have their votes counted.

• Promulgate an Executive Order instructing the Bureau of the Census to include a count of all pesons of voting age, by race, color, national origin and number registered to vote.

Vice Chairman Storey dissented to the first recommendation principally on grounds that "proposals to alter long-standing Federal-State relationships such as that incorporated in the Federal Constitution, declaring that the qualification of electors shall be left to the several states, should not be made unless there is no alternative method to correct an existing evil. Such is not the case today." Storeys dissent was joined by Commissioner Rankin for similar reasons. These were the last dissents to Commission recommendations or conclusions except a dissent by Commissioner Rankin on one of the 12 recommendations on education.

*Education.* In the introduction to the report dealing with Education, President Kennedy was quoted as follows:

> Our progress as a nation can be no swifter than our progress in education. Our requirements for world leadership, our hopes for economic growth, and the demands of citizenship itself in an era such as this all require the maximum development of every young mind. The human mind is our fundamental resource.[30]

John Hannah stated this critical role and conception of education many times before becoming Chairman of the U.S. Civil Rights Commission, during his eleven year tenure with the Commission, and frequently in speeches and other activities since resigning as Chairman of the Commission. Although there is no evidence that Hannah actually "ghost wrote" the comments of the President, there is little doubt that Hannah expressed these views in the several meetings which he had with the President. They were on the same "wave length" in their views of the prime importance of education.

After extensive examination of documents, field investigations, public hearings, federal and state court opinions, and other sources, the Commission made the following principal recommendations that:

• Congress enact legislation requiring every local school board which maintains any public school which excludes pupils on the basis of race to file a plan for desegregation within six months of the passage of the legislation.

• Congress provide Federal grants-in-aid to states for elementary and secondary schools on a differential formula basis depending on the extent to which school districts are operated on a non-discriminatory basis. Commissioner Rankin dissented to this recommendation on grounds that the net effect might be punitive and that schoolchildren should not be made to suffer for the errors of their elders.

• The President direct, and the Congress enact, legislation to authorize the Civil Rights Commission to serve as a clearing house to collect and disseminate information used by school districts to comply with Federal requirements to diminish segregated practices. And also to establish an advisory and conciliation service to assist local school officials to "mediate and conciliate disputes between school officials and school patrons regarding plans for desegregation and for implementation of plans already in operation."

• The President direct the Department of Defense "to make a complete survey of the segregated-desegregated status of public schools attended by dependents of military personnel living on-base or in the absence of sufficient housing on-base . . . and report its findings to them. And also to instruct the Commissioner of Education to make suitable arrangements for their education in public schools open to military dependents without discrimination because of color or race."[31]

Hannah personally conferred with the Secretary of Health, Education and Welfare and the Commissioner of Education to implement this and other directives to Education to deal with segregation practices in the public schools.

With reference to higher education, the Commission recommended that:

> The Federal government either by Executive order or Congressional action, take such measures as may be required to assure that funds under the various programs of the Federal government to assist higher education are disbursed only to such publicly controlled institutions of higher education as do not discriminate on grounds of race, color, religion or national origin.[32]

Four of the Commissioners, including John Hannah, expressed the belief that the above recommendation should also be applied to privately controlled institutions of higher education.

This recommendation was not intended to permit the government to interfere in such aspects of university administration as curriculum on which Hannah had strong convictions about the need for university independence.

*Employment.* Investigating an area not covered in the 1959 report, the Commission found extensive evidence of discriminatory practices in the training and employment of blacks particularly with respect to:

• Vocational as well as academic training.

• Labor organization apprentice training programs, particularly in the construction and machinists crafts.

• Referral service by State employment offices.
• Employment opportunities offered by the armed services including the civilian components.
• Government contracts, even in those on Federal projects.

Basic to these complex problems was the recognized factor of the "lack of motivation on the part of many Negroes to improve their educational and occupational status." Generally, of course, lack of motivation was thought to be, in itself, the product of long-suffered discrimination.

The following were the principal recommendations of the Commission in these areas of discrimination.

• That Congress grant statutory authority to the President's Committee on Equal Employment Opportunity to establish a similar agency to encourage and enforce a policy of equal employment opportunity in all Federal employment; in all federally assisted training and recruitment programs; and in the membership or activities of labor organizations operating under government contracts or Federal grants-in-aid.

• That Congress enact legislation to provide equality of training and employment opportunities for youths (age 16–21) and particularly minority group youths, to assist them in obtaining employment and completing their education.

• That Congress amend the Labor Management and Disclosure Act of 1959 to require labor organizations to cease discriminatory practices in membership because of race, color, religion or national origin.

• That the President issue Executive orders providing equal treatment and training opportunity for applicants or members of the Reserve components and other branches of the armed forces, making clear that employment supported by Federal grant funds is subject to the same non-discrimination policy as those applicable to employment by Government contractors, and that he direct that information be disseminated to make known the availability of non-discriminatory employment as indicated above.

• That Congress and the President take appropriate measures to encourage the fullest utilization of the nation's manpower resources and to eliminate the waste of human resources inherent in discriminatory denial of training and employment opportunities to minority groups . . .

• That steps be taken either by Executive or Congressional action to reaffirm and strengthen the Bureau of Employment Security policy to take a variety of actions to foster non-discriminatory practices in employment, referral and other services.[33]

The Commision was unanimous in making these far-reaching recommendations, using their direct access to the President and the Congress to use the expenditures and prestige of the Federal government for projects directly and indirectly, through contracts with the Federal government or on federally-aided projects, as a fulcrum for expanding non-discriminatory job and training opportunities for negroes and other disadvantaged groups.

Although in principle Hannah was opposed to expansion of Federal powers and involvement of the Federal bureaucracy in normally free enterprise activities, the compelling evidence of discriminatory practices in employment and training of negroes dictated the need to open up new opportunities for them and other disadvantaged groups. In the follow-up on Executive and Congressional action on the recommendations, Hannah met with and otherwise encouraged Cabinet officers and other Federal executives, directly involved in implementing the directives and legislative actions, to get on with their responsibilities.

*Housing.* Overt and covert discriminatory policies and practices in housing by government agencies, financial institutions, builders, labor unions, town planners, real estate organizations and agents and, to a degree, the general public in conforming to and choosing to ignore these discriminatory practices were all involved in this highly complex problem.

The critical importance of Federal public and Federally assisted or insured housing to private builders and financial institutions, and ultimately to the public, was singled out, after exhaustive study, to be the key to the complex of factors which made the initial recommendation of the Comission essentially inoperative. In its 1961 report the Commission elaborated on its views expressed in the 1959 report and unanimously concluded that:

> Denial of equal housing opportunity means essentially the deliberate exclusion of many minority group members from a large part of the housing market and to a large extent confinement in deteriorating ghettos. It involves more than poverty and slums, for it extends to the denial of a fundamental part of freedom; choice in an open, competitive market . . . For in housing, as elsewhere, the essence of freedom is choice. Nevertheless, Federal programs, Federal benefits, Federal resources have been widely, if indirectly used, in a discriminatory manner, and the Federal government has done virtually nothing to prevent it.

Consistent with this overall conclusion, the principal recommendations were directed to Federal policies and practices in the area of housing. They were:

• That the President issue an Executive order, specifically directing all Federal agencies concerned with housing and home mortgage credit to shape their policies and practices to make the maximum contribution to the achievement of the goals of equal opportunity in housing.

• More precisely that the President direct the FHA (Federal Housing Administration) and the V.A. (Veterans Administration) on a *nation-wide basis* (italics in the original text) to take appropriate steps to assure that builders and developers and lending institutions will not discriminate on grounds of race, color or creed in the sale or lease of housing built with the aid of FHA mortgage insurance or VA loan guarantees and that Government owned housing will be available on a non-discriminatory basis.

• That the Federal government, either by Executive order or Congressional action require all financial institutions engaged in mortgage loan business that are supervised by a Federal agency to conduct such business on a non-discriminatory basis.[34]

Commissioner Rankin concurred in part with the main objective which the Commission wished to achieve, but dissented in part with the method recommended which would involve the Federal government's intervention in the "right of financial institutions to pursue their economic policies free from unwarranted Federal control."

Vice Chairman Storey agreed with the views of the Commission that it is "not in keeping with American principles that a person be denied a housing mortgage loan solely on the basis of his race, religion or national origin" but dissented more fully than Commissioner Rankin in the intrusion of Federal influence on regulation in private affairs. Hannah clearly had a delicate job to achieve agreement on the recommendations and strategies to offset the discriminatory policies and practices in housing, which the research clearly showed, but at the same time to recognize strongly held dissenting opinions on some aspects of remedial measures which the majority of the Commissioners concluded were necessary. It was fortunate, in some respects, that the Federal government was, directly or indirectly, already critically involved in the housing area and thus provided a convenient means of attacking the problems.

*Administration of Justice.* The final part of the 1961 report comes under the general heading of administration of justice, involving some of the most flagrant, elusive and covert abuses of civil rights, not covered in the 1959 report. The major sections of the report were:

unlawful police violence; private violence; Federal civil sanctions; and exclusion of Negroes from juries. This part of the report also included treatment of the problems of the American Indians—a new dimension to Commission thinking—to which it gave serious attention.

Some of the major findings were:

• On the positive side, that the actions of most policeman demonstrate that effective law enforcement is possible without the use of unlawful violence, (particularly after some dimunition of the excessive violence was experienced after the earlier marches and other demonstrations and confrontations with the police). Nevertheless, police brutality by some states and local police continued with both white and Negroes as victims, but Negroes in greater number than other groups. Lynchings, however, which frequently involved police assistance, may be extinct.

• Police connivance in violence in contast to violence by private persons (in part by private persons choosing to ignore or condone violence which was clearly visible to them) diminished even though American citizens in some places, however, continued to live in fear of police violence and mob violence with police connivance.

• State and local officials who have the immediate responsibility of dealing with civil rights abuses are sometimes reluctant to use their power, even taking at times a protective attitude toward miscreant officers and local prosecutors rarely bringing criminal actions against them, many of whom are poorly paid and trained.

• Complaints are rarely made against Federal police agents and FBI agents (who are professionally selected and better trained) are sometimes placed in a difficult position when they must investigate allegations of misconduct against local policemen.

• The Federal Civil Rights Acts providing civil liability for unlawful official violence have not proved to be effective remedies, and several need to be clarified or amended.

• The practice of excluding Negroes from juries on account of race, color or national origin, still persists in a few states, and when it exists is a major deterrent to securing justice for Negroes charged with offenses. Criminal remedies for unconstitutional jury exclusion are available only to the Federal government which has only used such powers once since 1870. "Civil action instituted in the name of the United States would constitute a more effective method" of dealing with this problem.

Recognizing that the primary responsibility for administering justice rests with state and local authorities, with Federal resources and authority being important but secondary, the Commission couched its unanimous recommendations in a different style, namely that "Congress consider the advisability" of providing grants-in-aid to state and local governments upon their request, for programs designed to better select and train their police officers. The Commission did recommend more specifically that two sections of the United States Criminal Code be amended to make the prescribed Federal criminal penalties of those statutes available to state and local officials responsible for administering justice, and to "empower the Attorney General to bring civil proceedings to prevent the exclusion of persons from jury services on account of race, color or national origin."

## The 1963 Report: Challenge and Response[35]

The 1963 report differed from the voluminous five-part 1961 report by being only 268 pages in contrast to the 1380 pages of the preceding reports. The Staff Director, Berl Bernhard, was credited with persuading the Commission that a shorter report would be more readable and effective without the extensive tables of data which characterized the earlier reports. The Commission had moved beyond the mainly fact-finding stage, which formed the basis for previous recommendations, incorporated in the Omnibus Civil Rights Bill soon to be recommended for passage by the Congress by President Kennedy. All of the recommendations in the 1963 report were unanimous.

Although the report identified very slow progress in several areas of civil rights and a continuation of difficult programs, the Commission was clearly enthusiastic about the progress which had been made, prompting Hannah, on behalf of the Commission, to testify at a news conference following the issuance of the report "that every step taken by the Congress and the Executive Department in the field of civil rights in the past four years originated with the recommendation of the Commission or depended on facts it had gathered." This claim was disputed in an article in the *Wall Street Journal* but President Kennedy supported Hannah's uncharacteristically bold statement, declaring that the "Commission's recommendations have provided the basis for remedial action both by Congress and the Executive Branch."

In the introduction to the report, the Commission characterized the time as being of "increased awareness of the nation's civil rights problems" aided and abetted by "sharpened controversy and quickened hopes" which have created a "sense of futility, indignation" and an "avowed determination to see several principles translated into the practices of everyday life without further delay." Furthermore, the Commission had learned from its six years of study and investigation in all sections of the nation that the "civil rights of citizens continued to be widely disregarded." These conditions had inflicted "deep wounds upon the Negro community," and also tarnishes our image in the new and uncommitted nations, most of which are non-white and that "America is what it practices, not what it professes. To our enemies, our civil rights record provides a wealth of propaganda to persuade neutral nations that America practices hypocrisy." Although Hannah may not have actually written this language, he approved it and it is clearly compatible with his previous statements on the subject and on his future experiences and work in third world countries.

The report continued on a more positive note that the nation had shown a pragmatic realization that a greater, rather than a piecemeal, effort needs to be made and that the civil rights problems are "inextricably interrelated and none can be solved in isolation." Voting rights, education, employment and public accommodations were cited as being interrelated parts of the whole civil rights complex. Even though state and local governments were noted as being increasingly active, along with citizens groups, in creating a more favorable legal climate, the "full mobilization of America's moral resources is required at this crucial time to solve the problems."

*Voting.* An analysis by states of techniques of discrimination and difficulties of enforcement of civil rights laws, leading to disenfranchising many Americans of their voting rights on the "wholly arbitrary and irrelevant ground of race" led to the following major remedial recommendations for action:

> That Congress enact legislation (under provisions of the 14th and 15th Amendments) that only "failure to complete six years of formal education or its equivalent, legal confinement at time of registration, determined mental disability, or convinction of a felony, can be used as a basis for restricting the right to vote or to have one's vote counted."[36]

In a statement concurring with the above recommendations, Vice Chairman Storey and Commissioner Rankin, reaffirming their conviction that "the right to vote is the cornerstone of our democracy" but noting what actually happened under legislation embodied in civil rights legislation in the Acts of 1957 and 1961, wrote:

> Now, 2 more years have passed since the most recent of these acts. The core of arbitrary disfranchisement has not diminished materially. . . . For

these reasons we have concluded sadly, but with firm conviction, that without drastic change in the means to secure suffrage for many of our citizens, disfranchisement will continue to be handed down from father to son . . . Finally, we must state that the survival of the honorable doctrine of the states rights imposes coterminous obligations . . . As we have said on so many occasions, civil rights carry with them civil responsibilities. So, too, states rights carry with them state obligations to all its citizens.[37]

This statement would seem to be proof that all of the Commissioners had become accustomed, as a result, at least partially, of the Commission's deliberations under Hannah's leadership, to putting aside their prior convictions when objective facts demonstrated the need to change. It is also a tribute to the character of the persons involved and their belief in the rule of law.

*Education.* In its 1963 report the Commission went beyond previous recommendations regarding education in the following respects, based on the fact that even after ten years since passage of the Supreme Court decision requiring desegregation of schools, "Negro school children still attend segregated schools in all parts of the nation because of protests, hair-splitting legal definitions, pupil assignment practices and other delaying tactics." The principal recommendations to remedy this situation were:

• That Congress enact legislation requiring every school district "to adopt and publish within 90 days after enactment of such legislation a plan for prompt compliance with the constitutional duty to provide non-segregated public education for all school age children within its jurisdiction."

• That Congress authorize the Commission to provide technical and financial assistance to those school districts which are attempting to comply with the above requirement.

• That the President call a White House conference of educators and civil rights experts to discuss how the Federal government could assist state and local school boards solve the problem of segregated schools.[38]

*Employment.* Recognizing that our complex economy places a premium on skills which are created by job training and job generating programs, substantially financed by the Federal government, and that these programs effectively restrict enrollment of Negroes, the Commission recommended the following principal remedial measures:

• That Congress enact legislation to establish the right to equal opportunity for employment on projects assisted by the Federal government or which affects interstate commerce; to issue appropriate orders to enforce the legislation; and to provide funds to implement the program.

• That the President direct the Secretary of Labor and Secretary of Health, Education and Welfare to administer federally assisted vocational education programs on a non-segregated basis.[39]

*Housing*. Because of the fact that only one year had elapsed since the Commission had persuaded the President to issue an Executive Order to diminish segregation practices followed by Federal Housing agencies, the effects of which had not been evaluated, no further recommendations were made on housing.

*Administration of Justice*. Based on intensive case studies of infringement of the rights of citizens to "speak freely, to assemble peacefully and to petition government for redress of grievances" in four key cities in the South and Middle West, the Commission made four basic recommendations addressed to Congress to:

Empower the Attorney General "to initiate civil proceedings to prevent denials of such freedoms; to enact a program of grants-in-aid to states to increase the professional quality of their police forces; amend a section of the United States code to make county and city government jointly liable with officers employed by them who deprive citizens of these rights; and that Congress also amend another section of the United States Code to permit a change of venue from a state court to a district court of the United States when the defendant is denied his civil rights by laws of such states or by administrative action of the judges in such states.[40]

*Health Services*. Studies by the Commission staff and State Advisory Committees of segregation practices by hospitals and other health facilities provided from funds made available by the Federal government under the Hill-Burton Act, formed the basis for three recommendations to the President to:

Direct the Secretary of Health, Education and Welfare and the Surgeon General of the U.S. Public Health Service to: refuse approval of applications for grants submitted under the separate-but-equal provisions of the Hill-Burton Act; refuse approval for proposed construction of duplicate health facilities to be used on a "racially segregated basis," and to assure that grant recipients comply with non-discriminatory requirements of the Hill-Burton Act.[41]

*Urban Areas.* Based upon general observation that civil rights denials, although existing in all areas of the nation, are more apparent in heavily populated urban areas, the Commission directed the staff to make investigations and set up public televised hearings in four metropolitan areas in Phoenix, Memphis, Newark, and Indianapolis on discriminatory practices in public education, administration of justice, employment, housing, government facilities, and privately owned public accommodations. Although the studies and hearings revealed extensive discriminatory practices in all fields of civil rights, the major purpose of the hearings was largely educational for the large number of participating citizens, advisory committees, government officials and others of the interrelated nature of discriminatory practices and of ways to diminish such practices. Public exposure of these practices was believed by the Commission to be a constructive step in the process of increasing community awareness and responsibility. Accordingly, the recommendation to the President and the Congress was limited to the suggestion that "Presidential Awards of Merit" be presented annually to persons and organizations whose work has resulted in significant civil rights advances in their communities, such nominees to be submitted to the President by the Civil Rights Commission.

*The Armed Forces.* The Commission instituted a wide-ranging investigation of the treatment of Negroes by the several branches of the armed forces in terms of numbers, occupational assignment, recruitment and promotional procedures, treatment of servicemen and their families on bases and in neighboring communities, housing, education and public accommodations. Based on the results of these investigations, the Commission made several strong recommendations to the President and the Secretary of Defense to eliminate gross discriminatory practices in the armed forces and to foster a more congenial domestic environment for families of military personnel. John Hannah had been personally involved with the Secretary of Defense in eliminating discriminatory practices in the armed services under an earlier assignment by President Eisenhower as Assistant Secretary of Defense for Manpower.*

Some of the more far-reaching recommendations included:

• That the President direct the Department of the Navy to take corrective actions to assure that Negroes be given equal opportunity

---

*See Chapter I for more details.

to serve as officers and enlisted men to broaden their occupational assignment and promotional opportunities.

• That the President request the Secretary of Defense to reappraise testing procedures for the procurement of enlisted men and officer personnel; for measuring performance standards for promotion and reduction in force; and for discontinuation of ROTC programs at any college or university which does not accept all students regardless of color.

• That the Defense Department take measures to provide equal treatment for all members of the armed forces by establishing an office to direct its attention to the removal of vestiges of racial discrimination from military installations; insuring that in dealings with local communities that the policy of the armed forces of equal treatment prevails; that an affirmative program to encourage that open-housing opportunities be made available to military personnel and for equal treatment of military personnel at places of public accommodation.

• That the President and the Secretary of the Department of Health, Education and Welfare assure that the granting of federal funds for the construction and operation of schools in impacted areas be assigned to schools without regard for race.[42]

The 1963 report closed by detailing Congressional and Executive action on recommendations made by the Commission in the 1961 report. This summary undoubtedly provided the basis for the optimistic remarks made by Hannah in the opening paragraph of this section, regarding the constructive results of Commission activity in expanding civil rights for Negroes and other minority groups.

*Other Reports and Publications.* Other reports and publications of the Commission under Hannah's Chairmanship were typically on a single aspect of the commission's work. One exception of special importance was prepared at the request of President Johnson, commemorating the 100th Anniversary of the Emancipation Proclamation, written by Dr. John Hope Franklin, Chairman of the History Department of Brooklyn College, who was assisted by three distinguished historians, Dr. Allan Nevins, Rayford W. Logan, and C. Vann Woodward. This comprehensive report reviewed the court cases, literature, political and other movements and developments at significant intervals from before Lincoln to 1962. A comprehensive bibliography and list of Supreme Court and other legal cases was also cited. Several other important publications, sent to the White House and the Congress, included: *"Equal*

*Protection of Laws in Public Education,"* 1960; *"A Time to Act, Voices from the Ghettos of the Nation's Cities,"* 1967; *"Equal Opportunity in Farm Programs, An Appraisal of Services rendered by Agencies of the United States Department of Agriculture,"* 1965.

All of these required especially careful reading by Hannah and the other Commissioners because of their critical importance to the Executive and Legislative branches of the Government, as did the staff reports which provided the background for these reports.

A large number of representative reports by State Advisory Committees, transcripts of hearings and conferences, conducted by the Commission, Clearing House publications of the Commission and numerous other publications by organizations vitally interested in aspects of the Commission's work were also distributed.

## Hannah's Relationships With the Presidents

The three most important components in the success of the Commission's work were: (1) relationships and communications between Hannah and the Presidents under whom he served; (2) relationships and communications which he had with committees and members of the Congress; and (3) internal management and relationships which he had with the staff, and particularly the Staff Directors. In all three critical components, Hannah demonstrated his skill in organization and administration and in his attributes of friendly but objective and candid relationships with persons with whom he worked most closely and in his sustained motivation and genuine belief in the purposes of the projects which he directed in the public interest. All three of these components had to be artfully articulated and coordinated to achieve maximum possible results.

*President Eisenhower.* An important measure of Hannah's dedication to the cause of civil rights and his objectivity, non-partisanship and skills in conducting the work of the Commission, is exemplified in his relationships with the several Presidents to whom he reported, as may be seen in the following pages. President Eisenhower was generally supportive but somewhat conservative in embracing the whole program of the Civil Rights Commission but highly supportive of Hannah in his role as the Chairman and his open style of leading the Commission and the Commission's staff in their complex mission. He unswervingly supported Hannah in the selection of staff for the Commission on the basis of merit without reference to partisan affiliations or considerations. He was stout in his convictions regarding the need and necessity for all citizens to comply with basic provisions of the Civil Rights Act and the decisions of the Supreme Court and he acted quickly and firmly with reference to violence in defiance of these provisions. He gave strong support for recommendations of the Commission with reference to reforms in the military establishment to expand their policies and practices with reference to civil rights. Communications with President Eisenhower were relaxed, sufficiently frequent and personally comfortable, perhaps because of the confidence which the President had in Hannah's previous major appointments in the Federal government under his Presidential direction. Hannah and the President also had some relationships, as educational administrators, while Eisenhower served as president of Columbia University from 1948–53 and Hannah served as President of Michigan State University. They also had other mutual interests in education, public affairs and in fishing. They met informally for breakfast on January 3, 1958 before an official meeting with the whole Commission at a swearing in ceremony, on the same day. The official records show little or no contact between the two for the first six months of the Commission's existence. On June 13, 1958, however, Hannah requested a meeting for himself and Vice Chairman Storey to brief the President on some Commission conclusions regarding tentative policies and procedures. Eisenhower responded promptly on June 18, with a "Dear John," "With Warm Regards, Sincerely, D.E.," letter, indicating that he was "anxious to learn (of) the tentative conclusions reached by the Commission on Civil Rights and since I am shortly to visit Canada, I should like also to be brought up to date on the work of the Permanent Joint Board of Defense, Canada–United States."*

This meeting was held on July 22. A second meeting was held in December 1958 in Montgomery, Alabama before the critical hearing on voting rights. A joint meeting of the CRC and the President's Cabinet was held on February 27, 1959 to review the tentative recommendations of the Commission in its first public report scheduled for November 1959. The President was also persuaded by Hannah to make informal remarks to a national conference of the 50 states Advisory Committees, after which the White House issued a press release which quoted Eisenhower's warmly congratulatory extemporaneous remarks to the conference which previewed some of Hannah's and the Commission's own views.

---

*See Chapter II

On July 28, 1959 Hannah wrote to the President indicating that, in spite of delays in the confirmation of members of the Commission, it was prepared to issue its report to him on Sept. 9, 1959. He also apprised the President of rumors in the Congress and elsewhere that there was some dissension in the Commission and some ambiguity about extending the life of the Commission beyond 1959, and of possible resignations of Hannah and other Commissioners. To deal with these rumors the Staff Director prepared and submitted for Hannah's approval a strong statement on behalf of the Commission to the President and the press:

> The members of the Commission on Civil Rights accepted their appointments to serve for the statutory life of the Commission; under existing law this would terminate on November 9, 1959. Various conflicting reports have appeared in the press as to the intentions of the various commissioners to serve on the Commission if its life is extended and if they are invited by the President to continue to serve as members.
>
> The Commission has made no official statement in this regard, because we have felt it was presumptuous to assume what action might be taken whether by the Congress or the President.
>
> This reticence coupled with the fact that one or two members of the Commission accepted the original appointment with firm commitments not to continue after Nov. 9, has been misunderstood to mean that all of the members of the Commission would not be willing to continue because they were frustrated and discouraged at the prospect of accomplishing anything worthwhile. Some critics of efforts in the field of civil rights have been using this misunderstanding to argue against the extension of the life of the Commission on Civil Rights. Pending legislation may be affected by such an impression and it therefore seems desirable for me as Chairman to correct this impression.
>
> Not one of the Commissioners sought membership on the Commission. That it is an onerous assignment is beyond question but to say that our work is frustrating or that we share a sense of futility is not true. In many respects the work has given us real satisfaction. The association on the Commission has been rewarding.
>
> Our report which will be submitted on Sept. 9 will indicate that there has been some significant accomplishments, several of which have been gained with unanimity. I believe that the life of the Commission should be extended in the public interest. . . . I believe this feeling is shared also by other members of the Commission. There is no feeling of gloom or frustration.
>
> I expect to remain on the Commission if I am invited to do so, and if its life is extended. . . . I am satisfied that to the extent it is possible, every member of the Commission will remain so long as necessary to

assure that the work of the Commission will proceed without significant interruption, even if some personal inconvenience is necessary.

On September 23, 1959, the President wrote to Hannah praising Hannah's and the Commission's accomplishments reported in its first report:

I want to tell you how much I appreciate the splendid work you are doing and have done as Chairman of the Commission on Civil Rights. The overwhelming vote in Congress in favor of the extension of the life of the Commission emphasizes the value of your effort. Indeed, the free and candid expression of different views adds to the Commission's strength. I am more convinced than ever that if any agency of government can make a substantial contribution to advancing America toward a goal of equal opportunity for all, it is the Commission on Civil Rights. I hope very much that you will continue to serve as a member and as Chairman during the extended life of the Commission.

After thanking the President for his kind remarks, Hannah replied, "It is not a pleasant assignment, but on the other hand, it is of very great importance to the future of our country. . . ." He closed by indicating that he would discuss the question of his continuing to serve with the Michigan State University Board of Trustees at its next meeting. Eisenhower had also made an appeal to the Board of Trustees to approve Hannah's continuation as Chairman. The President's request was agreed to. The President wrote to Hannah another letter on Oct. 27, 1959 in which he said in part:

It is with a deep sense of appreciation that I write this letter for I understand full well the personal sacrifice involved in serving as you have on the Civil Rights Commission. . . . I am taking this opportunity to convey my gratitude and I am sure the gratitude of the country for you willingness to continue in this capacity and for the confidence which your membership will inspire.

With reference to the question of extending the life of the Commission, Senator Philip Hart of Michigan made a partisan, but politically understandable, speech at a Democratic party dinner on December 7, 1959 in which he criticized President Eisenhower on his inaction in support of the Commission's recommendations, while the Congress was considering an extension of the Commission's life. The Congress, however, even after hearing Senator Hart's criticisms, extended the life of the Commission for two more years.

The last session Hannah had with President Eisenhower on civil rights matters was on February 5, 1960 after the President's term had ended. But they continued to meet unofficially from time to time.

*President Kennedy*. Based on the record of competence and non partisan leadership which Hannah had demonstrated in leading the Commission through the shoals of producing the first report of the Commission, Hannah's relationships with President Kennedy were remarkably objective, straightforward, and effective, particularly in the beginning of their relationship.* They were less so in the middle of Kennedy's administration when Kennedy apparently became more calculating in terms of the political consequences of affirmative and sustained support for policies and actions with reference to civil rights. The lack of prompt response to Hannah's and the Commission's requests for actions on nomination of Commissioners to fill vacancies; delays in responding to Commission requests for guidance (e.g. a year elapsed at one period between meetings with the President); his lack of clear-cut support for even the Democratic platform on civil rights on which he was, partly at least, elected to the Presidency; the possible undue influence of his brother, Robert, the Attorney General, on the complex problems of drawing strict lines between fact gathering and compliance on civil rights issues; plus the increasing difficulty of taking effective action on some of the more complex recommendations of the Commission (e.g. withholding Federal funds from states which contin- ued to practice segregation in voting rights and other programs which were, in part, Federally financed); plus finally a different administrative style—all of these no doubt contributed to a strain on their relation- ships in the middle years of President Kennedy's tenure as President. Toward the end of his administration, and even shortly before his assassination, he became much more supportive of civil rights and in fact recommended the passage of an omnibus civil rights bill which was more inclusive of the wide spectrum of civil rights than had been previously initiated and supported by the White House. President Kennedy fully supported the non-partisan selection of staff of the Commission which Hannah had established with President Eisen- hower. But perhaps we should let the reader judge for himself, from an examination of some of the details of their relationship.

---

*See Note Number 2 for additional background on President Kennedy's relationship to Robert Kennedy and to the political considerations/actions and major civil rights confrontations (James Meredith, George Wallace, assassination of Robert Evers et. al) which influenced him to move more broadly in his support of civil rights legislation and the use of his presidential power.

Hannah met with President Kennedy on Feb. 7, 1961, less than a month after the President's inauguration, at which he talked to the President from a set of hand-written notes. Preceding the meeting with the President, Hannah and Hesburgh had met with Harris Wofford (who served as Hesburgh's legal assistant) to plan the session with the President. Wofford had a special interest in civil rights from his legal training at Howard University under Commissioner Johnson and later at Harvard University. Wofford had earlier been asked by President Kennedy to prepare a confidential memorandum on civil rights between his election in 1960 and his inauguration. This connection between the Commission and the White House provided a useful linkage on major issues and to the staff of the Commission as they later worked closely with a White House task force on civil rights headed by Harris Wofford.

Hannah wrote the President on the next day enclosing notes on the major topics of their wide ranging conference stressing major points as follows: (1) the need for strong presidential statements in support of the policy of non-discrimination and for the issuance of timely executive orders in the areas of voting rights, education, housing, armed services, transportation and health facilities; (2) the need for a full-time Presidential Advisor on race relations on the White House staff and another in the Civil Rights Division of the Justice Department; (3) the need for each Federal agency to appoint a civil rights officer to assure compliance with Federal policies on fair employment within the government and on projects generated by Federal funds; and (4) the need for the President to support legislation for elimination of literacy tests for voting and for the requirement that all school districts submit plans for first-step compliance with desegregation objectives. In his oral remarks, Hannah also reported the unanimous decision of the Commission to nominate Berl Bernhard as Staff Director of the Commission and a personal requirement to take formal action to retain him as the Chairman, if the President so desired.

The President wrote to Hannah on Feb. 24 that he was "delighted to have the opportunity to discuss with you recently the work of the Civil Rights Commission and the problems in this important field. I look forward to your continued leadership for the Commission and to the continuation of the informal exchange of views which marked our recent meeting."*

---

*He also took cognizance of a side point made by Hannah of his seven years as the

The President, On March 15, 1961, appointed Berl Bernhard to the position of Staff Director (on Hannah's strong recommendation) and Dean Griswold and Spottswood Robinson to fill the vacancies on the Commission. He took these actions in spite of rumbling published in *Newsweek* for Dec. 26, 1960 which predicted that President Kennedy would change the major personnel of the Commission "from top to bottom." Without the confirmation of the two Commissioners, the Commission "continues to be divided on substantive recommendations. Furthermore, if the Commission is asked to have a series of recommendations printed, and on your desk by Sept. 9, 1961, as required by law, the Commission must act on these recommendations not later than mid-June in order to allow time for review of preliminary work that has been done as a basis for making recommendations."

On March 21, Hannah wrote the President thanking him for his nomination of Berl Bernhard as Staff Director and of Dean Griswold and Spottswood Robinson to fill the two vacancies on the Commission created by the resignation of Carlton and Johnson. He also indicated that the Board of Trustees of Michigan State University had approved his continuation as Chairman of the Commission and as Chairman of the Permanent Joint Board on Defense. He also noted that wherever he went . . . "one of the first subjects discussed by the government officials and othes with whom I come in contact was their feeling of gratification and hope generated by the several actions you have taken since assuming the Presidency."

The President acknowledged Hannah's letter of March 21 in which he expressed his gratitude to the Michigan State University Board for their approval of his continuing to serve as U.S. Chairman of the Joint U.S.-Canadian Defense Board.

Kennedy in due course: (1) in April 1962 issued an executive order against discrimination in housing; (2) used his executive power to achieve civil rights advances in equal acces to voting, employment, education and public accommodations; (3) consolidated the various proposals of the Commission into one "package" as an inclusive proclamation on all Federal programs in all parts of American life—a

---

United States Chairman of the Joint American-Canadian Defense Board as follows:

I fully understand the tremendous demands being made on your time because of the heavy responsibility as President of Michigan State University and your other activities. If you feel that because of your other commitments you would prefer not to remain as Chairman of the Permanent Joint Defense Board we would seek to find a suitable replacement.

Hannah chose to continue at both jobs.

second "Emancipation Proclamation." Belatedly, on June 11, 1963 in a nationally released speech, Kennedy submitted an omnibus bill supporting major Civil Rights Commission recommendations on voting rights and five recommendations on education.

On May 11, 1961, Hannah wrote President Kennedy, after a meeting of the Commission on May 5, that "the Commission instructed me to write urging that an early decision be made as to whether or not the Commission is to be continued beyond Sept. 9, 1961." (The existing legislation terminated the life of the Commission on that date). Hannah continued:

> If it is the intention of the administration to recommend the continuation of the Commission, it is our judgment that this decision should be announced at an early date. Othewise, our able staff membes are soon going to be in the process of finding other employment . . . We have noted that in recent days there has been introduced into the Senate a series of civil rights bills including one proposing to extend the life of the Commission. The newspapers have reported, however, that the White House has indicated that these bills do not have the endorsement of the White House. The Commission on Civil Rights has from its inception taken the position that the extension of the life of the Commission is a matter to be determined by the White House and the Congress, and it has refused to take a position recommending its own continuance.

On August 11 the President telegraphed Hannah requesting him to extend his best wishes to the new members of the Commission, Griswold and Robinson, who were confirmed by the Senate in time for them to participate in the preparation of recommendations to be made in the forthcoming 1961 report of the Commission. He also indicated that "we are seeking extension of the Commission's life" and closed with "your work was never more needed. Cordially."

The President's statement that he was supporting an extension of the Commission's life was not, however, followed up by the White House even though Congressman Emanuel Celler, Chairman of the House Committee on the Judiciary recommended that the Commission be made a permanent agency of the Federal government. Hannah wrote Congressman Celler on May 12 that it was not the policy of the Commission to comment on pending legislation.

Disturbed by the continued delays and uncertainties of the Commission's future, Hannah sent a different kind of letter three months later to Senator Joseph Claren reporting that:

> The Commission has authorized us to depart from past policy in commenting on proposed legislation to the extent of suggesting that if the

Commission is continued it is convinced that its operations could be more
efficient and effective if it were put on a longer term basis. We have found
it very difficult to recruit competent personnel or to retain good personnel
when there is a fixed, limited two year life for our work and we are to
cease to exist after that period. It is very difficult to plan long-range
studies and to establish priorities when there is uncertainty about our
continued existence.

In spite of the President's expressed support for the work of the
Commission, his preoccupation with political matters and the consequences of civil rights demonstrations, including Martin Luther King's
monumental demonstration in Washington ("I have a dream" . . .
speech), apparently kept him from taking necessary executive actions
to help the Commission do its job. He took issue with some of the
recommendations of the 1961 report, particularly that to cut off Federal
funds from the state of Mississippi because of its segregation policies.
Schlesinger, in this *Thousand Days,** reports on the conversation in
the President's office about the 1961 report as follows:

> Bernhard said he gathered the President would prefer that the Commis-
> sion not publish the report. "That is correct," Kennedy said. After some
> going over of the statistics, he finally said, "I still don't like it. If the
> Commissioners have made up their mind, I presume they will issue the
> report anyway. I think they are off the track on this one, but I wouldn't
> try to suppress it. That would be wrong, couldn't do it anyway. It is
> independent, has a right to be heard, but I do wish you could get them to
> reconsider."

The Commission, however, did not revise the text of its 1961 report
and it was officially released. The reaction to the controversial recommendation on withholding federal support from states which continued
to practice segregation, was instant and highly emotional, both in
support of and in opposition to the Commission's recommendations.
Active debate continued in the Congress and in the editorial columns
of the press over the Commission's recommendations. Direct communications with the President, however, were very limited in 1962 on
these issues.

On Sept. 13, 1962, Hannah wrote to the President that he would like
to see him with reference to his work on the Joint Defense Board "and
at the same time I would like to discuss with you some of the concerns
of the Commission on Civil Rights." Toward the end of December

---

*Schlesinger, Arthur M. Jr., *A Thousand Days: John F. Kennedy in the White House,*
Houghton, Mifflin Company, Boston, 1965. (Page 953)

Hannah requested, through the Special Assistant to the President, an appointment with the President to secure his guidance before a meeting of the Joint Defense Board scheduled for early February. He also reminded the President's Assistant that . . . "It has been more than a year since the Civil Rights Commission last met with the President. While I am meeting with him, I would appreciate any advice that the President may wish to offer or any suggestions he may care to make with reference to the work of the Commission."

A meeting with the President was arranged shortly thereafter which was not attended by Hannah (who was abroad at the time), and which was thought to be unsatisfactory from the viewpoints of Hesburgh, Griswold and Bernhard, who exchanged letters particularly critical of the President's reactions to meeting problems in Birmingham. Hesburgh expressed his very critical thoughts to Griswold on March 22, 1963 with copies to Hannah in these words:

> This decision (to keep the Commission from forcing action on the Birmingham case) may be politically expedient, but I have the deep impression that they are de-naturing the effectiveness of the United States Commission on Civil Rights. Buffet dinners with many Negroes in attendance at the White House are impressive, but I find myself reluctant to continue in an organization that chooses Indianapolis instead of Jackson and Birmingham . . . I had the distinct impression that this was a situation in which we could have been very tough with the President, but instead were compliant and conciliatory.

Hannah responded to Hesburgh's letter after he returned from Nigeria:

> I was tempted to call or write after reading your earlier letter to concur in your unhappy reaction to the meeting with the President. Then I decided that since I had not attended the meeting, it was really inappropriate for me to comment. I have been troubled for some months about the possible future effectiveness of the Civil Rights Commission.

He then went on to suggest that he would not want to do anything to impair Bernhard and the Washington staff because of their good work; "were it not for this, I would be inclined to resign now if it would serve a useful purpose to indicate the ineffective role in which we are cast by the Attorney General and others."

The President was also obviously disturbed over the meeting with the Commission, particularly on the matter of withholding Federal funds from Mississippi as recommended in an interim report of the Commission dated April 16, 1963. He wrote to Hannah on April 19, which was made public by the office of the White House Secretary, asserting, inter alia, some of the highlights of the President's letter, the text of which was probably prepared in the Department of Justice, headed by Robert Kennedy.

> The deeply held views of the members of the Commission are fully appreciated . . . I share the Commission's stated goal of assuring for all citizens of the United States the full enjoyment of the rights guaranteed by the Constitution. The record of the Justice Department in promptly investigating any allegations of violation of Federal law and in prosecuting in those cases where there are violations is, I believe, outstanding . . .
> The Commission's suggestion that Congress and the Executive Branch study the propriety and desirability of legislation authorizing Federal funds to be withheld from any state which fails to comply with the laws of the United States raises difficult and far-reaching considerations.

The President then went on to spell out some of these considerations in water resource projects, construction of airports and other programs which, once started, require continuity. He also mentioned the hundreds of thousands of Negroes in Mississippi who receive Social Security and other Federal benefits.

On Oct. 10, Hannah wrote the President a tough but polite letter with copies to the Commissioners, the MSU Board of Trustees and Robert Kennedy, highlights of which follows:

> Several of the members of the Commission had contemplated resigning with the completion of the 1963 report. I am among the number. You are aware of the fact that Staff Director Bernhard is resigning from his post at the end of the month. I assume that you know that many of our ablest members of our staff have accepted positions elsewhere . . . The Commission should make some fundamental decisions almost immediately as to the work to be undertaken during the interim period. Before it can act intelligently, it needs to know what your desires are. If you would like the opportunity to appoint new Commissioners, I am ready to resign and I believe Father Hesburgh and Vice Chairman Storey are ready to resign . . . I have not discussed the matter with Dean Griswold or Doctor Rankin. If you wish me to stay with the Commission during the interim period, my willingness to do so will depend largely on the choice of a new Staff Director . . . I know of the great many demands on your time. Perhaps it would conserve your time if we might visit on the telephone for a few minutes at your convenience, but prior to the meeting of the Commission that is now scheduled in New York on Sunday, October 27. With great respect.

On October 21 the President affirmed that he wished Hannah to remain on the Commission as its Chairman. He concurred with Hannah's recommendation that an Acting Staff Director could be designated from the existing staff. He also suggested that the Commission consider various possibilities at their forthcoming meeting on October 27. "Then you and I could meet and together consider the various alternatives. Needless to say I appreciate your willingness to do this work."

Hannah met with the President for a long evening on Nov. 12, 1963 to discuss the results of the Commission's Oct. 27 meeting. He wrote a comprehensive four page letter (an uncommon length for Hannah's communications with the President) on Nov. 13 summarizing the high points of their discussion. In outline form, the major points on which they agreed were:

• That he (Hannah) would try to persuade Father Hesburgh to remain as a member of the Commission. With Griswold and Rankin being willing to remain, the Commission would have a quorum to do its work.

• Replacements for Storey and Robinson would be made at an early date. Hannah expressed a personal view that one should be a Negro and the other a "distinguished white person from the South."

• Wm. Taylor is worthy of your consideration as a permanent Staff Director. At the time when a Staff Director is to be finally selected, however, I think we agreed that there will be an opportunity to visit with you about the qualifications that the Commission feels are desirable attributes for the person with this important responsibility.

• The Civil Rights legislation (proposed by the President) under consideration by the Congress would give no problems for the Commission with reference to clearing house functions which are proposed. The proposal that the Commission be charged with the responsibility for investigating vote frauds, however, would need to be thought through with the possibility of creating a new division with appropriate personnel other than those then employed by the Commission for the programs which are currently being undertaken as Civil Rights functions.

• In addition to continued routine investigation and processing of complaints and conducting surveys on voting, education, housing, employment, justice, medical care and military service, the Commission will undertake field surveys in selected communities on various aspects related to "social unrest." Also to undertake a new research project designed to collect information on state and local anti-discrimination laws and to implement programs for civil rights progress by unions, community groups as well as governmental agencies.

• Acknowledged the President's interest in a study of civil rights pertaining to Eskimos in Alaska, American Indians, Mexicans, Puerto Ricans and possibly other minority groups.

• Hannah also indicated that it is the desire of the Commission to cooperate with the President, Department of Justice and other Federal agencies "but there is a feeling on the part of the Commissioners that the Civil Rights commission should be independent of other agencies of government and should always be in a position to exercise independent judgment. You agreed that this was a sound position."

• In conclusion, Hannah indicated that he would report the content of the conversation to the Commissioners and staff and to "indicate to them that your attitude was as I expected it to be, fully understanding of the work of the Commission. I came away from our session very much encouraged with the understanding that when the fate of the Commission is finally decided by the Congress, there will be another oportunity to visit with you."

*That opportunity never arose as President Kennedy was assassinated on November 22, 1963.*

*President Johnson.* We come to an almost complete turn-around in communications and relationships with the White House, considering the fact that President Johnson had been a strong supporter of civil rights while a Senator, Majority Leader and Vice President of the United States. His somewhat erratic, if not "flamboyant" administrative style (which differentiated him from his predecessors) coupled with his vigorous and sustained espousal of the "Great Society" (especially before getting bogged down by the Vietnam War), distinguished him for his articulate support of civil rights legislation and programs to alleviate poverty. However, he fully supported the Kennedy legacy, and the substance of Kennedy's "Second Emancipation" speech and program (the Omnibus Bill for Civil Rights) which he recommended to Congress. He also requested Eisenhower's support for the legislation which Eisenhower declined to give on grounds that it was a "whole bunch of laws."

The day after Kennedy's assassination, Hannah on the eve of a month's absence overseas, sent President Johnson a copy of the record of his last meeting with President Kennedy. He wrote that it was the Commission's intention "to proceed with its work with a minimum of visibility;" that the Commission assumed that it would be made a permanent agency by the Congress; that the Commission expressed its desire for such guidance as you wish to give them; and that after the first of January, the Commission would welcome a meeting with him. In closing, Hannah wrote: "We join all the citizens of this country in pledging to you our full cooperation and intention to be helpful as you assume the heavy burdens of your high office."

On Jan. 16, 1964, Hannah again wrote the President repeating the key points of the earlier letter and asked for the President's personal attention to the following: (1) the need for firm affirmation of the Congress for assured status of the Commission to eliminate the handicaps in continuity of the program and the retention of able staff resulting from the short one or two year terms of the Commission's life; (2) the need to nominate replacements for Vice Chairman Storey and Spottswood Robinson as Commissioners; (3) the previous availability of Presidents Eisenhower and Kennedy, to "receive the views and suggestions of the President and to present views and conclusions reached by the Commissioners;" and (4) of the proferred resignations of Father Hesburgh and himself which President Kennedy urged them not to do. Hannah made clear, in his forthright style, that:

> The Commission on Civil Rights has an assignment that does not increase the popularity of its members in many quarters. Nonetheless, its members have spent much time, effort and thought in carrying forward the work of the Commission because they believe in its objectives. By and large, I think even its critics will grant that the Commission has consistently contributed toward the solution of problems that are not easily solved.

President Johnson replied promptly, in a letter to Hannah dated Jan. 21, in which he expressed the hope "that the Commission would continue to operate under the policies that have guided you the past few months as set forth in your letter to President Kennedy of November 13" and that "I believe the most important consideration is enactment of the civil rights bill (Kennedy's omnibus bill) and that all of our efforts should be undertaken with that objective in mind." He then reminded Hannah and the other Commissioners of his chairmanship of the Committee on Equal Employment Opportunity, set up by President Kennedy, in which he devoted "a great deal of effort to the elimination of discriminatory practices in employment and related fields." He also mentioned that he knew of the "good work of the Civil Rights Commission and, of course, take a good deal of personal pride in its existence since it came into being during my tenure as Majority Leader of the United States Senate." He closed by predicting that "we will be able to set up a meeting while the Commission will be meeting in Washington on or about Feb. 15."

But it was not until July 24 that Hannah did meet with the President following a Commission meeting on the same day, at which time the following points were discussed, most of which had been previously discussed by the Commission: (1) the importance of nominating a Staff Director and the Commission's unanimous view that they would like to see William Taylor appointed to the position, but that "they would be interested in reviewing the qualifications of any persons who might be suggested to him;"* (2) the need to expedite confirmation by the Senate of his nomination of Mrs. Freeman and Mr. Patterson whom the President had appointed to fill the vacancies on the Commission: (3) the President's expressed hope that Father Hesburgh and Hannah would continue with the Commission "indefinitely;" (4) the need that the President designate someone in the White House to coordinate the civil rights activities of the Federal government, which Harris Wofford had done in the Kennedy administration.

On December 2, President Johnson requested his old colleague, Senator Hubert Humphrey, to perform this function.

On Oct. 15, 1965, almost 15 months after Hannah had met with President Johnson, Hannah requested a meeting with him to bring him up to date on a number of investigations and reports which the Commission had been actively undertaking during these months. Hannah asserted that "this Commission has been inspired by your leadership in the field of civil rights" and commended him for his "eloquent address" at Howard University. He mentioned the work which the Commission was undertaking on the problems of deprivation and discrimination in urban areas, which the President had stressed in the Howard University address.

On Nov. 17, 1965, the President, in a letter to Hannah, requested the Commission to undertake a massive study of the quality of education in the nation, especially as involved Negro children. In addition to his own personal concern (deriving in part from his experience as a classroom teacher in the South but also from facts brought out by earlier Commission reports and recommendations), the President said:

> Although we have made substantive progress in ending formal segregation of schools, racial isolation in the schools persists, both in the North and in the South and because of housing patterns, school districting, economic stratification and population movements. It has become apparent that

---

*President Johnson instructed his assistants, Messrs. White and Dungan, to prepare a list of names by July 25th (possibly to include some party loyalists) but the President later acquiesced in the Commission's unanimous suggestion of Taylor.

such isolation presents serious barriers to quality education. The problems are more subtle and complex than those presented by segregation imposed by law. The remedies may be different. But as a first and vital step, the nation needs to know the facts. I trust that the task may be completed expeditiously, and that your findings may provide a basis for action.

Hannah responded two days later assuring the President that the Commission would meet on December 2 "to assess the additional resources that may be needed to carry out adequately the program you have requested." He assured the President of the Commission's complete cooperation . . . and that "we hope that our studies will make a contribution to the goal you have articulated."

President Johnson made another significant speech to Congress on April 28, 1966, in which he included strong references to facts such as:

• Overcrowded ghetto schools produce thousands of ill-trained citizens for whom the whole community will be responsible.

• Negro Americans comprise 22% of the enlisted men in our Army combat units in Vietnam, and 22% of those who have lost their lives in battle there. We fall victim to a profound hypocrisy when we say that they cannot buy or rent dwellings among citizens they fight to save.

• No civil rights act, however historic, will be final. We would look in vain for one definite solution to an injustice as old as the nation itself, an injustice that leaves no section of the country and no level of American life unstained.

In addition to the firm rhetoric on civil rights issues, President Johnson supported specific Commission recommendations on establishing advisory and consultive services to help reduce discrimination, facilitate the use of Federal registrars in areas where voting rights were denied, and other specific measures.

On Jan. 20, 1967, Hannah and the other Commissioners met with the President to brief him on the Commission's "Race and Education Report" and on other plans and programs of the Commission. The major findings of the report included data and generalizations as follows:

• Racial isolation is intense and has been increasing.

• Negro students are harmed when educated in racially segregated schools.

• White students often are damaged by attending isolated schools. They are more likely to develop fears and prejudices based on lack of contact and information.

• There are solutions that will not only remedy injustice but also will improve the quality of education for all children, white and Negro.

• Education is the critical place to intervene to bring about improvement in race relations. Although housing also is critical, it is the area of greatest resistance; contact through the schools will help to bring about the attitudes necessary to solve the housing problem.

The Commission presented six recommendations identifying necessary legislation, needed funding for construction of facilities, and clarification of responsibility of states, local communities and the Federal government in the field of education.

On Nov. 2, 1967, Hannah wrote President Johnson (after he and Hesburgh had served almost ten years as members of the Commission, and having been encouraged by President Kennedy and him to extend their tenure), that it was now time to offer their resignations with the thought that they had done their "stint" and had made "some slight contribution toward the solution of America's most difficult domestic problems." Hannah closed with a request that he and Father Hesburgh meet with him on November 15 or 16.

The President did not accept their resignations and Hannah and Hesburgh continued to serve. More than two years later, Father Hesburgh and John Hannah wrote separate, coordinated letters, requesting President Johnson to accept their resignations on the eleventh year of their service on the Commission, which coincided generally with the end of Lyndon Johnson's presidency and with the expected Congressional approval of an extension of the Commission's life for five years.

Hannah closed his letter with appreciation of support which the President had given the Commission, and for his "success in promoting the passage of much of the needed legislation which will be long and gratefully acknowledged."

*President Nixon.* But that last letter to President Johnson didn't end Hannah's and Hesburgh's service on the Civil Rights Commission, as President Nixon came into office. Relationships with President Nixon were relatively easy and generally supportive, especially in the early years of Nixon's presidency but they declined rather sharply in the last months of Hannah's chairmanship.

On Jan. 3, 1969, Hannah wrote to President-elect Nixon stating his and Father Hesburgh's previously expressed desire to resign to President Johnson on two occasions which were not acted upon. However, when President Johnson announced that he was not a candidate for re-election "there was no alternative but for us to serve at least until after the November election."

On Jan. 23, Hannah wrote President Nixon saying that he and Father Hesburgh would remain with the Commission for a few months, complying with what they understood was the President's wish. He informed the President concerning relationships which the Commission had with each of his previous presidents. He also reported on the status of interim appointments of two members of the Commission and for the Acting Staff Director. As he had done with all previous presidents, Hannah requested the President's suggestions on the appointment of a permanent Staff Director which he noted, by precedent, was largely determined by the Commission—perhaps a subtle effort to make the point that the directorship should be professional rather than political. He further suggested that the President meet with the Commission on their next scheduled meeting on Feb. 6 or at a mutually convenient date.

The meeting was actually held on February 15th which Hannah was unable to attend. At the meeting the President apparently offered the Chairmanship of the Commission to Father Hesburgh. On Feb. 17, Father Hesburgh wrote to the President with reference to the "proposal you made to me" with a copy to Hannah. When Hannah returned he responded to the copy of the Hesburgh letter expressing some disappointment that he, Father Hesburgh, had not acted in accordance with the agreement which they had reached earlier to coordinate their relationship with the President. Nevertheless, Father Hesburgh accepted the appointment as of Feb. 17, 1969 and remained as Chairman until 1972 when he resigned after policy differences with the President.

## Hannah's Relation to and Hearings Before the Senate and House Committees

Hannah testified before two hearings of the Senate Committee on the Judiciary, two meetings of the House Committee on the Judiciary and seven meetings of the House Appropriations Committee for a total of eleven hearings between February 1957 and April 1968. The principal themes which Hannah stressed were; (1) the importance of the task of the Commission as set forth in the several acts on civil rights plus his personal views and those of his fellow Commissioners on their sense of their duties and responsibilities to uphold the statutes and the

Constitution; (2) the independent character of the Commission; which reported directly to the President and the Congress; (3) the importance of getting the *facts* about infringement of the rights of citizens, especially Negroes and other minority groups; (4) desirable remedial legislation, executive orders and other actions by the administrative branch of the government on the policies, programs, and organization of the work of the Commission and requests for funding of its activities. As Hannah had told to others, neither he nor any of his fellow Commissioners had sought the positions. On several occasions, particularly when a new President took office, their resignations were offered.

Three additional policies of the Commission were clearly articulated by Hannah in several of the hearings:

• The Commission took no initiative in proposing extensions of its tenure, which he emphasized was the responsibility of the Congress. He took this position even though living from two-year to two-year extensions clearly made it difficult to plan work and retain staff. Not until five years had elapsed, and the results of the Commission were clearly positive and support for its continuation was fairly widespread did Hannah, speaking for the Commission, with Presidential support, openly advocate extension of four more years of legislative and financial support.

• The Commission aimed at unanimity in its recommendations to the President and the Congress but in the event of failure to achieve this highly desirable result, especially in the first (1959) report, the objections, dissents or comments on the recommendations were to be fully reflected in the published reports.

• The importance of the extension of civil rights for citizens of the United States as an end in itself was always supported by consideration of the international implications of a humane and progressive American civil rights record.

*Format of the Hearings.* As the head of an independent agency Hannah was called upon first to make such introductory statements as he cared to make personally or on behalf of the Commission. He invariably introduced himself as President of Michigan State University and then introduced the Commissioners and staff members who accompanied him at the hearings. Congressmen were free to ask any questions or make any comment which they cared to make. Hearings before the Judiciary Committees of the Senate were principally concerned with the views and policy positions of persons appointed by the President as Commissioners or Staff Directors, subject to the consent of the

Senate, whereas Committees of the House were concerned principally with budgetary and fiscal matters. The usual procedures of the Senate and House prevailed and only twice in 11 years were the records of the hearings closed for executive sessions. Hannah persisted in a polite and dignified manner and was never criticized for his manner of presentation or responses to questions, even though he was firm in expressing Commission views on various issues.

In the early years Hannah reminded the congressional bodies of the responsibilities assigned to the Commission by the statutes and of the immense task which they were asked to undertake. This approach set the parameters of the discussion and questions which followed in a serious, if not always sympathetic, mood. Hannah urged the members of Congress to direct questions which they had of a legal nature to his fellow Commissioners and/or the staff directors, who may have been present and were lawyers, like many of the Congressmen. This approach forestalled Hannah's involvement in areas of potential or real hairsplitting legal disputes and thus contributed to his effectiveness as Chairman. The early hearings were more concerned with procedures of fact-finding and relationships, particularly relationships with the Department of Justice and State-Federal relations. Later hearings in both the Senate and the House were more concerned with the provocative findings which the Commission's research had turned up in the reports and recommendations which the Commission had made to the President and the Congress. By 1959 and after, the number and character of complaints of violations had begun to shift from a preponderance of questions of voting rights and segregation in education, which primarily focused on Southern states, to violations in housing, employment and other areas of civil rights, which more often occurred in the Northern cities. The reports of the Commission, based solidly on factual data, supported by 50 State Advisory Committees made up of non-paid leading citizens drawn from varied occupations, races and religious backgrounds, diffused the initial focus on Southern violations of civil rights and made vivid the national problem of improving living conditions for all citizens, North and South, East and West, with varying political preferences and loyalties.

The format for the more numerous appropriation hearings of the House always included a comprehensive general program statement printed for the committee and an oral summary by Hannah. Appropriations requested ranged from a low of $750,000 to a high of $3,782,000 and for staff ranging from 73 to approximately twice that number. Most of the budget was spent on salaries of staff for the conduct of investigations, hearings and conferences. The assignments were on an expanding number and complexity of problems in the civil rights area, which the earlier reports and recommendations of the Commission, supported in varying degrees by the President and the Congress, precipitated. The hearings in the House invariably included: information on size and salaries of staff, Commissioners, and consultants; contracts for services; number and types of complaints received by states and other information having a bearing on the size of the appropriation request.

The mood and attitudes of members of Congress, initially skeptical or hostile, changed over time as a result, in part at least, of the overwhelming evidence provided by the Commission reports and recommendations, and of Hannah's skillful handling of the discussions. Several of the most articulate opponents of legislation passed by the Congress, and of the creation of the Civil Rights Commission itself became, if not stout advocates of progress in civil rights, at least less obstructive in their tactics and more inclined to be generous in financial support of Commission requests. Hannah was never personally criticized and one Senator, (who personally objected to the whole idea of the creation of the Civil Rights Commission), even referred to Hannah as an able man whose only fault was that he didn't know about "Southern conditions."

Hannah, usually in response to questions and comments by the Congressmen, made a point of emphasizing the frugal nature of Commission operations and its efforts to avoid useless expenditures. But in a meeting of the House Appropriations Committee on April 30, 1959, responding to Congressman Rooney's comment on the size of the appropriation request, which was quite modest compared with later requests when the scope of the Commission's research and advisory programs were greatly expanded, Hannah was polite but firm as he said:

> It is a lot of money, Mr. Rooney, but this is a very real problem . . . I came into this business with no more interest in civil rights than other citizens. I had an idea that this was a matter which had to do with a gang fight in some of our big cities and equal educational opportunity in the South, but I have come to the conclusion that there is no more important domestic problem that faces the United States in 1959 and in the years ahead than the problem of civil rights, first from the standpoint of maintaining tranquility at home and secondly, the effect this has on our status and stature in the world. I have devoted a good deal of time on it and if the tenor of the questioning is whether this is a problem that is

worthy of substantial support from the Federal government, there is no question about it. This is a very important problem.

Hannah reiterated his conviction, and those of his fellow Commissioners, in several key speeches, articles, many letters and comments to the Press, with even stronger emphasis as he and the Commission got more deeply into the problems and possible solutions. His early and unambiguous testimony on the needs for financial support were critical in sustaining the work of the Commission.

Highlights of some of the key hearings by the Senate and House Committees provide some indication of issues which were discussed and of Hannah's viewpoints.

*Judiciary Committee of the Senate.* The initial meeting of the Commission with the Judiciary Committee of the Senate was held on February 24, 1957. Appointees John S. Battle. Doyle Carlton, Father Hesburgh, Robert Storey, Ernest Wilkins and John A. Hannah, and Gordon Tiffany, named as Staff Director, were being interrogated by the Senate Committee for confirmation of the President's choices for these positions as required by Public Law 85-315.

John Hannah began the testimony after opening remarks by Senator John Eastland. Hannah indicated that the group had held four preparatory meetings prior to the hearing. Funds in the amount of $200,000 for launching the work of the Commission had been provided from the President's Emergency Fund, but a request for funds for the balance of the fiscal year 1959 were being prepared by the Commission. He then outlined the duties of the Commission, as referred to earlier.

In conclusion to these opening remarks, Hannah expressed the hope that the Commission would have the benefit of the Congressmen's judgment and guidance "to make a useful contribution to our country it is willing to do our best of which it is capable, and now submits itself to you for your consideration."

A second meeting of the Senate Judiciary Committee was held on June 16, 1961. Nominations had been made for Dean Griswold of the Harvard Law School and Spottswood Robinson to fill the vacancies created by the resignations of George Johnson and Doyle Carlton, and for Berl Bernhard as Staff Director.

Dean Griswold was questioned closely to ascertain whether he supported a recommendation of a rare split vote of the Commission by Hannah, Hesburgh and Johnson to amend the Constitution of the U.S. which would "deprive the States of their power to prescribe qualifica-

tions for voters subject to the limitations of the 15th Amendment."
Senator Ervin interpreted the proposed amendment as giving every
person an absolute right to vote in any election conducted in any of
the 50 states "regardless of his intelligence and regardless of his
character." Dean Griswold hedged his response by indicating that the
process of passing an amendment was too long a process to worry
anyone. He comforted the Senator by commenting that: "I would
think the question of mental capacity and citizenship were entirely
relevant to a matter of voting. But I have not given careful consideration to the question, not having regarded it as one which was really an
immediate question." On the more immediate question of whether the
life of the Commission should be extended or not, he was firm in his
response in saying: "I should think the life of the Commission should
be extended and it is my hope that it should be extended in order to
help with the study and education which is involved in working out
appropriate answers in this area." He advocated a four year extension.
Although Griswold's testimony did not forthrightly support Hannah
and two other Commissioners in advocating an amendment to the
Constitution, he did advocate an extension which was twice the length
of other and previous recommendations and went on to be a valuable
member of the Commission and a supporter of Hannah's leadership.

With reference to the confirmation of Spottswood Robinson, the
Committee cross-examined him on his work with the National Association for the Advancement of Colored People (NAACP) and the influence which such association would have on his participation in the
deliberations and recommendations of the Commission. Robinson
readily admitted that the Legal and Education Fund of the NAACP
with which he was specifically associated "does lend legal assistance
to persons who have a claim of denial of their civil rights on the ground
of race or color where they are unable to, for financial reasons, supply
their counsel." Robinson's supporters on the Committee indicated that
Senator Ervin had voted to confirm Arthur Goldberg in spite of the
fact that Goldberg had represented large labor unions; Joseph Swidler
as a Federal Power Commissioner even though he was a strong advocate of public power; and Douglas Dillon as Secretary of the Treasury
even though he had previous business connections. Robinson affirmed
that he did not expect to "be a member of the Civil Rights Committee
and an advocate at the same time." In effect, the case was closed and
Robinson was confirmed by the Senate.

The case of Berl Bernhard who had the unanimous support of the
Commission for the position of Staff Director, who had previously

served as Assistant Staff Director, was smooth by comparison. In addition to his superb legal qualifications, his attitude toward his role as the chief staff officer and in effect the administration of the day-to-day operations of the Commission, as expressed in his testimony to the Committee, further affirmed his qualifications for the position and the spirit in which the Commission carried on the work. His statement follows:

> While Commission members and staff personnel can be expected to hold diverse views, we all recognize that our minds and actions must be accomodated to the professional standards of objective fact finding. This is our assignment. We must locate the problem, document it factually, study the law surrounding it and recommend such actions as the Commission may deem warranted.

Hannah clinched the discussion by reporting that at a conference with President Kennedy he informed the President that Bernhard had the unanimous support of all six members of the Commission, three of whom were native Southerners with divergent views.

*House of Representatives Committee on Appropriations.* The first two meetings of the Commission with the House Committee on Appropriations were held after the Commission had met for several sessions. These meetings were significant in setting the tone of future hearings, particularly in describing and explaining basic policies and viewpoints of the Commission toward its job. Hannah customarily was joined by some Commissioners and key staff members, who responded to specific detailed questions. His initial statement at each hearing typically covered a recital of the legal obligations of the Commission, the organizational structure and functions of the staff, number of staff, program priorities for the year, number and distribution of complaints, and the appropriation requested.

The most important result of these early meetings was related to the clarification of Commission policies as indicated in the following areas: The need for Congressional action on the budget; the delegation of authority and responsibility to the Staff Director for operations, personnel appointments, relations with the Justice Department; decision making procedures and program priorities of the Commission; evaluation and interpretation of statistics; and relationships with other governmental agencies.

Hannah's testimony on these matters follows:

• Although the Commission started operating on $200,000 made available by the President from his Emergency Fund, Hannah expressed the belief that the Commission would prefer to have an appropriation for the fiscal year 1959 "so as to give us Congressional sanction when we incur these expenses rather than to have us continue on an emergency basis. . . . We assure you we will be thrifty and frugal in our operations and will not spend the money that is provided just because we have the money."

• With reference to Commission policies on the vital matter of delegation of responsibility to the Staff Director, which was followed throughout his tenure as Chairman, Hannah testified that the Staff Director was responsible for:

> Planning, organizing, operating and reporting on all programs or activities of the Commission. He is responsible for securing or recommending the selections of supervisory officials of the Commission and for initiating and carrying to completion under the general directions of the Commissioners the statutory duties and responsibilities of the Commission.

This clear authorization and delegation made it possible for the Commission to focus on policy questions, liaison with the White House, Congress, and interested organizations. This was not abdication of responsibility on the part of the Commission, but a delineation of functions. As a matter of record, individual Commissioners and Hannah gave immense amounts of time in reviewing staff reports (especially recommendations), in making speeches on the policies and activities of the Commission, meeting with the Press and other media organizations, responding to vast amounts of mail in representing the Commission at the higher levels of government often at the suggestion of the Director and Staff.

• In addition to the general statement on personnel policy indicated above, Hannah made a more specific statement about the employment of numerous consultants for special problems which would have opened up a possible Pandora's box of politically or other partisan appointments. His words:

> We would not like to put any of them to work until we have them across the board so that we do not get into a lot of commotion as to whether we have any balance between Republicans and Democrats or other groups that think they ought to be represented.

President Eisenhower agreed with the personnel policy recommended by Hannah and thus set the tone and style of his successors by not imposing his perogatives in the selection of the first Staff Director. Hannah reported that at the first meeting of the Commission with the President, that "he had no intention of imposing a Staff Director of his own choosing," but rather to invite the Commission to participate in the selection. With reference to relationship to the Justice Department with particular reference to possible overlapping, Hannah said:

> My answer would be, if the Justice Department is carrying on an investigation and an inquiry that would seem to meet the needs, it would not be our desire to go in and add to the expense with no gainful result likely to come from it. . . . it is our intention to operate a sensible operation and not waste our time, energy or money in fruitless enterprises.

Although this statement set the tone and general parameters of relationships, problems emerged in later years regarding jurisdictional boundaries and authorities.

• Recognizing the composition of the Commission with an equal number of Republicans and Democrats, from the North and the South, Hannah took the initiative to explain how the Commission got on with its work as follows:

> I think you might be interested in knowing how we got started with a Commission of widely divergent views on this whole matter of civil rights and by frequent meetings, surprisingly, we finally arrived unanimously at the judgment that since we did not have time to go into all the areas that the Commission might go into, that we should devote our energies principally to three areas of the act itself: the area of housing, public education and voting.

• After much discussion of the validity and interpretation of some statistical reports on deprivation of voting rights in some Southern and Northern states and cities, Hannah, in a sense, put a closure on the possibility of endless debate by stating that "In my personal view it is not very significant because if a person is deprived of voting in Alabama or Mississippi or somewhere else, this is a very real deprivation of an important right."

Subsequent meetings of the Subcommittee on Appropriations in 1961, 1966 and 1968 (during Hannah's tenure), were largely devoted to reports on program developments; hearings on voting rights, housing, employment, and administration of justice; and protection of rights of Spanish Americans, American Indians and other minority groups; and on complaints of deprivation of civil rights in various areas. Frustration and a certain amount of restlessness on the part of the Commission and staff over Congressional inability to extend the life of the Commis-

sion for satisfactory periods of time made it difficult to do a better job
of planning and developing work projects. Ambivalence on the part of
President Kennedy to move from general political affirmations of
approval of civil rights to executive actions led to some mentions of
offers of resignation. For example, in a meeting of the Appropriations
Committee on April 17, 1961, Hannah reported: "I offered my resignation (on Nov. 8, 1960) with a good deal of vigor and hope that it
would be accepted, but it was not until February (1961) that the
President prevailed upon me to continue."

Two problems of intergovernmental relations and jurisdiction were
reported and discussed, one with the Department of Health, Education
and Welfare and one with the Department of Agriculture. The problem
with the Office of Education was with reference to a possible overlap
between the Commission and the Office of Education on a study of
"Racial Isolation in Education." Hannah's comments:

> I do not know the motive that prompted the President to ask the Commis-
> sion to undertake the study, but I assume that it was the feeling that this
> Commission, over the nine years of its existence has been charged
> generally with what the facts are in the whole field of civil rights. . . . I
> assume that the President was influenced by the fact that the Commission
> was pretty objective and does not start off with a predetermined position.
> We do not start off with the idea we are going to defend what we have, or
> criticize what we have, but we find out what the facts are.

The confusion over the question was satisfactorily resolved after
staff discussions between the two agencies and a conference between
Hannah and John Gardner, Secretary of Health, Education and Welfare.

A similar temporary "hassle" involved relationship between the
Department of Agriculture and the Commission over the contents of a
Commission report on the compliance of the Department of Agriculture under Title VI of the Civil Rights Act which alleged to be critical
of the Department of Agriculture. Title VI required equitable treatment
of farmers in programs in which Federal funds were involved in
financing the program (Title VI also applied to housing, employment
and other areas which involved Federal, state and private expenditures). A member of the Committee from Iowa requested Hannah's
views, to which he responded:

> Because as you may now know, I came out of Agriculture and I have
> been pretty familiar with the Department of Agriculture . . . There were
> rumors in the press prior to the election and during the campaign a year

ago (1963) indicating this report had been suppressed. This was not so. The report was not finished and we wanted to be sure that everything in the report was true. The Department was informed from the beginning and copies of the report were submitted to Secretary Freeman and others. It is true that they moved substantially before the report saw the light of day, but it should be understood that this was instigated to a degree, at least, by the work of the Commission. Having been Chairman of this Commission from the beginning, we have always followed the policy of never embarrassing anybody. There has never been a report by the Commission on a department or agency that has not been discussed with them before a report was put in final form.

In the sometimes "jungle" of disputes between Federal governmental agencies, Hannah's clear and affirmative statement of the principle of prior collaboration on potentially disputable issues (with the focus on the objective facts of the case instead of political considerations) was a wholesome departure and contributed to the prestige of the Civil Rights Commission.

## Growth of Hannah's Convictions on Civil Rights and Dedication to the work of the Civil Rights Commission

An examination of Hannah's testimony before Congressional committees of the House and Senate shows a definite growth in the depth of belief in and the increasing positive results of the work of the Commission in alleviating injustices in American society of Negroes and other minority groups in the exercise of voting rights and availability of nonsegregated education, housing, employment, and evenhanded administration of justice. This growing conviction of the usefulness of the Civil Rights Commission and its activities took the forms of more affirmative views of the extension of the life of the Commission, and in the positive results which were being achieved.

Hannah started out in February 1958 with the belief that there were a considerable number of reasons why he should not undertake this assignment but nevertheless with a philosophical belief that "few if any problems facing our country are of greater importance than the problem of civil rights." By hearings in 1959, after one year of work, he expressed the modest, but informed, view that ". . . we do not have all the answers to all of the problems in the field of equal protection of the law. But we believe that we have made some progress in understanding the problems . . ." By 1963, after he had been immersed in the gross violations of civil rights brought out in the research of the Commission's staff, and in the poignant and frightened testimony of witnesses who had been deprived of their civil rights in various parts of the country and in the violent demonstrations resulting from these injustices, Hannah was prompted to address the Senate Committee on Constitutional Rights in these strong words:

> These actions and the feelings which prompted them must be understood. Instead of being overly critical of leaders who now demand action, we should be grateful to the American Negroes for their patience, forebearance and tolerance over long years of slow progress. Violence cannot be condoned, but we should understand why some feel that they are driven to it. . . . I would ask those who plead for gradual alleviation of the Negro's miserable lot to put himself in the place of the Negro and ask himself how patient he would be if nine years after the Supreme Court's desegregation decision he saw that fewer than 8% of Negro children in the South attended integrated schools . . . if he saw equal opportunities for employment denied him, if he saw himself without a vote 100 years after the Emancipation Proclamation, if he saw good housing denied him even if he could afford it, and if he saw his fellows receive a different kind of treatment by police officers than accorded whites.

With reference to the speed, or lack of it, which had characterized changes in the above-stated views and actions, Hannah extended his remarks:

> Philosophically, a slow tedious advance toward equality in education, employment, voting, housing and justice may be best but the individual Negro cannot be philosophical. He has but one lifetime; who can blame him for wanting to enjoy his rights within that lifetime?

Furthermore, inaction would have highly undesirable results:

> If when the current struggle is over we have been drawn into opposite camps and are left with a legacy of hate, fear and distrust, nobody will be the victor. This it seems to me is the real danger. In many places, tensions are now so great and feelings so bitter that it is difficult to see how they can be alleviated. Binding up the nation's wounds may well be a task almost as difficult as when Lincoln spoke of it almost a century ago.

In conclusion, on this occasion Hannah supported the legislation introduced by Senator Hart of Michigan for a four-year extension of the Commission on Civil Rights which he saw as providing "sufficient continuity for the Commission to plan its operation efficiently and effectively. But it is my own judgment a permanent extension of the agency is amply warranted by the facts. No one can foresee the day when the guarantees of our Constitution will be fully secured for all citizens, much less the time when prejudice and mistrust will be replaced by understanding and harmony. . . .''*

By 1966, Hannah testifying before the House Appropriations Committee in celebration of the Commission's achievements after nine years which he and Father Hesburgh were the only members of the Commission who had the privilege to witness, reminded the Congressmen that:

There were people who said folks were denied the vote because they were black; other people said it was not true. There were people who insisted there was inequality in education. . . . others said this was not true. There were people that felt that employment opportunities were unequal; other folks said that this was not true. It was claimed that Negroes got a different kind of treatment so far as the enforcement of laws and administration of justice; other folks said this was not true.

The Civil Rights Commission started off as a very unpopular agency and we had dead cats thrown at us from both sides and they hit us on both sides of the head. In the nine years, the whole series of reports have come to the President and the Congress; no one has validly demonstrated that there was anything in our reports that are alleged to be the facts that were not factual. So they have not found much fault with our recommendations. I do not say that they like them but they concede that there was some logic in them.

Hannah reiterated these basic convictions and accomplishments a year and a half later to the same House Committee and added that he had "witnessed enough progress in the field of race relations to convince me that this nation is capable of solving the problems . . ." But after ten years the Civil Rights Commission must assess anew its role and programs to adapt its program to changing needs. . . . "We have concluded that there is a continuing imperative need for voices of reason in the field of race relations."

## Evaluation of Progress in Civil Rights in the United States and Problems Yet Unsolved

The Civil Rights Commission, during Hannah's chairmanship from 1957–69, constantly evaluated the progress that was being made and

---

*Permanent continuity is not now advocated under conditions with which the current Civil Rights Commission now operates.

the problems yet unsolved. These evaluations made public in the several official statutory reports of the Commission to the Presidents and Congresses were widely distributed and commented upon by the Press and other media; in legislative hearings on revision of the Civil Rights Acts and the several extensions of the tenture of the Commission and on the appropriations for the Commission. The reports and evaluations of the 50 state Advisory Committees were also widely referred to in key hearings and conferences from 1957–59 on voting rights, desegregation of public schools and housing, improvements in employment, administration of justice, public accommodations, health services and other aspects of the work of the Commission. Some references to these evaluations have been noted in the preceding parts of this chapter. Generally the evaluations were quite positive on the extension of voting rights (particularly in the Southern states), but less so in the more complex areas of civil rights which are more enmeshed in the social, economic and political forces in all parts of the country, namely housing, employment and education. The Commission, however, used the direct involvement of the Federal government in these and other activities as a fulcrum and demonstration of how the job of civil rights could be done. A very direct area in which the Federal government was solely responsible was in all aspects of civil rights in the armed services. Not only were the changes in the armed services initially fostered by President Truman, but followed by President Eisenhower and his successors, dramatic in and of themselves but useful as demonstrations of the feasibility of changes in the civilian economy.*

A comprehensive historical analysis of progress of civil rights was provided in the remarks of Professor John Hope Franklin, a distinguished Negro scholar, of Duke University and the author of a book previously cited *("Freedom to be Free")*.[43] He updated his previous comprehensive survey of historical factors in an address on June 27, 1984 before the "Joint Center for Political Studies" on the subject of "The Civil Rights Act of 1964; a Modest Achievement." On this occasion which celebrated the 20th anniversary of the Civil Rights Act, Professor Franklin saw a major change in education since the Supreme Court Decision in 1954, ("Brown vs. the Board of Education,") first in the legislative branch and then in the executive branches of the Federal government. Further legislative acts were:

---

*See also expanded remarks on desegregation of the armed forces in Chapter I, pages 7–10.

Stressed rather courteously by President Kennedy and prodded relentlessly by his successor Lyndon B. Johnson, Congress finally passed on an act whose comprehensive nature was indicative of the denial of basic human rights from which Negro Americans had long suffered. Despite its comprehensive nature, the Civil Rights Act of 1964 proved inadequate. . . . (However) it strengthened and made more independent the United States Commission on Civil Rights.

He went on to express the opinion that "during the past year (1983), the independence of the Commission has been seriously compromised and its status reduced to that of a political arm of the present administration" which among other negative results led to the resignation of Father Hesburgh who succeeded Hannah as Chairman of the Civil Rights Commission.

On a more optimistic note Professor Franklin, reflecting on changes which he characterized as "significant," created in part as a result of the work of the Civil Rights Commission under Hannah's chairmanship, said:

By the end of the sixties, the changes in the status of blacks in American life were apparent even to the casual observer. A Negro American could expect civilized treatment and accommodations . . . Under the protection of United States marshals and with the blessings of the federal judiciary, Negro Americans could vote and hold office anywhere. There were some significant breakthroughs in the area of employment, although the spectacular appointment of a few blacks in high places in the public and private sectors tended to obscure the inability of vast numbers of them to obtain even consideration for employment. As Martin Luther King, Jr. said so often, 'we have come a long way, but we still have a way to go.'

John Hannah would agree with this overall appraisal and often expressed the same view, even though Professor Franklin chose not to comment on some achievements in the desegregation of public schools; the creation of better opportunities for Negroes in higher education; massive improvement in access to public accommodations; reduction in housing restrictions; more employment opportunities in public and private projects; massive changes in the armed forces and other improvements in civil rights for Negroes and other disadvantaged persons. Nevertheless, John Hannah did not believe that the millenium had arrived in the field of civil rights.

## Appraisal of Hannah's Leadership and Style of Work

• *Ex Governor John S. Battle*—Commissioner from 1957–1959

. . . I have learned a lot since I became a member of the Commission. I hope and I believe that some other members feel the same way about it. When we disagreed it has been with scrupulous regard for the opinions of others and we have been forgiven for having taken what have appeared to be rather strange positions on some occasions. . . . (MSUAHC)

• *Dr. George Johnson,* former Dean of the Howard Law School, staff member and Commissioner from 1962 to 1967. (Letter to the author dated May 1984)

I believe that Dr. Hannah joined other members of the Commission in recommending that I be appointed as Wilkins' successor. It is my understanding that Dr. Hannah was at that time aware that some Southern Senators would object to my appointment. . . . Because of my open opposition to racial segregation, I had incurred the wrath of several Southern Senators, including Senator Eastland. In any event, Eisenhower, upon the recommendation of the remaining members of the Commission, did nominate me to the Commission. Although Senator Eastland and other Southern Senators blocked my appointment for several months, Dr. Hannah and the other Commissioners permitted me to sit as a Commissioner-designate until the Senate finally confirmed my appointment. The three Southern Commissioners were all lawyers but Dr. Hannah was not disturbed by this. When the Commission's voting rights hearings in Louisiana were enjoined by a Federal Court, a delicate legal issue was raised. The U.S. Department of Justice was asked to represent the Commission and appeal to the U.S. Supreme Court. The temporary restraining order (T.R.O.) which was granted by the lower federal court was eventually reversed by the U.S. Supreme Court in *Hannah v. Larche* with two Justices dissenting. When the time came for the Commission to submit its first report to the President and to the Congress, I am sure that Dr. Hannah was aware that the three southern Commissioners would be opposed to any meaningful recommendations. Under Dr. Hannah's leadership, however, agreement was reached to submit the report in two parts; findings and recommendations. By adopting this approach, it was possible to get either unanimous or majority support on some very important issues. I think Dr. Hannah demonstrated real leadership and ability to compromise in the development of the Commission's first report.

• *Dean Erwin N. Griswold,* former Dean of the Harvard Law School and Commissioner from 1961 to 1967 (MSUAHC)

In my experience and judgment, Dr. Hannah was an extraordinarily fine Chairman of the Civil Rights Commission. He was very faithful in his attendance at meetings. I do not recall that he ever missed a meeting, despite his responsibilities as President of Michigan State University. At meetings, he presided fairly and effectively, and he gave excellent leadership. There were a number of difficult problems, such as the time (in 1963, I believe) when the Attorney General "ordered" the Commission not to hold hearings in Mississippi. We did delay the hearing a few weeks, but then went ahead and held it, successfully.

In this case, as in others, Dr. Hannah gave wise leadership. He was always tolerant, always composed. I do not recall that he ever raised his voice at any meetings. I should say, though, that there was a good deal of harmony among the members of the Commission, and between the Commission and its staff.

• *Eugene Patterson,* former editor of the *Atlanta Constitution* and *Washington Post,* Commissioner from 1961 to 1963. (Letter to the author dated March 6, 1986.

John Hannah's strength of character translated itself into strong leadership of the U.S. Civil Rights Commission during his chairmanship. He was a forceful leader—big-shouldered, crop-haired, icy-eyed, with the boom of finality in his deep bass voice. He ran a brisk meeting with no room for nonsense. Yet he deferred sufficiently to his strongwilled fellow commissioners to permit full expression of their own views.

Appointed by President Eisenhower, he was one of the three Republican members on a commission supposedly balanced by party. The other two on that side of the "aisle" were Dean Erwin Griswold of the Harvard Law School and Father Theodore Hesburgh of Notre Dame. Whether these three were in fact Republicans mattered no more than the political flavor of the three who were supposed to be Democrats—Professor Robert Rankin of Duke University, appointed by President Kennedy, and Frankie Muse Freeman and myself, appointed by President Johnson. I chose then and now to wear no party label but partisanship did not figure at all in the Commission's deliberations under Hannah anyway.

The over-towering mission—to find facts that would serve justice and convey them to Congress and the President—caught all of us up and dwarfed such relatively inconsequential considerations as politics. Under Hannah, we prized our little agency's utter independence and guarded it effectively. John Hannah liked it that way and his example set the course for the rest of us; personal honor and public service, not power politics, were his guides.

Not all politicians appreciated this independence. Robert Kennedy as Attorney General under Kennedy and Johnson treated the Commission with some contempt and made plain to Chairman Hannah that he expected the Commissioners to take their lead from, and extend their deference to the Civil Rights Division of his Justice Department. Hannah coolly declined to accommodate him. . . .

Hannah was an extraordinarily articulate chairman who spoke rapidly and firmly, with a judge's conclusive inflection. For all his forcefulness, though, he could turn gentle and fatherly when heated argument required conciliation. Particularly in public hearings this peacemaking aspect of his personality often restored composure and civility to emotional moments. He also insisted on fair treatment of even the unfriendliest witness by our staff lawyers. If he hadn't been a university president he'd have made a fine judge . . .

Whether presiding over our hearings in dim chambers from Rochester to Oakland, or leading us into the Cabinet Room to make arguments to the President, John Hannah was a commanding chairman guided by clear moral insight into the requirements that the suffering of the minority placed upon the decent majority in an ethical American society in the last half of the 20th century. Few Americans served that cause more effectively, or helped more of us find the right way.

• *Father Theodore Hesburgh,* President of Notre Dame University and Civil Rights Commissioner during the twelve years of Hannah's chairmanship*

In the fall of 1957 I had a call from Sherman Adams asking if I would serve on the Civil Rights Commission. He mentioned that John Hannah was going to be chairman and that there would be three Republicans and three Democrats as required by law, also because of the decision of President Eisenhower, three of the members would be Southerners and three Northerners . . . I had another call from Sherman Adams asking if I were a Republican or a Democrat since they had to be divided evenly. I told him I was neither because I have always been independent in politics, and he said that was no problem, he would put me into the open slot which I believe was Republican at that time since most Southerners tended to be Democratic.

As anyone can see from the disposition of the membership, John was going to have a very difficult time bringing any unity out of a group divided both politically and geographically and one might say especially in point of view. It would take a kind of genius to bring anything out of this commission by way of unanimous report and everyone thought it impossible anyway since the Congress had fillibustered and argued about the civil rights situation all during the summer of 1957 and their legislation establishing the Commission was a kind of compromise position. It has been said that when no one can agree on anything, you appoint a commission to find an answer. In this case, they appointed a commission

---

*Supplements previously cited quotations on other aspects of the Commission's work and Hannah's leadership. This material is excerpted from a tape dictated by Father Hesburgh while sailing down the Danube River. In addition to judgments expressed, the excerpts provide some light on the inner workings of the Commission.

that agreed on very little outside the Constitution of the United States. Anyway, as we began our work I was convinced that if anyone could bring unity out of this Commission it was John Hannan because he had the respect of all of us and was a fair and intelligent and well balanced human being. . . .

We had the usual problems of assembling a staff. One of the first things John and I insisted on was that we have an assistant since neither of us were lawyers and I believe all the others were. Subsequently, we put together a very bright young staff of assistants who were very influential, especially the one who served me, Harris Wofford. . . . We also had very little money since we were given a few hundred thousand dollars out of the President's emergency fund. What we lacked in resources and facilities we made up for in the dedication of our staff and our own personal convictions, with John's good leadership all along the way, to do something about a situation in America which could only be described as comparable to apartheid in South Africa. . . .

One of the most interesting events that brought success to the first two years of the life of the Commission was the matter of a hearing in Shreveport, Louisiana, and the ensuing effort to produce a report for the President and the Congress. We had a series of partial reports from all of our public hearings. . . . At the end of each of these individual public hearing reports we would have a section indicating what our findings were in a factual matter, from the testimony that had been received. We would then have a section on our conclusions regarding equality of opportunity following these facts. And then finally we would have a section of recommendations for Federal law to correct the matter of denial of equal opportunity involved in this particular matter under hearing. As can be imagined, there were long discussions on each one of these reports but we gradually achieved a consensus based on the facts. One of the most interesting strengths of the Commission was that we were never found misrepresenting facts. Faced by the startling facts that emerged from our hearings, it was difficult not to agree with our findings, our conclusions and our recommendations for new legislation, even though they were all very controversial in the public mind and especially in the Congress. . . .

With reference to the final preparation and review of the 1959 Report I suggested to John that we change the situation completely and thanks to a good trustee of Notre Dame, Mr. O'Shaughnessy, we were able to get his DC-3 airplane to fly us to Northern Wisconsin where Notre Dame has a lodge at Land O'Lakes. It is hard to describe the change of atmosphere when one goes from what we had been enduring in Shreveport to the pine-setting north woods where we took the whole Commission and staff out to a Notre Dame lodge for cocktails and charcoal broiled steaks on the lawn overlooking a beautiful lake. I should say that half our Commission were non-drinkers but at least they got cold cokes. After dinner we arranged for everyone to go fishing. I guess the good Lord was on our side because everybody caught a lot of bass and walleye and when we arrived back at the lodge at sundown around 8:30, everyone was in a completely mellow mood. We fixed up a table on the screened-in porch of the lodge and then between 8:30 and midnight as the full moon was rising over the lake and the loons crying in the distance, and everyone feeling good about the world generally and relieved to be out of Shreveport, we were able to get a practically unanimous decision on the whole report. As I recall, there were 12 recommendations and 11 of them passed unanimously. On one of the recommendations on education, the former governor of Virginia decided to vote contrary since he thought it was too sociological. I recall at breakfast the next morning the southerners looked at each other and said, "we were had last night," but then the governor of Virginia said, "yes, we were had, but we agreed and we will be gentlemen about it." Perhaps it was one of the best testimonies to John Hannah's leadership. He had really brought order out of chaos and we had a very strong report to present to the President and the Congress, the result of which the Commission was renewed for a few more years and that went on for many years yet to come. It was always a precarious existence though I recall once when we were renewed and kept from going out of existence at the final act of legislation in the dying Congress, the only way we were saved was by hooking the renewal of the Commission onto the peanut subsidy bill which no southerners would dare to vote against. . . .

Perhaps the real breakthrough for the Commission came in 1964 following the assassination of President Kennedy and the presidency of Lyndon Johnson. When John and the Commission met with Lyndon Johnson right after he became president, he said that he would like the test of his presidency to be the number of poor people who were deprived and suffering at the beginning of his administration and what he hoped would be a much smaller number of people following his administration. However, to solve that problem structurally and organically and systemically, we simply had to change the law and we simply had to create new laws and new structures for equal opportunity. This happened with the omnibus civil rights law of 1964 which was passed after Lyndon Johnson addressed the joint session of Congress and with great courage for a southerner finished his speech by quoting the battle cry of Martin Luther King, "we shall overcome." Johnson has been greatly criticized for many things, particularly for Viet Nam, but he has not received anywhere near the praise he deserves for passing that omnibus civil rights act in 1964 which was followed by the voting rights act in 1965 and subsequently the 1968 law on housing which had been fillibustered to death in 1967 . . .

In his relationship with all of the commissioners, John was both fair and friendly. It was very hard to disagree with him when he stated a basic principle in very clear and forceful language. Also, he was most fair in giving those who dissented ample time to speak and that included the witnesses at all our hearings but he was both fearless and courageous in confronting the difficult kinds of people we would call for testimony and were totally against everything we were doing. The whole matter was not without physical danger either because I recall at Jackson, Mississippi, the local redneck group called the hotel and tried to get the numbers of our hotel rooms so we could be bombed. In Nashville, Tennessee, we were staying in the Heritage Hotel and we got word in the middle of the hearing that a bomb was going off in the next ten minutes so we had to clear the room. When the FBI couldn't find a bomb we decided to rub it in and we went back in the same room for lunch and continued the hearing in the afternoon. . . .

I am sure there are not too many people who have accused John of having a deep sense of humor but I must say that he has a great laugh and he could laugh heartily at some of the almost impossible opposition that faced us to an extent that seemed ludicrous at times. He could keep his cool in arguing with inimical senators and adversarial congressmen; there was no doubt that there was steel in his voice and when he was right and knew he was right; he did not suffer fools gladly. I think he had great character in keeping his temper under control and I am sure he has a considerable temper when aroused by injustice . . .

When I talk to the South Africans, I say you've got to believe that one can live without apartheid because we had it and we destroyed it utterly, root and branch, and we introduced a completely new system that precludes apartheid ever returning to America, and we still have a better country and it works. John Hannah should get the credit for that.

## Staff Director—Berl I. Bernhard

Berl I. Bernhard, who served with distinction as Assistant Staff Director and Staff Director, during the formative period of the work of the Civil Rights Commission from 1961 to 1963, appraised the work of John Hannah on the occasion of a testimonial dinner for him on the 25th anniversary of Hannah's presidency of Michigan State University, as follows:

As Staff Director of this bipartisan agency, I can testify personally to the burdens of service in the field of civil rights . . . The Commission has always been a group of men from different sections of the Nation, holding strong and often divergent views. Without strong leadership, such an agency would inevitably have drifted into disunity and ill will. Instead, in the past five years it has been a strong and effective instrument for protection of our constitutional freedoms. This strength and the ability of the Commission to reach a consensus on highly controversial issues has been due in great measure to the stewardship of its Chairman.

Bernhard concluded his remarks with these words:

Dr. Hannah is a highly intelligent man, but many men are intelligent. Dr. Hannah has an inquiring mind, but many have this gift of interest in the new and challenging. Dr. Hannah has great energy, but others, too, display physical strength. These are natural attributes which we admire— for seldom are they found in a single man . . .

But the man whom we honor tonight has two further attributes which we can do well to ponder. One is an iron discipline of self which manifests itself in a dedication to service. Dr. Hannah literally finds and makes time which he selflessly devotes to the public welfare. The second attribute could be characterized as an unwavering belief in the uniquely American method of accomplishing things through the processes of democracy. It is this quality which I personally find to be magnificent and instructive, for it embodies a lesson for us all.

Dr. Hannah seeks the counsel of others because he recognizes that in a free society there is no limit to intellectual expression. He is never reluctant to ask for the labor of others, because he assumes that in a democracy all those who can help have an obligation to do so. He chooses his colleagues in the public service on the basis of competence, rather than color or creed, because he knows the history of those who subscribe to the theories of the master race. And, finally, he is unafraid to assert his own views because he has faith that, if they are valid, they will survive the test of examination and criticism. These, I believe, can fairly be called the qualities of leadership.

*John W. Macy, Jr.,* a former Chairman of the U.S. Civil Service Commission, Presidential Assistant to President Kennedy and former President of the Public Broadcasting Corporation. (Letter to the author dated March 18, 1986.)

He was remarkably successful as Chairman of the Civil Rights Commission. His judgments were statesmanlike. He displayed compassion and understanding in evaluating the civil rights revolution that occurred during those times. An avowed Republican he worked in such a fashion that he gained the respect of the Kennedy and Johnson administration. He was looked upon as committed to justice and progress. Because of my own intensive involvement in equal employment opportunity matters I looked to him and his Commission for reinforcing support in guiding the civil service system onto the paths of true equal opportunity. He established a high standard of character and performance for that position and his standards were followed by his distinguished successor until there was a total change of outlook in the current administration.

## Chapter IV

# Administrator of the Agency for International Development (AID)[1]

John Hannah was appointed as Administrator of the Agency for International Development (AID) on April 2, 1969, by President Richard M. Nixon,* this position being the first full-time position which Hannah held after resigning from the Presidency of Michigan State University. Hannah was the fourteenth person to serve as head of the various agencies which carried on the United States programs of economic aid and military and technical assistance to foreign countries since 1948. These included the Institute for Inter-American Affairs (IIA), the Economic Cooperation Administration (ECA), which was the first foreign-aid agency to administer the European Recovery Program, known generally as the Marshall Plan. Concurrently, and to some degree overlapping with ECA, the Technical Cooperation Administration (TCA) was established in December 1950. The Mutual Security Agency (MSA) succeeded the TCA for approximately two years and was in turn succeeded by the Foreign Operations Administration (FOA), which also had an organizational life span of approximately two years. The International Cooperation Administration (ICA) was the first agency to show some organizational stability, lasting for twice the life span of its predecessor agencies. Not until 1961, with the

---

*The President-Elect was supported in the selection of John Hannah by the Secretary of State, William Rogers and by Elliott Richardson, Under Secretary of State.

creation of AID, did the executive and congressional branches of the Federal government settle on a relatively permanent organizational framework for administering the wide-reaching U.S. foreign aid program.

Quite clearly, one can conclude that the United States was groping for and experimenting with an administrative framework which would be a more appropriate organization to meet the needs of developing countries and the interests of the United States. Although the Marshall Plan for the rehabilitation of Europe after World War II was highly successful, and varied and flexible policies and programs were necessary to meet the changing needs of developing countries and our national and international interests.

The situation had settled down somewhat by the time Hannah took office; but there were still considerable confusion as to objectives, program priorities and methods of accomplishing the varied purposes of the foreign aid programs.

Hannah's predecessors included several distinguished Americans: Paul G. Hoffman, business executive and United Nations official; W. Averill Harriman, ex-governor of New York, business executive and diplomat; Harold E. Stassen, Governor of Minnesota and frequent candidate for the Presidency; Henry Bennett, President of the University of Oklahoma; Henry R. Labouisse, United Nations official and Nobel Prize winner; and David Bell, former Director of the Office of Management and Budget in the White House and Vice President of the Ford Foundation.

Hannah's early interest in foreign peoples and governments, especially in developing countries, and in ways in which U.S. resources and skills could help them help themselves to reach higher levels of education, health and well being were basic to his background qualifications for the position. The creation of social and economic conditions which would lead to stability and peace were integral parts of his established long-time values and global outlook. It is, therefore, difficult to apply a specific beginning date or event which one can point to to prove this generalization. Some of the elements in is background which qualified him for the position of Administrator of AID were:

• His early interest in foreign students and international affairs as President of Michigan State University and his continuing personal involvement in establishing and supervising the University's extensive campus and overseas programs of education and technical assistance. Included in these activities was the creation of the first University-wide organization, headed by a Dean, for International Studies and Programs.

• His active participation in committees of the American Council on Education on international development problems and on the relationship of University programs to the policies and procedures of the Federal Government.

• His service on the Education Committee of the International Cooperation Administration (ICA).

• His support for and participation in the creation and funding by the Ford Foundation of the Midwest University Consortium for International Affairs (MUCIA) composed initially of the Universities of Illinois, Wisconsin, Indiana, Minnesota and Michigan State University, all of which were actively involved in campus and overseas international programs.

• His membership on the Board and active participation in Education and World Affairs, a foundation-funded New York-based organization which focused on campus programs on international affairs and on their overseas projects. (See Chapter VI for details)

• Although not precisely focused on international affairs, his chairmanship of the United States Civil Rights Commission, which was motivated in part by his concern with the international implications of our race relations practices on our international relations.

• His service as Assistant Secretary of Defense for Manpower and Personnel, especially as related to the global impact which desegregation of the armed forces of the United States had on our national prestige abroad. His chairmanship of the United States Section of the Joint United States/Canadian Defense Board also had relationships to international security.

• And perhaps most directly of all was his initiative as early as 1949, while President of the National Association of State Universities and Land Grant Colleges, in persuading his colleagues in the Association to offer the services of the member institutions to President Harry S. Truman to help him implement his memorable Point 4 Program.*

• Shortly thereafter, his service on the International Development Advisory Board, chaired by Governor Nelson Rockefeller, which produced the framework for the celebrated program "Partners in Progress" focused on the needs and possibilities of collaboration with Latin American countries in their social and economic development.

---

*Hannah's letter and President Truman's response are reproduced in Appendix B, pp. 215–216.

Hannah's deep and growing concern with international affairs is poignantly stated in a note written by his personal assistant, James H. Denison, in September 1971:

> . . . It might be established at about this time (1965–66) that he began to lose interest to a degree in the University itself and its on-campus operations, and transferred that interest to international projects. This loss of interest, if substantiated, could be attributed to many things: he had accomplished so much, and comparatively little of consequence remained to be done, or was well in hand, in the areas of planning and building . . . and he had attained most of the honors available to men in his profession, and had taken a liking to official Washington.
>
> So it came as no great surprise to those who knew him well when he resigned unexpectedly and accepted appointment as the Administrator for the Agency for International Development, an assignment which both represented a change of scenery, and offered a great challenge in the area which had become his major interest.[2]

## Background, Research and Recommendations for Policy and Program Changes in AID

Several years before Hannah became Administrator of AID and all during the four years and a half of his administration, numerous scholars and practitioners flooded the market with reports, books and journal articles and other communications which analyzed policies and programs favorable to and critical of the past performances and future needs and prospects for international development. Among these were reports of the Pearson Task Force[3] of the World Bank and that of the National Planning Association.[4]

Highlights of some of the publications and policy recommendations which issued from this period of inquiry and which influenced Hannah, his staff and national opinion leaders, are summarized in Appendix B.

Of more direct influence on the policies, priorities and programs of AID, however, were two personal experiences of Hannah, prior to his becoming Administrator of AID, and actions taken by newly elected President Nixon.

*Report to the National Association of State Universities and Land Grant Colleges (NASULGC).* Approximately ten years before Hannah was appointed Administrator of AID, he chaired the task force of the Association to review the experience of American universities during the previous 20 years in research and training and institution-building projects abroad. The task force included educators from nine universities active in international activities. A Michigan State University Professor, George Axinn, served as Research Director for the study. The Task Force's mission was:

• To restate the philosophy and objectives which justify and obligate our nation's commitment to the assistance of developing nations.

• To state its views on ways the effort should be organized and administered, on the levels and conditions under which funds should be appropriated, on the functions which universities are peculiarly fitted to perform and the conditions under which universities can best perform such functions.

• To propose remedial legislative and executive measures to achieve needed results.

The Task Force made an extensive review of recent studies and discussed key issues in development assistance work in developing nations with experienced persons in government, foundations and private organizations. It published a bibliograpy containing more than 150 titles of books and pamphlets, almost 70 major articles in periodicals, relevant speeches and other sources of information. Included in these were several reports by Hannah to the Association of prior committees which he had chaired on the general subject of the participation of American universities in developmental activities abroad.

The Task Force considered, inter alia: (1) the need for a fundamental reassessment of the U.S. position in international affairs; (2) the loss of meaning of the old Cold War split of the world into two camps; (3) the fact that poor people of the world have learned that poverty and deprivation are not necessarily inevitable and that the gap between have and have not peoples is growing wider; and (4) the responsibilities of the universities to foster understanding the problems and to suggest possibilities for improvement of the situation.

The major conclusions of the Task Force, some of which were much later reflected in the policies and recommendations of the Nixon administration, were the need for:

• Increased emphasis on technical assistance and institution building.

• Involvement of a multiplicity of institutions, political, economic, and social, private and public in the development of less developed countries on a sustained, long-term basis, to be funded by host countries and from external agencies.

• Applying the full range of analytical and research resources, public and private, domestic and foreign, to improve understanding of the problems of each overseas area, biological and physical resources, and economic, social, political, and psychological obstacles at work in achieving development.

• Establising a limited number of high-quality research and training centers in developing countries to concentrate on food and population problems.

• Appointing experienced people in international finance to administer human resource and technological development projects and to make funds for such programs available through international agencies.

• Encouraging American business organizations to invest in development projects abroad and to be a source of professional and technical personnel for overseas projects.

• Increasing substantially the annual investment of the United States in the development of people in disadvantaged areas from the then 1/30th percent of its gross national product to something more in line with the investments of other developed countries. (This point was associated with the need for a grass-roots nationwide understanding of why support of international development assistance is in the long-range national interest).

• Dispelling the myth Americans had the know-how to solve all the world's development problems.

*Senate Committee on the Foreign-Aid Program.** Seven years after the report of NASULGC in 1976, Hannah was invited by Senator J. W. Fullbright, Acting Chairman of the Senate Committee on Foreign Relations, to serve on a committee to study all aspects of the U.S. Foreign Aid Program. The components of the review involved: (1) Eleven research projects conducted by international centers or institutes of Columbia University, Massachusetts Institute of Technology, the University of Chicago and the Brookings Institution, National Planning Association and others; (2) Hearings conducted over several months by approximately 50 knowledgable persons in the field of international affairs including Max F. Millikan, Benjamin Fairless, John Foster Dulles, John Hannah and newspaper editors and representatives of widely varying organizations including the military establishment, League of Women Voters, National Farmers Union and several organizations having a substantial interest in the foreign-aid program

---

*By Senate Resolution 285 of the 84th Congress, second session.

and (3) Comprehensive on-the-spot surveys of results, problems and values of the foreign aid programs in ten regions of the world including Korea, the Phillipines, Japan and Taiwan, which were assigned to Hannah. His study team included Dr. Emory Morris, President of the Kellogg Foundation plus an international specialist from the Library of Congress.

Of special relevance to this account were the remarks of Hannah before the Special Committee on the results of is observations on the four countries assigned to him and more generally on the tentative conclusions which he had reached regarding foreign aid programs. Among his comments which, in retrospect, foreshadowed some of the principal concepts and convictions which he embraced in his adminis-tration of AID, were:

• While no one could maintain that foreign aid projects have been uniformly successful, yet the implementation and administration have been successful in general . . . Benefits accrue to both the American people and the people of the Far East, which is the way it should be.

• With reference to the area of military aid and assistance . . . the United States "is well advised in its policy of helping to build strong defense forces in Korea, the Phillipines and Taiwan-Japan. They should be encouraged, however, to develop a military force for defensive purposes and a very serious effort should be made in concert with other free nations to help Japan find markets for her products."

• The "flagrant" North Korean violations of the terms of armistice between North and South Korea supports the position that "we are morally obligated to give our own military forces and our allies the weapons with which to defend themselves should they be at-tacked."

• The mix of economic, political, psychological and military consid-erations . . . "must be taken into full account and treated with all the intelligence and ingenuity at our command as a means of combating Communist infiltration and influence."

• The time lag between appropriations by Congress and allocation of funds to the area concerned should be substantially reduced. Fur-thermore, more flexibility and delegation to local administration was needed for efficient operations.

• Higher education in these countries needs to be liberalized to admit more able students rather than to continue in their elitist tradi-tions.

• Operations under our Public Law 480 in which surplus commodi-

ties are made available (mostly agricultural products) for humanitarian
and developmental purposes "needs to be reexamined by Congress."

  • Assignments of personnel to foreign projects should be made on
"competence to perform specific tasks rather than on a policy of
rotation" which was currently followed.

  • Use of private consulting firms by the United States was commended.

  • The planning of and local cooperation in administration of projects
to meet fundamental needs should be the modus operandi of American
involvement. "Cooperation, not coercion, is the key to achievement
of maximum benefits and long-enduring relationsips."

  • "That the necessary legislative and administrative action be taken
to keep funds allocated for military and for civilian programs definitely
separated."

Hannah closed his testimony with a characteristic conviction which
motivated his concern for a broad and sensitive approach to the
problems for feeding the world's poor.

> But I venture to suggest that there is a place in decision-making (in
> addition to "practicality") for what might be called sentiment, or perhaps
> better, moral obligation, not spelled out in all detail, but all the more
> important because it is felt in the consciences of men. Nations, no less
> than the people who constitute them, have moral obligations to fulfill if
> they are to measure up to those occasional tests by which destiny makes
> its determinations.[5]

The full Senate report made specific recommendations on the need
for: (1) clarification of the nation's foreign aid objectives and policies;
(2) separation of the military, non-military and technical assistance
components of the foreign-aid programs; (3) more effective personnel
policies and practices; (4) closer coordination of the policies and
administrative practices between the Secretary of State and the Secretary of Defense and (5) legislation to clarify the objectives and to
provide more support for the foreign-aid program.

Hannah's oral testimony and written report were consistent with
these recommendations and had a significant influence on their formulation.

In 1968 Congress, aware of the checkered history of foreign aid and
its recurrent problems, passed the Foreign Assistance Act of 1968
which, inter alia, requested the President to report to Congress before
March 31, 1970 "his recommendations for achieving such reforms and
reorganization of future foreign assistance programs as he determines

to be necessary and appropriate to the national interest in light of such reappraisal.'' In addition, the President was requested to submit to the Congress, on or before July 1, 1969, ''an interim report presenting any preliminary recommendations formulated by him.''

Pursuant to this Congressional directive, President Nixon appointed a special task force in September 1969, to guide him and the Congress on the subject ''U.S. Foreign Assistance in the 1970's.'' The task force was chaired by Rudolph A. Peterson, President of the Bank of America and included 15 distinguished leaders from business, law, research organizations and academia. Included in this group were Professors Samuel P. Huntington and Edward S. Mason from Harvard University, David Rockefeller, Chairman of Chase Manhattan Bank and General Robert J. Wood, president of Sears Roebuck. The task force was assisted by a staff of assistants which acknowledged help from several important prior reports on the same subject.

The Peterson report summarized much of the current thinking concerning development assistance.[6]

The substance of the ideas and proposals was consistent with and reinforced the recommendations of previous reports, but were in a form which could be acted upon quite promptly. Furthermore, Nixon's appointment of John Hannah as the soon-to-be Administrator of AID gave further assurance of the prospect of action on the recommendations.

## President Nixon's Response

The President actually beat the deadlines proposed by Congress by several weeks, sending his initial message, which was titled ''New Directions in Foreign Aid''[7] to the Congress on May 28, 1969, a few months after John Hannah took office.

He pointed out in the introduction to his strongly worded message that the value of the programs rested essentially in our own national self interest:

• Efforts to help nations feed millions of their poor helped ''avert violence and upheaval that would be dangerous to peace.''

• Military assistance to allies helped maintain a world ''in which we ourselves are more secure.''

• Economic aid to developing countries ''helped develop our own potential market overseas.''

• Technical assistance created "respect and friendship for the United States in the court of world opinion."

The President continued, but all of the above—

do not do justice to our fundamental character and purpose. There is a moral quality in this nation that will not permit us to close our eyes to the want in this world, or to remain indifferent when the freedom and security of others are in danger . . . We have shown the world that a great nation must also be a good nation. We are doing what is right to do.

The three main conclusions arrived at by President Nixon as the components of his "New Directions" were to:

• Enlist and expand private enterprise in part by establishing an Overseas Private Investment Corporation to be headed by a Board of Directors who will be drawn from private life and/or will have had business experience.

• Expand and give new emphasis to technical assistance—with priority given to programs in agriculture, education and family planning, but also to meet needs in health, public administration, public safety and other areas. The new emphasis on technical assistance was to be given new organizational status by the creation of a new Technical Assistance Bureau which will devise new techniques, evaluate the effectiveness of programs, and seek out the best possible people in universities and other private groups to direct the programs.

• Increase U.S. contributions to international development banks and provide support for the United Nations technical assistance program[7]

He saw this increased support for multilateral programs as providing a cushion to political frictions between donors and recipients and "to bring the experience of many nations to bear on the development problem."

On September 15, 1970, approximately 17 months after his first message to Congress, President Nixon sent a second message generally reaffirming the ideas in his first message but adding some ideas generated by the Peterson report, the views of Henry Kissinger, his newly-appointed Secretary of State, and by the work of John Hannah and his staff developed during the preceding 15 months.[8]

In this message, the President proposed six basic changes in our international relations, which he characterized as "a set of fundamental and sweeping reforms to overhaul completely our foreign assistance operations to make it fit a new foreign policy,'' taking account of the emergence of new nations in the aftermath of World War II, and the widespread sense that foreign assistance programs had not kept up with these changes.

More specifically, the Nixon proposals involved:

• Creating separate organizations for the three major components of the program: security assistance, humanitarian assistance, and development assistance.

• Persuading other countries to assume the responsibility of their own defense and thus help us reduce our presence abroad—the ''Nixon Doctrine.''

• Channeling an increasing share of the U.S. development effort through multilateral institutions including: (a) a U.S. International Development Corporation to deal with lower income nations on a businesslike basis, and (b) a U.S. International Development Institute to ''bring the genius of U.S. science and technology to bear on the problems of development and to help build research and training competence in the lower income countries themselves.''

• Negotiating an international treaty for ''utilization of the vast resources of the sea beds to promote economic development.''

• Encouraging all donor countries to take steps to end the requirement that foreign aid be used to purchase goods and services produced in the nation providing the aid. As an initial implementing step the President proposed that U.S. aid be ''immediately untied from procurement in the lower income countries themselves.''

## Preparation of Hannah's Response to the Congressional and Presidential Mandates

Hannah took his time about reorganizing and reorienting the large staff and multi-million dollar program which he inherited. For the most part, authorized projects and commitments in the pipe line were continued. He did, however, in his first months as Administrator, size up the personnel which he had inherited and set up several working committees to examine crucial issues and to make recommendations as to needed policy and procedural changes which would have a factual and realistic basis for adoption. In addition to top key staff which he retained,* he promoted Maurice J. Williams as his Deputy, to whom he delegated major responsibility for coordinating the staff work and to perform a wide range of other administrative duties.

At Hannah's directive, field personnel submitted their appraisals of existing policies, programs and organizational arrangements with thoughtfully prepared memoranda. Among the suggestions for changes which emerged were the need for a quicker response to needs for assistance identified by local leaders, and for better guideposts to help less-developed countries (LDC's) establish more realistic priorities for institutional and manpower development. In research the greater need was said to be in the area of indicators by which to describe existing situations in terms which are meaningful to the home audience and against which goals could be established and performance measured, a point that had been stressed in Congress in the Tunney amendment. The country programming process (to determine needs and priorities from the host country's point of view), "has shown itself particularly inept in dealing with less developed countries" and, broadly speaking, the basic problem with AID is that it is "over-administered and under-managed."*

By October 13, 1970, 17 staff reviews were underway on key aspects of two of the recommendations of the President for the creation of an International Development Corporation and an International Development Institute.

An additional problem was put on the agenda for staff study by William P. Rogers, the Secretary of State, when he wrote to Hannah in January 1970, regarding relationships of AID to countries which had "graduated" from receiving assistance from AID or developing countries which had not received assistance from AID. He wrote:

> Our December 11 discussions with Lee DuBridge (Science Advisor to the President) clearly illustrated that the United States is not now taking advantage of the increasing opportunities for useful technical cooperation especially with former AID and non-AID developing countries. Such association could serve to promote U.S. commercial interests as well as our interests in improved international relations and understanding while also being of value to a wide variety of U.S. Government agencies and private organizations.

---

*Hannah had an understanding with President Nixon that AID would not be an organization to which politically deserving, but professionally unqualified, Republicans would be appointed. He had a similar understanding with other Presidents under whom he served.

*Quoted from Peter F. Drucker *The Age of Discontinuity*. Harper and Brothers, New York 1969.

At present there is no adequate institutional mechanism for identifying such opportunities and for facilitating relationships at the technical level among government agencies, universities, industrial concerns and other private organizations of the U.S. and the post-war countries.

Furthermore, there is apparently a need for statutory authority and a funding source for such relationships. I consider the repair of these deficiencies to be a matter of some urgency. I understand that this problem is encompassed in an assignment levied upon AID last December by the Interagency Council on Education and Cultural Affairs, and that AID is currently chairing an interagency working group.

Hannah assigned this special problem to a group of four staff members. This group prepared a report based on studies of 19 "graduate and phased down countries" such as Mexico, Spain, Venezuela; "phased-down, regional and self-help project support countries" such as Ivory Coast, Niger and 22 other African countries; and four non-aided LDC's.

A third comprehensive staff review of the legislative background of Title IX was presented to Hannah under the title of "Increasing Participation in Development—A Primer on Title IX." Hannah's foreword explains the purpose of Title IX as follows:

Title IX of the Foreign Assistance Act enjoins the Agency for International Development to seek new approaches to improve the quality of life for the people of the less developed countries. It encourages us to place greater stress on social and civic developments and take steps to ensure that the broad masses of the people both participate in and benefit from the development process. Title IX is a significant injunction. We must always remember that man does not live by GNP (Gross National Product) growth alone, that an equitable and widespread improvement in the lives of people is the overriding aim of development.

The Primer then went on to elaborate on the spirit of Title IX as articulated by Congressional leaders who authored the Title and on further background material from a six-month's study authorized by 25 Republican Congressmen in 1966 which had considerable influence on subsequent legislation for Title IX. The Primer closed with brief descriptions of specific regional and long-range training seminars for AID and host-country personnel focused on development case studies by the Brookings Institution and the Fletcher School of Law and Diplomacy of Tufts University.

The ideas and recommendations which were received from a wide spectrum of the AID organization in Washington and the field were initially reviewed and assembled by Hannah and his immediate staff and then forwarded to the Reorganization Executive Study Group. In a memorandum transmitting the draft paper to this group, Hannah characteristically kept the door open for their thoughtful but prompt review in these words:

> I have made some changes in it, added to it, and subtracted from it. Rather than trying to polish the language, the attached is presented as a working paper for tomorrow's meeting. It is our expectation that the members will act frankly to what is proposed and give us the benefit of their judgments and suggestions. . . . After the meeting, we will welcome written expressions of views. At the end of the week we hope to be able to put something in final form.

The principal topics covered in the 23 page working paper included:

• Purpose and importance of economic assistance.

• Progress of reforms to date which included: (a) references to the creation and operation of the Auditor General's program "which have improved management and provided strict accountability throughout the Agency;" (b) clear separation of security economic assistance from economic and humanitarian assistance; (c) reshaping of technical assistance programs to give greater emphasis to agriculture and food production, education, public health and population and public administration while terminating weak projects; (d) reduction of AID staff by approximately 30%; (e) beginning of centralizing AID lending operations in Washington.

• Need for further major reforms including: (a) modifying the administrative structure which had remained essentially unchanged since 1961 to reflect changes in AID operations. The structure had been designed to directly manage large assistance programs by semi-autonomous regional bureaus with "strong emphasis on foreign policy objectives in specific countries;" (b) adjusting programs to deal with increasingly complex problems; (c) modifying programs in light of decreased U.S. funding and increasing funding from other developed countries to provide "increasing emphasis on man's relations with the environment."

• Further reforms included: modification of program operations to reflect a "more collaborative style of assistance which include greater participation of American private groups."

• Creating a new Bureau of Humanitarian Assistance which included: (a) the upgrading of disaster relief capability; (b) greater emphasis on population growth and birth control; (c) "programming economic assistance more directly for basic human needs in sectoral terms" (agriculture and food production, shelter etc.) combining capital, technical assistance, food and other assistance resources.

• Creating a new Bureau for Program and Administrative Services support.

• Giving greater emphasis to research and innovation, including greater emphasis on adaptive research on critical developing country problems.

• Revamping sectoral programming techniques which combine bilateral capital loan and technical assistance grants with greater support for World Bank led consortia for providing sectoral loans.

• Substituting a series of policy determinations from the Administrator to augment "Manual orders" by separate autonomous Regional Bureaus for large operational programs.

• Creating an "Administrator's Advisory Council" and other Washington-based organizations "to develop and coordinate policies and operational guidelines, coupled with appropriate decentralization of operations, to put the Administrator in a stronger position to give guidance to the whole operation internally and externally with the White House, Congress and other outside bodies with a strong delegation, to a Deputy Administrator for day-to-day coordination and administration of the Agency policies and procedures approved by the Administrator."

The staff studies helped significantly to make it possible for Hannah to assure the President in September 1971 that:

> he was pleased to be able to report that AID had made solid progress in moving in the direction of your foreign assistance concepts and approaches. Despite the uncertain legislative proposals submitted to the Congress earlier this year which continuously plagued the operation and financial support for the organization, we are, within the constraints of existing legislation, moving to translate your announced policy objectives into effective operation.

Hannah also indicated to the President that AID had:

• separated economic-security assistance from development programs within the AID structure.

• substantially reduced AID direct-hire American staffs abroad.

• implemented promptly the President's decision to untie aid financing from procurement in the developing countries, and materially simplified AID's procurement policies and procedures.

• made substantial progress in concentrating our technical assis-

tance programs in priority sectors, eliminating weak projects, and achieving further reductions in related staffs abroad and
• moved in the direction of centralizing lending operations in Washington. (They had been spread around the world in country missions.)

He reported further, that:

We are well along with a number of special studies in other areas designed to further streamline operations and to improve our responsiveness to development requirements abroad. There is every prospect that these studies will produce equally encouraging results in advancing your foreign-aid policies.

Finally, Mr. President, I am pleased to be able to assure you that our AID staff, both here and abroad, are working towards these objectives with a dedication and creativity I find gratifying.

The President in a reply thanked Hannah for his letter commenting further that he "strongly believed in the importance of assisting development in lower income countries. You have undertaken significant reforms which increase the efficiency and effectiveness of AID's operations and thus strengthen the ability of this nation to contribute to the development process."

As to the "uncertain legislative proposals," on Oct. 30 Hannah released a statement to the Press indicating that the Senate action on Oct. 29 would "have the effect of bringing the AID program to a halt on Nov. 15, 1971." More specifically, it would: (a) end U.S. assistance to help solve the population problem; (b) eliminate the disaster-relief program; (c) cause the collapse of the Vietnam economy; (d) strand 15,000 students from abroad who are enrolled in U.S. and third-country educational programs funded by AID. He closed his press release with the

hope that thoughtful Americans will take a hard look at today's world . . . and recognize that before we put 100% of our attention on our domestic problems, we remember that polluted air and poluted water flow freely across national boundaries. Social unrest results from hunger, or from seeing one's family die because there is no health care, or no hope that through education one's children may have better lives than their parents because there are no schools, no teachers, no books for them. Social unrest flows across national borders too.

## Decisions Reached by Hannah

After review by the Executive Study Group of the responses of the staff to the memorandum noted above and Hannah's report to the

President, a copy of the finally adopted, reorganized plan was distributed as a General Notice memorandum for all AID employees with an indication that Hannah's Deputy would be in charge of the implementation of the plan.

Hannah believed in the function and values of committee work on complex problems by those who are knowledgable about the substance, options and issues involved and who are to take responsibility for action on the proposals agreed to. But he was not interested in protracted discussions. When it was clear what actions should be taken he acted promptly taking into account their suggestions and his conclusions.

Excerpts from this General Notice to implement the decisions taken to take effect on February 1, 1972, follows:

> During 1971, this Agency began a number of programs and administrative reforms to initiate a transition toward a full response to the President's policy for U.S. assistance in the 1970's . . . In the fall of 1971, when it became clear the Congress would postpone action on the President's proposed legislation, we embarked on an accelerated and basic internal reform. This report contains our decisions on immediate program and related organizational changes. The paper outlines goals and directions for the Agency and takes the beginning steps down the road toward these goals. We expect the changes called for in this report to be implemented quickly. Some can be instituted immediately . . . Your attention is directed to a statement we made concerning AID personnel. The need for reorganization and change is due to external circumstances and not to lack of performance on the part of AID employees. Throughout this reorganization, we will insist that equity and full regard for past loyal performance and employee rights will be strictly observed.

Hannah's specific decisions follow:

1. *An organizational structure.* An organization chart was attached which clearly showed the principal line and staff positions.

2. *Administrator's Advisory Council.* The members of this council included Hannah as Chairman, the Deputy Administrator, all Assistant Administrators, General Counsel, Auditor General, Directors of Offices of Legislative Affairs and Public Affairs. An Executive Secretary informed the members of the agenda for the meetings and distributed decisions made by the Administrator in the course of or as a result of Council deliberations. Hannah stated:

> . . . that while there will be no rigid restrictions on the subjects to be considered by the Council, its considerations will normally be devoted to

major Agency and development-related issues within the U.S. Government and in international organizations. These include overall program policies and sector strategies, positions on issues before international financial and development institutions; overall programming, budgeting and Congressional presentation matters; and major operational and administrative issues. Senior Agency officers should inform the Executive Secretary of issues which may be appropriate for consideration by the Council.

3. *Project Approval Committee.* A major operating procedure to implement Agency policies formulated by the Administrator's Advisory Council was the creation of a Project Approval Committee. The function of the Committee was:

> to assure that the proposed projects support Agency policy and objectives. As part of its function, the Committee will review loans, grants, PL480 (surplus grain exports for sale on concessional terms or as gifts) and housing investment guaranty proposals to assure that they conform to Agency guidelines for sector concentration (eg. agricultural production, family planning etc. which were determined to be priority programs), contribute to key problem-solving objectives, infuse applicable research and training, and achieve maximum efficiency in the delivery of AID resources.

The members of the Committee included: (a) the Bureau office making the proposals, (b) all Regional Bureaus, (c) Bureau of Technical Assistance, (d) Bureau for Program and Management Services, and (3) other Bureaus or offices as appropriate.

4. *Bureau for Population and Humanitarian Assistance.* This Bureau brought together under one organizational unit a number of functionally-related programs. Clearly defined responsibility for policy, programs and operations was made possible by putting these functions under one Assistant Administrator. The establishment of this Bureau had the further value of emphasizing priority programs recommended by the Congress and the President. The language of Hannah's memorandum follows:

> The new Bureau for Population and Humanitarian Assistance will consolidate activities which concern the post urgent needs of people—help in immediate disasters, hunger, and overpopulation. It will reinforce the humanitarian efforts of the United States, both public and private, through improved coordination and working relations with the varied and numerous nongovernment organizations with overseas humanitarian and development programs.

5. *Bureau for Programs and Management Services.* Another organizational unit for the purpose of consolidating a number of important service functions and to fix responsibility for the administering of these services was the Bureau for Programs and Management Services. The function of this Bureau was described as follows:

> The Bureau for Program and Management Services will consolidate and centralize Agency program and management support services. This service-oriented Bureau will provide responsive central support to the Agency as a whole in the areas of participant training, contract services, commodity procurement, engineering, controller, personnel, management planning, data systems, and administrative support services.
>
> The Bureau also will administer the Agency's worldwide programs for housing and for American schools and hospitals abroad.

As before, the designated Assistant Administrator was instructed to submit a detailed reorganization plan for the unit to be submitted to the Deputy Administrator for his approval.

6. *Bureau for Asia.* The principal change in the field office structure of AID was authorized by Hannah in the creation of a new Bureau for Asia.

7. *Transfer of Functions to the Bureau for Program and Policy Coordination.* In order to administer the complex functions and far-flung geographical operations of AID, Hannah transferred functions previously performed by the Office of Program Evaluation and those functions in the Office of the Controller concerned with budgeting. The Assistant Administrator for Program and Policy Coordination was instructed to collaborate with other agency-wide organizations such as the Office of Program Evaluation and the Offices of the Controller and General Counsel in the development of organization and staffing plans and to submit to the Deputy Administrator for his approval the plans and actions necessary to give effect to this assignment. The organization as set up in 1972 remained essentially unchanged for the balance of Hannah's administration.

### Some Illustrative Follow-up Steps Taken on Structure and Policy Reforms Announced on Feb. 1, 1972

*June 28, 1972.* Losing very little time the Deputy Administrator addressed a memo to the eight top officials requesting their responses (by July 7) to the following questions: (1) "what issues, questions and problems have arisen which need resolution before further progress can be made? (2) what further major tasks are necessary to achieve the goals we have set? and (3) what position do you believe the Agency should be by December 31, 1972?"

The Deputy Administrator further indicated that as a by-product of this assessment, management was planning a report to the President to bring up to date Dr. Hannah's previous reports including actual changes made to achieve reform objectives, manpower and project statistics, program trends, contract and grant activity, and other data useful in assessing the pace of change."

*July 26, 1972.* The results of the survey request of June 28 were reviewed by the Administrative Council. The highlight accomplishments reported were:

• Beginning steps had been taken toward a more concentrated program.
• Centralized service for management and program support had been organized.
• Staff levels were well down, below the OMB (Office of Management and Budget) ceiling.
• Some increased effectiveness in collaborating with client countries and with other international organizations had been achieved.

In addition to a review of achievements, there was considerable discussion regarding other problems which had emerged in the reorganization.

*August 14, 1972.* As a follow-up on implementing policy statements and directives which were anticipated when the basic structure and program reforms were launched in Feb. 1972, Hannah sent a long cable to all field locations under the general title of "collaboration style of project monitoring" which summarized the work of several working committees on various aspects of this difficult mode of operation, with cooperating countries, private organizations, funding agencies, etc.

*September 13, 1972.* On this date, the Executive Secretary of the Administrator's Council sent a memorandum, approved by Hannah, on "Guidelines on strengthening the innovative and research thrust of AID programs." This comprehensive guideline covered such topics as: (1) basic policy, (2) role of central technical office and country level offices, (3) identification of global priorities, (4) project design and management for optimum payoff, (5) budgeting for research, and (6) project review procedures.

*January 12, 1973.* Reflecting the concern expressed by some advisors and his own sense of priorities, Hannah sent to all members of the

Agency a policy paper on "Aid and the relatively less-developed countries." In the opening paragraphs Hannah asserted that the justification for special measures to help these least-developed countries is compelling:

> Their poverty, the critical nature of the problems they face, the fact that they have not been able to benefit greatly from existing programs and measures designed to assist the developing countries in general are lagging behind. For developmental, humanitarian, moral, political and economic considerations, the U.S. strongly supported the resolution to make a special effort to assist this group of countries.

In support of this broad policy position, Hannah provided specific information and guidance on multilateral approaches and support for the United Nations Development Program (UNDP), and the Development Advisory Committee recommendations and related development and funding organizations; on new types of research and evaluation efforts addressed to this type of country; and on increased collaboration with non-government organizations (NGO's). He closed with specific suggestions on interim measures which should be taken as a step toward more priority attention to this area.

In keeping with AID's responsibilities affecting U.S. foreign policy, Hannah submitted reports on AID organizations and staffing to the Office of Management and Budget (OMB). In a memorandum on Oct. 12, 1973 regarding personnel ceiling requirements, Hannah reported, inter alia, that:

• In four years (June '68–June '72) AID's employment has been reduced by fully 33% from 17,569 to 11,710 and that over-all projected employment will be reduced by almost 44%.

• By June of 1974, AID's American staff will have been reduced by approximately 15% of the number on board when we began the AID reform organization last February. That figure approaches the goal to which AID made a public commitment when the reform program was announced.

Hannah took no pleasure *per se* in these required staff reductions in compliance to personnel ceilings mandated by Congress and the Executive. None, or very few, employees were dismissed but many took advantage of accelerated retirement options which were offered generally by the U.S. government. Hannah believed that "leaner" is sometimes "better" in government operations.

## Budget Requests During Hannah's Administration of Aid

The format of printed, formal fiscal-year* presentations to United States House and Senate committees was very similar in each of the four years of the Hannah administration. Oral presentations were ordinarily made by Hannah in person before committees which were sometimes friendly, favorable and sometimes hostile and unfavorable. Unlike many government programs which had strong constituent and lobbying support, AID had very limited popular support, so that it was an uphill struggle in most years to receive adequate appropriations for the projected programs. Furthermore, as previously indicated, the period of Hannah's tenure (and before and after) saw many scholarly and media analyses and congressional debates about the rationale for foreign aid and of methods for getting the job done. Hannah was sympathetic with President Nixon's response to Congress which directed various reforms in the AID program, some of which required smaller appropriations. He continued to make budgetary requests, however, which were based on his strong belief in the need for and value of providing aid to developing countries which made strenuous efforts to help themselves.** Besides budget requests to Congress which were prepared under Hannah's supervision and supported orally by him, Congress also had available the annual budget message and other messages of the President as well as a variety of newspaper stories and editorial comments, magazine stories, press releases, radio and TV and other sources of information. But the bottom line is that Congress has not been generous in support of foreign aid, as measured by the small percent of our Gross National Product which has been appropriated, particularly in comparison with the support for foreign assistance provided by some other developed countries. Excerpts from the FY 1970–73 appropriation requests are provided in Appendix C.

## The Chronicle of Hannah's Administration of Aid

Hannah said in connection with the preparation for "A Memoir"* that he had never kept a diary of his life-time of leadership of Michigan

---

*Fiscal years for the Federal Government were then from July 1 to June 30.

*Hannah also responded to the expressed interests of individual members of Congress. For an example, see his letter to Chairman Inouye of the Subcommittee on Foreign Operations in Appendix D, page 228.

*Previously cited

State University nor of the varied activities described in that volume. His colleagues in AID, particularly in the Office of Public Affairs of the AID Publication Office, which published a tabloid-size paper under the title of *Front Lines,* took care of this deficiency. On the occasion of his retirement, he was presented with a bound copy of the issues of the publication covering the period of his tenure as Administrator. The hand-lettered inscription to the volume follows:

> Nothing tells better the story of AID during the four and a half years under your leadership than these one hundred and ten consecutive issues of *Front Lines,* whose pages bear honest witness to what the Agency has tried to do during that time, and how it fared in the process. Most of all, there is recorded herein the faces and characters of the people you have led, and the faces and character of the people you have helped, people who esteem you greatly and who view your departure with regret.

The chronicle was replete with pictures of Hannah and his associates from the swearing-in picture of him with his friend William Rogers, Secretary of State, to a pictorial resumé of events and personalities throughout his tenure as Administrator. Included were pictures and stories of his several trips abroad to visit AID projects, sometimes with Mrs. Hannah, and to meet with field staff members and various heads of state to a picture of him with President Richard Nixon and Henry A. Kissinger in the Oval Office to review Nixon's 1970 foreign-affairs message to Congress.

The chronicle emphasized *people,* a central interest of Hannah both in his leadership of the Agency and his devotion to improving the lot of the millions who live in the underdeveloped world. This was not a sentimental approach to his association, or the "clients" of AID in the third world, but a stout conviction that was what life is all about! Accordingly, pictures of people in all their various activities was the striking feature of the chronicle.

But the account was more than pictures; it was a full accounting of the principal events of Hannah's tenure. Included were:

• Verbatim accounts of several messages to all employees about the job that was theirs to do; of organizational and personnel changes; of celebration of honors presented to employees; of one potential moral crisis in November 1971 when Congress failed to act promptly on the Agency's appropriation request to keep the Agency operating, temporarily with one of several "continuing resolutions." On this occasion Hannah met with all of the Washington employees to tell them "You do your job and let me worry where the money is coming from to buy pencils."*

• Brief notes and resumés of Hannah's eight to ten meetings with committees of the U.S. Congress. On one session with the Foreign Relations Committee of the Senate in 1971, after he had become well acquainted with the key officials of the Agency, he reported: "There is more competence in AID than in any other development organization in the world." These and other tributes to the quality of work of the employees, of course, had a healthy impact on the morale of the organization.

• Brief notes and resumés of President Nixon's 10 to 12 messages to Congress to report on major program and organizational developments and appeals for financial support.

• Pictures and accounts of agricultural, family planning and other programs in progress in all parts of the world, and of natural disaster relief in several distressed countries.

## Notes and Letters to the Author on Hannah's Leadership of Aid

• *John W. Macy, Jr.,* former Chairman of the United States Civil Service Commission, Presidential Assistant under President's Kennedy and Johnson, University President and Chairman of the Corporation for Public Broadcasting (March 18, 1986).

... By all accounts he was the most effective AID administrator in the history of that benighted agency. He possessed a global understanding. He was clear sighted in identifying the priorities for aid to the developed world. He attracted top professionals, totally without ideological leanings, to serve in headquarters and in the missions abroad.

• *R. T. Ravenholt,* former head of the AID family planning program (Nov. 2, 1983).

He was surely the best Administrator AID had during my 14 year tenure there. He had a greater sense of mature wisdom than the others, and delegated responsibilities well. . . .

Dr. Hannah would carefully weigh the evidence and alternatives, make the key decision, and delegate responsibility for implementation.

---

*He expressed similar views at Michigan State University when, during the depression, he had to arrange personally for a loan from a large Lansing bank to tide the faculty and employees over until the Legislature found a way out of the financial crisis.

• *Elliott L. Richardson,* former Under-Secretary of State (November 9, 1983).

As I recall, I was principally responsible for finding and recommending Dr. Hannah as Administrator of AID. Thereafter, and as long as I remained at State (i.e., until May or June of 1970), we met from time to time at senior staff meetings and whenever some problem, usually on the Hill, required our getting together. What I recall best about him was his tenacity. He spent enormous amounts of time and energy talking to individual Congressmen about the needs and opportunities of AID. His down-to-earth approach, reinforced by detailed knowledge and laced with humor, was very effective.

• *Erving Long,* long-time AID official who worked with Hannah during all the years of Hannah's tenure as Administrator (Telephone conversation January 18, 1984).

General
• Hannah had the longest tenure of any AID administrator.
• Generally speaking AID has been blessed with able administrators but very different in personality and style.

Leadership of staff
• A+
• Great man—"father figure."
• Enjoyed better relationship with staff than any other administrator.
• Had very high respect for the staff as the most knowledgable persons in international work. This attitude had a very positive effect on the staff.

Administrative Methods
• Was not very interested in administrative details and procedures. He delegated administration to his deputy.

Major Policies
• Major emphasis was on people—believed that indices for cutting off AID to certain countries because of having reached a certain GNP level did not reflect the fact that many people in those countries were still below the poverty level.
• Had a conviction that AID was essentially a Congressional responsibility, especially in light of the fact that AID does not have a constituency for its support. His success in getting the 1974 revisions in AID legislation was evidence of this conviction.
• Hannah was not interested in abstractions and slogans about development . . . The purpose of AID was to make people better off. His brain was ¾ heart.

Relations with Congress

- Hannah maintained very close working relationship with the Appropriations and Authorizing Committees and other key persons in Congress.
- His testimony at hearings was very much appreciated. He was fully trusted.
- His habit of taking key staff members to hearings to respond to detailed questions was appreciated by the staff.
- His testimony to Congress emphasized that Congress should be proud of AID's accomplishments. The dialogue was easy and relaxed and to a degree anecdotal.

Major Achievements
- Revisions in the Foreign Service Act in 1974.
- Stimulation of professionalism in AID.
- Major contribution was in the prestige which he brought to the position.

Relations with White House and Relevant Departments (Treasury, etc.)
- Was under the impression that Hannah had an understanding with President Nixon that there were to be no "ward heelers" appointed. Believes that relationship with the White House (Nixon, Ford) was good.

- *James P. Grant,* Executive Director of UNICEF (29 March 1986).

First, it is of note that John Hannah made more of a major contribution to the revamping of the aid legislation by Congress in 1973 to make the U.S. foreign assistance much more responsive in meeting basic human needs than is generally known . . . The emphasis on giving priority to meeting human needs was both very much in line with his own long-term interests and with his own view of the revamping required if the foreign aid legislation, increasingly unpopular with Congress, was not to die as a major tool of development cooperation.

My second point is to mention my one criticism of John Hannah—this may be more valuable than adding further to the well earned kudos for him . . . My criticism is that during his years as administrator of USAID he had far greater prestige with Presidents Nixon and Ford than he was prepared to use. In short, I think he should have been more forceful with both Presidents in presenting his own much wiser views at critical policy junctures. Both Nixon, when he was Vice-President, and Ford, when he was a Congressman from Michigan, looked up to John Hannah and, in my judgment, would have seen him far more frequently at his request had he only asked. As a consequence, the views of other officials often prevailed when John Hannah might have had his own wiser views adopted by capitalizing on his potential access to the Presidents.

*Samuel H. Butterfield,* a key official in the Technical Assistance Bureau of AID (Aug. 28, 1984).

During its first 20 years the U.S. foreign aid program wavered between the proponents of capital transfers as the key element of effective development assistance and those who argued that changes in technology, institutions, and behavior were the keys to change. Capital assistance proponents were in control from about 1958 to 1968. Dr. Hannah's entry into AID signaled to all of us that the pendulum was swinging the other way, as it should have. Dr. Hannah's establishment of the Technical Assistance Bureau as a strong leader of agency technical assistance work world-wide was, to my mind, the most important thing that he did. He had to push hard against the senior career officers in most of the agency to put personnel and resources into the new bureau at the expense of the geographic bureaus. . . .

• *Princeton Lyman,* the U.S. Ambassador to Nigeria, formerly Director of the Title IX Office of AID (March 11, 1988).

. . . Dr. Hannah, to those of us in "middle management" in those days, was a formidable figure. When he was appointed, he was expected to be a partisan of the universities and therefore relatively negative toward the role of career AID programs and implementors, but that proved untrue. He was thought of as a master of congressional relations, and that was true. And he steered us through one of the most serious crises in our relations with Congress, when the Senate actually defeated the aid authorization bill. Out of that crisis grew the New Directions of AID and the emphasis on Basic Human Needs.

My personal experience relates to this restructuring of AID's priorities. I was, from 1968–71, Director of an office originally known as the Title IX Office, later Office of Civic Participation. It was created in response to an amendment to the FAA calling on AID to facilitate popular participation in development and to examine in that respect the political as well as economic aspects of development. In carrying out our mandate, we looked at two forms of participation, economical and political. With regard to the former, we concluded after many months of exploration, that if AID was serious about fostering economic participation, it could not be done through some rejuvenated efforts with cooperatives or some nicely visible but separate community development efforts. It would take a reordering of overall AID priorities. I wrote a memo to the then Assistant Administrator for Program and Policy Coordination, Ernest Stern, suggesting that if AID really wanted to promote popular, i.e. equitable, participation in development it would have to make such participation a major criterion of all its projects, e.g. agricultural loans, education projects, etc., i.e. the big money items not just some separate "show" programs. Ernie Stern passed the memo to Dr. Hannah with a note saying, "This is not practical, but it is interesting." I never heard back from Dr. Hannah. But later when the New Directions emerged from his negotiations with Congress, these principles became enshrined. I do not know if the memo had any effect. But clearly, Dr. Hannah understood that new winds were blowing, and that a whole new approach to equity was required.

• *President Nixon's "Dear John" farewell letter to Hannah (September 19, 1973, MSUAHC)*

It is with deep gratitude for your five years of splendid service as Administrator of the Agency for International Development that I accept your resignation from the post as you have requested effective October 1, 1973.

As we both know, I have long been convinced that major improvements were needed in our foreign assistance program. Over the past five years, we have made substantial progress in increasing the efficiency of our aid by focusing on a few key areas where we have a high degree of experience and expertise, and by coordinating our efforts more closely with other nations and international bodies. Your outstanding contributions to these efforts have not only my own high respect and that of your colleagues, but also the enduring thanks of all Americans. I hope you will always look back with great pride on the service which you have given your country.

Hannah was replaced by Daniel S. Parker, a Business Executive President of the firm which bears his name. At Administrator Parker's request, Hannah made a field study of the nine Agriculture Research Centers in as many parts of the world which Hannah strongly endorsed. He then returned to Michigan State University for a brief time before becoming Deputy Secretary of the World Food Conference and Executive Director of the World Food Council.

Chapter V

# The World Food Conference (WFC), World Food Council and The International Fund for Agricultural Development (IFAD)[1]

John Hannah was a key figure from 1974–78 in the coordinated efforts of three United Nations (UN) organizations to come to grips with the world food crisis. The successful performance of all three of these interrelated UN agencies was clearly called for if the monumental world food problem was to be dealt with to alleviate massive starvation and malnutrition, especially in the developing countries. By this time, Hannah's reputation and demonstrated competence as a leader in agriculture and education and in the administration of large and complex organizations to deal with problems of this magnitude (even though not in the U.N. framework) were well known to the Secretary General of the U.N. In discussing his potential role (initially with the WFC) at a meeting called by Kurt Waldheim, Secretary General of the U.N., Hannah showed definite interest in the task but had to be satisfied on two important conditions: (1) the role and relationship which the U.N. Food and Agriculture Organization (FAO) would have with the Conference and (2) whether sufficient resources would be available to employ a competent and independent staff to supplement the FAO in developing a factual basis for deliberations of the conference on the complex issues involved in increasing agricultural production and in arriving at realistically possible solutions to the problem.

On the first point it was necessary to get FAO, which was generally regarded as having a poor record of practical accomplishments in agriculture, (which was well known to Hannah) to take a subordinate role in the preparations for and in the conduct of the Conference. This problem was made easier by the attitude of the Director General of FAO, Mr. A. H. Boerma, who was aware of the deficiencies of his organization for the kind of high-level staff work which was essential to guide the Conference to constructive and manageable ends. He quite readily acquiesced in the decision to set up the Conference as an independent UN body.

As to the second point, when Hannah was told that there was insufficient unencumbered funds in the Conference budget for employing a high-level staff, he sought and secured additional funds from his friends in several organizations to make up for the deficiency. He then was authorized to employ a special staff to work with FAO staff members in preparing the necessary technical papers for use in the Conference.

Having been satisfied on these two points, he accepted appointment as Deputy Secretary General of the Conference. This appointment, on Feb. 1, 1974, by Secretary General Waldheim, was concurred in by the Secretary-General of the Conference, Mr. Sayed Marei, a distinguished Egyptian. Hannah was then ready to go off to Rome, with Mrs. Hannah to make his contribution. After the Conference had created the World Food Council, he was appointed its Executive Director. The Council in turn established IFAD as its operating body to administer a variety of practical activities in cooperation with the developing countries to improve agricultural production and nutrition.

Hannah spent approximately four years in these three international organizations before returning to MSU as President Emeritus, where he had continued to be active on University and Michigan problems and on the Boards of Directors of organizations having an interest in international development.

## The World Food Conference

The World Food Conference, like all major UN activities, was not entered into without full and deliberate participation of all relevant parts of this complex organization. What was, perhaps, a bit unusual for the U.N. was the relative speed with which the WFC was finally created out of the complex jigsaw of consultations and resolutions, tentative agenda, appointment of a Secretary-General, and preparatory work which went on from Sept. 1973 to the opening of the Conference in Nov. 1974. This accelerated action was no doubt influenced by the world food crisis which had been predicted but not addressed until the Conference was actually convened.

The origin of the idea of a World Food Conference is attributed to the Fourth Conference of Heads of State or Government of Non-Aligned Countries held at Algiers form Sept. 5–9, 1973. The rationale for an emergency conference was the extraordinarily serious food crisis confronting vast areas and populations of the world. The conference was to be convened at the ministerial level, by the UN, the Food and Agriculture Organization (FAO), and the United Nations Conference on Trade and Development (UNCTAD) to "overcome the increasing shortage of food and other commodities and to maintain stable prices."

Very shortly thereafter (only thirteen days), the Secretary of State of the United States, when addressing the UN General Assembly, formally proposed that a World Food Conference be convened under the auspices of the United Nations to "harness the efforts of all nations to meet the hunger and malnutrition resulting from natural disasters."

The UN organization on Oct. 4, 1973 proposed an agenda item for the 28th session of the General Assembly, which specifically recommended a World Food Conference.

The question was referred to the Economic and Social Council, which recommended to the UN General Assembly on Oct. 18 that such a Conference be held sometime in 1974 and that the responsible UN agencies consider this question as a matter of high priority and submit their reactions to the Economic and Social Council.

The FAO responded by welcoming the proposal for a conference in 1974 under the auspices of the United Nations and suggested that efforts should be focused . . . "to bring about a commitment by the world community as a whole to undertake concrete action towards resolving the world food problem within the wider context of development problems." FAO authorized, from its funds, up to a maximum of $500,000 to cover costs connected with the preparation for and servicing of a conference, a sum which was soon seen to be insufficient.

Favorable responses were also received from the United Nations Conference for Trade and Development (UNCTAD), the International Labor Organization (ILO) and the United States Government, which responses were recognized in a resolution of the UN General Assembly on Dec. 11, 1973.

With this support from the UN specialized agencies, the Social and Economic Council recommended that the conference be convened by the United Nations for about two weeks in November 1974 in Rome with the Social and Economic Council taking overall responsibility for the Conference; also that the UN Secretary General appoint a Secretary General for the Conference. On Feb. 1, 1974, the Secretary General appointed Mr. Sayed Marei and shortly thereafter Mr. John Hannah as the Deputy Secretary and Mr. Roslow, from the Soviet Union as the second Deputy Secretary.

The basic structure of leadership and some working funds having been established, the Council set in motion the creation of Preparatory Committees, which met for three working sessions in New York, Geneva, and Rome in February, May and September/October to prepare specific documents for consideration by the Conference. The Preparatory Committee took account of the suggestions made in: (1) a paper prepared under Hannah's supervision which provided a preliminary assessment of the world food situation, present and future; (2) a second conference secretariat document entitled "The World Food Problem: proposals for national and international action;" and (3) ideas generated in a meeting, held before the opening of the Conference, of interested delegations recommended by the Secretariat concerning the need for an 'integrated approach in tackling various aspects of the world food problem and the need for follow up action to be effective." The viewpoints expressed and the priorities recommended by this Group of 77 interested nations focused primarily on the food deficits of the poorest nations. The positions taken by the Group of 77 were also highly influential on the thinking of the Preparatory Committees and ultimatley on the resolutions and recommendations of the Conference.

The U.N. Social and Economic Council (SEC) acted on the recommendations of the Preparatory Committees by passing several resolutions with respect to participants in the Conference, rules of procedure, provisional agenda, and proposed work of the Conference. Of special importance to the structure and participants of the Conference was the resolution requesting the Secretary General to invite as participants:

(1) All states belonging to the United Nations (including the Soviet Union which was not a member of the FAO);

(2) Representatives of "liberation movements recognized by the Organization of African Unity and/or the League of Arab States," but without vote—a strategical action which probably encouraged later financial contributions by the Arab states;

(3) The interested organs and specialized agencies of the United Nations, the International Atomic Energy Agency (IAE) and General Agreement on Tariffs and Trade (GATT);

(4) Other interested non-governmental organizations to be represented as observers;

(5) Non-governmental organizations (NGO's) which were in consultative status with the SEC or with the FAO, as observers;

(6) Other organizations which might make specific contributions to the work of the Conference, as observers.

The organizational structure, rules of procedure, participants and a framework of ideas and data having been created by the Preparatory Committee and endorsed by the SEC, the Conference was scheduled to be convened in Rome from Nov. 5–16, 1974, by the Secretary General of the Conference. A little more than a year after the first recommendation to convene such a conference had elapsed was probably a record for the United Nations in bringing an idea of a humanitarian, technological and political effort into being.

The Conference was attended by ministers, or other official representatives of 136 countries from the smallest nations to the largest; representatives of 6 liberation movements such as the PLO, National Front for the Liberation of Angola; the Secretary General of the United Nations and the organizations associated with the Secretariat such as UNICEF, FAO and ILO; 26 representatives of intergovernmental organizations such as the African and Asian Development Banks, various international commodity organizations such as the Wheat and Olive Oil Councils; and representatives of 161 international and national nongovernmental organizations. The United States delegation was headed by Secretary of Agriculture Earl L. Butz and included among others Senator Hubert Humphrey and Congressmen Dick Clark and Clement Zablocki.

The grand total of conferees numbered approximatley 350, most of whom were designated as observers, as defined by the resolution of the SEC. The Conference was officially opened by the Secretary General of the United Nations who performed all of the protocol requirements and then defined the mission of the Conference as follows:

The World Food Conference is the last of the great conferences and debates that have made 1974 a year of unprecedented United Nations activity in the economic field. Food was not only the major economic and social problem faced by the international community . . . but it was without question the most immediately important. Less dramatic than actual starvation, but perhaps for this reason even more insidious were the tragic effects of prolonged malnutrition . . . It was difficult to review the sequences of events that had led to the current food crisis without being discouraged by the lack of foresight and common interest shown by individuals, governments and the international community . . . There had been a general failure to meet the target of 4% annual increase in overall agricultural production . . . As a consequence, many developing countries had become heavy importers of food . . . Together with the higher prices that had to be paid for other imports, including fuel, fertilizer and other agricultural needs, that was one of the reasons for the current severe drain on the foreign exchange reserve of many developing countries. . . .

The Secretary General then went on to mention other aspects of the food problem, broadly defined, including the inadequacy of emergency measures which had been taken to improve nutrition "for those who need it most;" the imbalance between the production of food and the rate of increase in a nation's population; the need for increased production of fertilizers and pesticides and for expanding and strengthening research facilities. He admonished the Conference that "while it is important to analyze problems, it is now necessary to enter the realm of action" . . . with concrete proposals for national and international action to meet short-term, mid-term and long-term needs. He also pointed out the overriding need "for the creation of international monitoring procedures to ensure that the world did not drift into crises without understanding or warning." He urged a "coherent, efficient and equitable global strategem" . . . and stated that there was not the political will to create it through the United Nations.

Many of the same topics were commented upon by the Secretary General of the Conference, who added:

. . . the food crisis had been aggravated by other disruptive factors, including runaway inflation, the energy crisis, unemployment and monetary instability, which had shaken the foundations of even affluent nations and spread despair among the poorer nations. But the deeper causes of the world food problem lay in rural poverty and in traditional, as opposed to modern agriculture in developing countries. The necessary changes would take time and could not be made without help from the developed countries.

The Secretary General said that he was greatly influenced by the reports of the three sessions of the Preparatory Committee which were produced under the general direction of himself and the specific direction of John Hannah and the key staff members he had recruited. These comprehensive background papers, some of which numbered several hundred pages of data and clearly reasoned and objective recommendations, constituted the substance of the debates and ultimate recommendations and resolutions which were distilled in the many plenary sessions which occurred during the eleven days of the Conference. The staff members recruited by Hannah had worked closely with FAO, UNCTAD, ILO and other staff members from United Nations agencies who had made earlier studies of the problems.

The Conference then proceeded to hear from the host to the conference, His Excellency Mr. Giovanni Leone, President of Italy, who added an important political note to the Conference proceedings.

> The tasks before the Conference were difficult and urgent, since it was being held in a general context characterized by profound imbalances in the individual economies of the world and in their mutual relations. The problems could not be faced within a merely technical perspective, but must be seen within a political context requiring concrete measures for providing the poorest populations with their food needs. The solution of problems of such great complexity provides the opportunity to establish new and closer cooperation between countries, both bilaterally and multilaterally.

The keystone address was presented by the United States Secretary of State Henry A. Kissinger at the Second Plenary session on Nov. 5, 1974. Highlights of this address, which focused on United States' appraisal of the world food crisis and on ways in which the United States was prepared to contribute to immediate and long range solutions to the problems are included as Appendix E.

After adoption of rules of procedure and agenda, and election of officers, the Conference created three working committees which were assigned responsibility for discussing papers produced by the Preparatory Committees, hearing experts, organizing the debates, preparing summaries of proceedings, formulating policies, priorities and programs, and formulating recommendations to the plenary sessions of the Conference in the form of draft resolutions. The primary foci of the three main committees and working parties were briefly described as follows:

*Committee No. 1*—Measures for increasing food production in developed and developing countries; policies and programs for improving consumption patterns and nutrition in all countries, aiming at ensuring adequate availability of food in developing countries, particularly to vulnerable groups, with appropriate programmatic subheadings. This committee met for 16 sessions before submitting its 15 draft resolutions to the Conference.

*Committee No. 2*—Measures to strengthen world food security. This committee also met for 16 sessions and submitted five draft resolutions to the Conference.

*Committee No. 3*—Specific objectives and economic measures in the area of international trade and adjustment relevant to the food problem, including measures toward stabilization and expansion of markets for exports from developing countries. This committee met for 15 sessions and submitted one comprehensive draft resolution to the Conference.

A fourth committee on Credentials apparently provided opportunities for various countries to vent their political biases with reference to participation of several countries such as Viet Nam under rules adopted by the Conference. Although there appeared to be considerable dissension and discord on marginal cases, these did not appear to make any major differences in the final resolutions adopted by the Conference.

*Resolutions.* The twenty-two resolutions of the Conference represented a comprehensive diagnosis of the many complex factors in the production of food and nutrition to meet world needs. Resolution No. 22 is of special importance to this account because it established the basis for creation of the World Food Council, to which responsibility was given for following up on most of the actions recommended by the Conference. The most important features of this resolution, couched in the typical form and language of United Nations resolutions, follows:

> *The World Food Conference,*
> *Recognizing* that an assurance of adequate world food supplies is a matter of life and death for millions of human beings.
>
> *Appreciating* the complex nature of the world food problem, which can only be solved through an integrated multi-disciplinary approach within the framework of economic and social development as a whole,
>
> *Considering* that collective world food security within the framework of a world food policy should be promoted and its concept further defined and elaborated, so that it should foster the acceleration of the process of rural development in developing countries as well as ensure the improvement of international cooperation,

*Appreciating* the need to coordinate and strengthen the work of the international agencies concerned, and to ensure that their operational activities are coordinated in an effective and integrated world food policy.

*Recognizing* in particular the need for improved institutional arrangements to increase world food production, to safeguard world food security, to improve world food trade, and to ensure that timely action is taken to meet the threat of acute food shortages or famines in the different developing regions,

*Calls upon* the General Assembly to establish a *World Food Council* at the ministerial or plenipotentiary level, to function as an organ of the United Nations reporting to the General Assembly through the Economic and Social Council, and to serve as a coordinating mechanism to provide over-all, integrated and continuing attention for the successful coordination and follow-up of policies concerning food production, nutrition, food security, food trade and food aid, as well as other related matters, by all the agencies of the United Nations system.

## World Food Council

The World Food Council was officially established in January 1975, when John Hannah was appointed as the first Executive Director by U.N. Secretary General Waldheim. Concurrently, Sartaj Aziz, a Pakistani, who had previously served as one of three Deputy Secretaries General under Hannah in the World Food Conference, was appointed Deputy Executive Director. Even though Hannah had performed most acceptably as a Deputy Secretary of the Conference under Sayed Marei, who became the first President of the Council, the Group of 77 underdeveloped countries protested Hannah's appointment as Executive Director, not on grounds of his personal qualifications or demonstrated competence, but because he was a citizen, and thus a symbol, of a world power which the Group of 77 conceived to be insufficiently sympathetic to their cause. However, after a very frank expression of their objections to Hannah's appointment, in a meeting in which Hannah and Sayed Marei participated, the Group of 77 withdrew their objections and Hannah was formally appointed by the Council.

Hannah agreed to serve first on a short term basis to get the Council underway, but later agreed to an extension until 1978.

The Council consisted of 36 ministerial level members: 9 from Africa, 8 from Asia, 7 from Latin America, 4 from socialist states and East Africa and 8 from the western states, including one from the

United States. All members were nominated by the Economic and Social Council and appointed by the General Assembly of the United Nations. One third of the members were succeeded each year by other ministers. The Council elected its own President, the first being Sayed Marei, two Vice Presidents and a rapporteur. This organization assured wide representation and a world view of food, agriculture and related matters, which slowed up its deliberations but doubtless improved the breadth and possible workability of its decisions. Members of other specialized agencies of the United Nations and other invited persons also participated as observers. The Council made annual reports to the UN General Assembly of the problems encountered and the progress or lack of it.

Annual meetings of the Council were held while Hannah was Executive Director, in Rome, the Phillipines, Sri Lanka and Mexico. The deliberations were based on factual material provided by the same research staff which had served the WFC. Council meetings were preceded by preparatory sessions, followed by official meetings which usually concluded with declarations and recommendations for follow-up work by the Council such as:

• to review periodically major problems and policy issues affecting the world food situation, and the steps being proposed or taken to resolve them by governments, and by the United Nations system . . . and recommend remedial action as appropriate . . .

• to establish its own program of action for assuring that appropriate United Nations agencies . . . focus attention on the problems of the less developed countries.

• to receive reports of a committee to be established by the FAO on "World Food Security," the functions of which were spelled out on four critically important areas.

• to provide a forum for intergovernmental consultation on national and international food aid programs and policies with particular reference to possibilities of securing improved coordination between bilateral and multilateral food aid . . .

• to coordinate its program with the United Nations Conference on Trade and Development (UNCTAD) . . . .

In addition, the Council was requested by the U.N. Secretary General to obtain information and follow-up views on the Conference from "interested countries." The Group of 77 was the most active and vocal of the countries, particularly in the first year of the Council when they wanted to influence the Council early on with their views with reference to the selection of an Executive Director, and other procedural as well as substantive matters. They prepared a comprehensive resolution (which was included in the report of the Council and the General Assembly) including the need for: a sharper focus on the needs of countries with severe food problems; identification of food priority countries, landlocked and island developing countries and those most seriously affected by economic constraints on increasing production; and attention to a variety of other problems. The expressed views of the Group of 77, and other interested countries, understandably took considerable time of the Council in their early meetings. As the Council settled down to topics and issues which incorporated the views of the informal advisory groups, but also others which mandated consideration by the Conference, the records of later sessions appeared to be more directly focused on possible solutions to the food crisis.

As an example of the more significant work of the Council, the records of the Fourth Ministerial session of the Council in Mexico City in June 1978, the last which Hannah attended, may be cited. The "Mexico Declaration," issued by the Council, had much the same appearance and content as the World Food Conference resolutions, but it was important in reaffirming some of the major resolutions and recommendations of the Conference and in bringing the whole United Nations system a bit closer to coming to grips with the problems previously identified such as stimulating contributions for the international emergency reserve of food grains from 82,000 tons to 425,000 tons. The lack of accomplishments on other objectives, however, was candidly acknowledged. But its major accomplishment was in establishing the International Food and Development organization, with a projected initial working capital of one billion U.S. dollars, the assembly of which required Hannah's principal actions for the rest of his tenure as Executive Director.

## International Food and Agriculture Development (IFAD)

In a comprehensive study of the operation of the whole United Nations system focused on the world food crisis, James Dickinson Grant[2], an Harvard University honors student, identified several components in the international complex of factors which he characterized as a "unique success story in the annals of the United nations."

The funding of IFAD was a last step in this dramatic story of

international collaboration. If one billion dollars of working funds for
the operations of IFAD had not been assembled by Hannah from the
donors to the initial fund—OPEC oil exporting countries (400 million),
the United States (200 million) and the important balance from European countries and the relatively smaller contributions from developing
countries—all the talk and debate which transpired in the Conference
and Council to improve agricultural production and nutritional levels
would come to naught, as was the case of previous World Food
Conferences in 1963 and 1970. Neither of these had succeeded in
creating an operating organization. John Hannah's role in the creation
of the initial IFAD fund—especially the key contribution of the United
States Government to the fund—was uniquely critical as will be
developed later.

Background factors in this fascinating and complex story included:
adjusting to and helping create more effective organizational relationships; novel domestic and international policy formulations and compromises; strongly and ably articulated positions and projects of the
representatives of developing countries; and extraordinarily good staff
work which produced a factual basis for discussion and debate.

The setting in which this drama was played involved several significant interrelated elements, most important of which probably were:

• The unparalleled world hunger and malnutrition situation affecting
millions of people, chiefly from the Third World, which shook the
world conscience and cried out for global cooperation.

• The world oil crisis, and the attendant world economic crisis.

• The presence in the White House of President Gerald R. Ford,
who was greatly influenced by John Hannah as a result of their long
standing relationship during which he generated great confidence in
Hannah's judgment and in his broad-gauged motivation to help solve
the international food crisis. He expressed his trust in Hannah's
request for assistance (described later) by taking strong stands within
his administration and calculated political risks with the Congress.

• The presence of Henry Kissinger on the scene in his early years
as the United States Secretary of State. Kissinger welcomed the
opportunity to exercise his considerable diplomatic talents in the
international arena. He combined food and oil issues in his strategy.
He also wanted to seize the initiative for the United States to take
world leadership in dealing with the understandable unrest in the group
of 77 nations to achieve a better degree of global equity previously
referred to and articulated in the "New International Economic Order" of the United Nations.

• John Hannah's demonstrated competence to coordinate and administer complex organizations.

### Important Milestones in the Evolution and Clarification of United States Policy and Commitment

• President Ford addressed the General Assembly of the U.N. on September 18, 1974, in the following forceful language:[3]

> Today the economy of the world is under unprecedented stress. We need new approaches to international cooperation to respond effectively to the problems that we face. Developing and developed countries, market and non-market countries are all part of one interdependent market system . . . The food and oil crisis demonstrates the extent of their interdependence . . . The United States believes in four principles to guide a global approach:
>
> *First*—All nations must substantially increase production.
>
> *Second*—All nations must seek to achieve a level of prices which not only provides an incentive to producers but which consumers can afford.
>
> *Third*—All nations must attack the abuse of man's fundamental needs for the sake of narrow or block advantage. The attempt by any nation to use one commodity for political purposes will inevitably tempt other countries to use commodities for their own purposes.
>
> *Fourth*—The nations of the world must assume that the poorest nations among us are not overwhelmed by rising prices of the imports necessary for their survival. The traditional aid donors and the increasingly wealthy oil producers must join in this effort.

Referring more specifically to the food issue, Ford continued:

> Americans have always responded to human emergencies in the past and we respond again here today. In response to Secretary General Waldheim's appeal to meet the long-term challenge of food, I reiterate: to help developing nations realize their aspirations to grow more of their own food, the United States will substantially increase the assistance to agricultural programs in other countries.

President Ford went on to indicate his support for: a world wide effort "to negotiate, establish and maintain an international system of food reserve; increased shipments of food from the United States; and for the comprehensive proposals to the World Food Conference in November, to be made by Secretary Kissinger. In closing the President made a firm challenge to the oil producing countries:

> Now is the time for oil producers to define their conception of global policy on energy to meet the growing need and to do this without imposing unacceptable burdens on the international monetary and trade systems.

• Kissinger's Plenary Stirring and Provocative Speech to the World Food Conference, given on November 15, 1974, has already been referred to. Excerpts are included in Appendix D.

• International Food Review Group. The importance of the international political and economic issues which were surfacing within the administration and the Congress was recognized by President Ford in Nov. 1974, when he created an International Food Review Group, chaired by the Secretary of State. Other members of the group included the Secretaries of Agriculture and Treasury, the Deputy Secretary of State, the Assistants to the President for Economic Affairs and National Security Affairs, the Chairman of the Council of Economic Advisors, the Executive Director of the Council of International Economic Policies and the Director of the Office of Management and Budgets. The Food Review Group advised the President on all national and international aspects of the proposals which were emerging in the World Food Conference and the World Food Counsil and the projected effects which the creation of IFAD would have on the U.S. economy and on agricultural policy.

The President not only had to listen to his staff advisors and other officials in his administration but also to the suggestions which were coming to him from interested citizens and organizations concerning what was being proposed in the Conference and in the United Nations but also to the views expressed in Congress by both his supporters and detractors. Specifically, the President had to satisfy the Secretary of Agriculture, Earl Butz, and the farmers and the Congressional spokesmen for the farmers that efforts to increase food production in developing countries would not seriously *diminish* markets for their surplus production. The other side of the coin was that he had to persuade the Secretary of the Treasury that the United States' economy could manage with a reduction in the income from export of surplus grains as a result of improved production by developing countries, and also from making more surplus grain available to food deficit countries on concessional terms or as gifts. The Office of Management and Budgets was concerned with the volume of funds which were already being expended for agricultural assistance and food aid, and whether additional appropriated funds would be needed for the program being proposed. Others in government and elsewhere were fearful that creation of an independent agricultural development organization (IFAD) would duplicate or overlap the international organizations already involved in increasing food production, notably the FAO and the World Bank. Moreover, the world didn't need another international bureaucracy. A fourth event in the evolution of United States' policy regarding the funding of IFAD occurred at a White House luncheon on April 12, 1975 concerned with international food policy. The conference was attended by President Ford, Daniel Patrick Moynihan, soon to be the United States Ambassador to the United Nations, Donald Rumsfeld, on President Ford's staff, and Dale Hathaway. Secretary Kissinger was interested in discussing the question of what initiative the United States could take in the food areas. Hathaway responded by offering the idea of committing 200 million dollars to the funding of IFAD, a figure which had been discussed in the deliberations of the Council. James Grant reports that "Kissinger at that luncheon backed White House support for the Fund."

*White House Conference on April 21, 1975.*[4] In preparation for the White House Conference Hannah followed closely the speeches and other comments of the President and Kissinger in support of the Conference and Council and concluded that it was timely to request a meeting with the President and his staff in the White House. The meeting, presided over by the President, was attended by John Hannah, Earl Butz, Secretary of Agriculture, William Seidman, Assistant to the President for Economic Affairs, James Cannon, Assistant to the President for Domestic Affairs and Robert Hormats, Deputy for International Economic Affairs in the National Security Council.

Hannah explained the mission of the Conference and the Council, which he did in characteristically succinct style, commenting on the highlights of the resolutions of the World Food Conference. In response, the President said:

> . . . .Well at the end of the (World Food) Conference, two things were agreed upon. Everyone agreed on the importance of increased food production, especially in deficit countries. And they agreed that it was essential to increase food security to help victims of an actual disaster. They agreed on 10 million tons per year for three years. I was able to get international agreement to provide the amounts. That has not been difficult. But people are also concerned with future food reserves. We definitely need to establish a food reserve scheme and (turning to Secretary Butz) we should not get lost in argument about who controls it. At the same time, I recognize that we need incentives to maintain production in the U.S. The last part of the recommendations was to establish a mechanism for initiating, monitoring and coordinating to get countries and the UN to implement other recommendations of the Conference.

At this point, the President called on Hannah to explain the organization of the Council, the preliminary expressions of support from

OPEC and other countries for funding IFAD, and some of the issues which were emerging; also the schedule of meetings on the strategy to collect the funds which would be needed to get the program started, to which Hannah replied:

> I want to get OPEC to provide 50% of the funds. The total will be $1 billion per year for three years and they will provide half of it. Most of the aid will go to the very poorest countries. The May 1975 Council meeting will talk about whether or not it is feasible to establish this fund. Actually, it is . . . Countries which put in the money should have a say on where it goes. There will be a Board of ⅓ OPEC, ⅓ developing countries, ⅓ developed countries. This is the OPEC formula. At the meeting, 61 countries will be involved, 18 Western countries, 15 OPEC, 6 Communist and 22 LDC's (less-developed) countries . . . The money will be channeled bilaterally. I know (Senator) Passman feels strongly about this and so do most of the other countries including the Saudis . . . Anything above the assistance to food and agriculture development provided in 1974 will count toward a country's contribution, but the money will not be put in a fund, but go through bilateral channels.

Hannah also asked and answered the question "Why is this important?"

> For the first 175 years of our 200-year history, the U.S. was seen as a friend of poor countries. But we have lost this. There are not going to be many chances. Five months after the food conference is over the world is still looking for ways to help meet food needs of poor countries. The U.S. has to do its fair share.

In response to a question from Earl Butz as to whether the U.S. contribution could be identified as a U.S. contribution, Hannah responded:

> Yes. The contributions will be bilateral but fit into a multi-lateral framework. There will be no funds for countries which do not make decisions to help themselves . . . At the May meeting, I do not need a U.S. pledge except that I would like the U.S. to say that it will do its "fair share." Between May and October, we will work further in setting up the fund. In the interim, we will try to get other countries to commit themselves, but no formal commitment will be needed until October.

The discussion then became very specific as to how to handle the problem.

*The President:* But if OPEC doesn't put up all of its money, ours will be less?

*Dr. Hannah:* That is right, Mr. President.

*The President:* What is the possibility of funding?

*Mr. Hormats* (National Security Council): The U.S. has increased its funding for agricultural development from $306 million in FY 74 to $476 million in FY 75. Plans are to increase it further to $679 million in FY 76, but this depends heavily on Congressional appropriations. The action taken by the Congress on the present aid bill, cutting this category from $546 million to $300 million, is a negative sign. But it is likely that we will have a $200 million increase above 1974 levels.

*Mr. Cannon* (Asst. to the President): My concern, Mr. President, is that after you veto the agriculture bill, this sort of assistance to farmers in developing countries might be criticized.

*Secretary Butz:* Yes, but the money is being appropriated anyhow. This is not really a new program.

*Dr. Hannah:* Yes, you should be able to make the $200 million (increase) figure.

*The President:* It would be helpful if you could testify before Otto (Passman).

*Dr. Hannah:* If that is what it takes, Mr. President, I would be delighted.

*The President:* Basically, this idea makes sense. I think that it is feasible in the Congress and that it can be sold in this country. Tell me when the meetings are again—May 5 and 6 in Geneva?

*Dr. Hannah:* And another meeting on the 25th of June. The whole idea for this World Food Conference came from the Declaration of the group of 77 in Algiers and Kissinger's U.N. speech. The U.S. needs to establish a basis of support in the Third World. We cannot afford to alienate them now.

*The President* (to Hormats): Will you tell Henry about this and indicate that he may want to use this in his food speech. I understand he wants to give that but has not decided where.

*Mr. Seidman:* Yes, he wants to give a food speech but I don't think he has set the place yet.

*The President* (to Hormats): Okay. This can be something he can use in his speech.

*Mr. Hannah:* Well Mr. President, thank you very much. I am glad to have the chance to discuss this with you and I think there are some important benefits for the U.S. in this plan.

The actions which followed this important meeting formented considerable confusion. Although Hannah had presumably acquiesced in the idea that the U.S. contribution could be made from previously committed funds, when he got back to Rome for further discussions and before the May meeting in Geneva, he firmly announced that the U.S. would contribute 200 million dollars of *new money* over and above funds already designated for foreign agriculture support. This caused consternation in certain quarters of the State Department and elsewhere, because they construed Hannah's statement at the Geneva meeting as premature since Congress had not yet passed the necessary appropriations. Grant's interpretation of this complex matter was contained in his comprehensive report referred to earlier:

> But one should not view Dr. Hannah's actions as a simple act of disobedience to the President; he felt he had a commitment from President Ford on the Fund and he acted accordingly. "I wanted a commitment from the President that the U.S. would do its fair share," Hannah said in a telephone interview, and got that commitment.[5]

Hannah's interpretation of President Ford's commitment was also verified in a conference which the author had with President Ford at his home at Beaver Creek in Colorado in August 1987.

Hannah's commitment of United States' support for the Fund at the May 5–6 meeting in Geneva certainly did not bind the United States government but it did, however, place the United States in a position from which it could not gracefully back down. Hannah's action created increased incentive for supporters of the Fund to follow through with their support.*

Most of the questions raised in U.S. deliberations with the administration and the Congress regarding the organization, governance (especially the willingness for all countries to delegate decision-making to a new international instrumentality), funding, policy making and other components, were paralleled by arguments raised by the 77 countries,

---

*Grant devotes almost 100 pages to a discussion of the debate within the administration and the Congress on the funding and other issues involved in the creation of IFAD. Hannah's belief in the President's basic commitment and the sure knowledge of the unacceptability of any arrangement except a firm commitment of U.S. dollars as the only means of "uncorking" the OPEC and other contributions, (which was reinforced at a meeting of the ad-hoc working group meeting on the IFAD in early July 1975), led him to forge ahead with the difficult task of getting all other contributors to achieve the goal of creating a one billion dollar fund which was the *sina qua non* of the whole enterprise. It was the keystone on which the whole edifice of IFAD rested as well as the whole international efforts of the World Food Conference and the World Food Council.

Germany, France, OPEC countries, World Bank, FAO and other interested parties. The bottom line facts are that Hannah, by diligent and indefatigable effort, was able to resolve the issues and to forge and launch a new and novel international organization to work at the problems of world hunger, an objective to which he had a passionate motivation.

The most emphatic and final public endorsement of United States cooperation in funding IFAD occurred at the Seventh Special Session of the United Nations on September 1, 1975 when Kissinger announced a specific commitment of the United States for funding IFAD:

> To mobilize massive new concessional resources for these purposes of expanding agricultural production in developing countries, the United States proposes the early establishment of the new International Fund for Agricultural Development. President Ford has asked me to announce that he will seek authorization of a direct contribution of $200 million to the Fund, provided that others will add their support for a combined total of at least one billion dollars.[6]

This commitment, however, did not settle the matter until John Hannah began to "beat the international bushes" for actual commitment and payment to the billion-dollar fund. But it did help in demonstrating to the nations of the world that the Ford administration was firmly behind genuine United States' participation in a large scale international program. In the process of soliciting funds from the OPEC countries and the developed countries, Hannah encountered all the problems previously mentioned including the two principal objections: (1) the questionable need for another "international bureaucracy" independent of the World Bank and other established international organizations and (2) a governance system which gave developing countries a two-thirds voting power over the developed countries. The French and German governments, particularly gave Hannah a hard time. Nevertheless, Hannah was persuasive in dealing with these problems and with the help of Sayed Marei and Sartaj Aziz with the OPEC countries successfully garnered in the billion dollars necessary to get IFAD underway. More precisely, the following commitments were firmly made by the following countries. The United States 200 million dollars plus contributions from 19 other developed (Category I) countries for a total of almost 600 million dollars; from Iran, Saudi Arabia and 10 other oil-exporting countries (Category II) of nearly 436 million dollars; and from 98 so-called underdeveloped countries (Category III) of almost 17 million dollars for a grand total of over a billion dollars. IFAD formally came into being in June 1977.

## Organization and Operations of IFAD

A brief analysis of the reports of the two presidents of IFAD from 1980, the third year of its creation, to 1986, reveals that the organization has remained faithful to the major purposes and program priorities which were defined in the resolutions of the World Food Conference. The influence of the Group of 77 underdeveloped countries is clearly reflected in IFAD actions as are the policies which were established by the World Food Council. The principal components of organization policy and program which the founding fathers created are:

• The work of IFAD is guided by the policies determined by a Governing Council, the members of which are called Governors who are selected by the 13 member countries of the Council. The Council is presided over by a Chairman elected by the Council.

• The operating decisions of IFAD are made by an Executive Board of 18 members, 12 of whom are from developing and oil-exporting countries and six from developed countries. The United States has one member on the Executive Board and one alternate. The President and Vice President are the chief operating officers, who are assisted by fewer than two hundred persons, about half of whom are professionals from 44 member states. The balance are support staff.*

• The primary program focus is on the rural poor in developing countries by using loans and grants to achieve higher levels of agricultural production and nutrition and general welfare of rural people. Emphasis is given to a comprehensive attack on the complex components involved in achieving the purposes of IFAD, relying chiefly on their supporting institutions. To achieve these purposes, changes in governmental policies and priorities favoring agriculture, land reform and governmental organization are stressed.

• IFAD is a specialized agency of the United Nations. It collaborates with and receives assistance from the World Bank and other organizations of the United Nations system as appropriate.

• IFAD has had only two Presidents, Mr. Abdelmushin M. Sudeary from Saudi Arabia, who served from 1977 to 1984 and Mr. Idriss Jazairy, an Algerian who was elected in 1984 for a six-year term.

The annual reports of IFAD programs are comprehensive, factual and attractively illustrated. Topics included are case descriptions of loans to small farmers in developing countries for irrigation, rural

---

*1985 Report of IFAD

development, credit, marketing and other purposes. Preliminary grants are typically made to governments of developing countries for assistance in preparing grant requests for research and other purposes and to assist them more generally in accelerating agricultural production. IFAD reports reveal its growing grasp of the difficulties of working with mostly landless rural people and demonstrate ingenuity and dedication in organizing, motivating and educating them to adopt and finance more productive practices and to participate in decision making.

Through December 31, 1985 almost two billion dollars in loans were made available for projects initiated by IFAD and by cooperating agencies. These were made to 177 African, Asian and Latin American developing countries. In addition, technical assistance grants (not to be repaid) in the amount of 88.6 million dollars were made to the same developing countries for planning purposes and to national and international agricultural research organizations.

The loan repayment rate and project completions have been considered generally satisfactory.

The 1985 report,[7] prepared by President Jazairy, discussed, candidly, some of the problems encountered by IFAD as it struggled to achieve its difficult goals. The following were stressed: (1) increased debt of developing countries; (2) falling oil prices for oil-exporting countries; (3) drought conditions in some countries; and (4) the reduction of concessionary aid available to alleviate the worst hunger conditions. Furthermore, replenishment of IFAD resources was at only about one half of the billion dollars agreed to by contributing countries in February of 1985. Criticism of donors included the need for better control of aid allocations, fiscal accountability and the sometime neglected technical assistance component in production practices. The highly desirable concept of participatory decision-making by farmers and agricultural organizations came under realistic scrutiny in these words: "The concept of participation is invariably advocated at the stage of rhetoric but before it reaches the stage of implementation it tends to get lost in technocratic blueprints or dissolve in bureaucratic labyrinth."

On the positive side, the 1985 report stated that IFAD (1) continued to persevere in its basic mission to provide substantial sums for loan guarantees and technical assistance grants; (2) continued research on traditional crops notably wheat and barley in semi-arid countries, improved varieties of sorghum for Latin American countries; bean production in Egypt and the Sudan and livestock and fisheries improvement in other countries and (3) relations with non-government organizations and the involvement of women in the development process were thought to have improved.

A study of 70% of IFAD funded projects under implementation were appraised as making good progress and only 30% encountered serious problems in implementation.

*Other Appraisals of IFAD.* In 1984 the Agency for International Development (AID) made an appraisal for the U.S. Government of IFAD's mandate and performance record in reaching the difficult target group of low income farmers and concluded that "IFAD's efforts to define, identify and reach the poor have been generally successful and that all the projects visited benefitted small farmers or the landless." Other aspects of the program such as credit, integrated rural development, irrigation, agricultural production, involvement of women in the development process and in monitoring and evaluation of projects were found to make some progress but to have varied weaknesses or defects, which, however, were believed to be remedial.[8]

The results of the World Food Conference, Council and IFAD continue to be evaluated by scholars, notably Carl Eicher, Professor of Agricultural Economics at Michigan State University and a knowledgable expert in food production programs, particularly in Africa. The Society for International Development devoted a section of a recent conference to the subject "Ten Years After the World Food Conference." The watchdog of the United States Congress, the Comptroller General and his staff have prepared the following reports: (1) an examination of the legality of the initial commitment of 200 million dollars to IFAD, which they concluded was legal;* (2) a comprehensive 50-page report to the Congress entitled "World Hunger and Malnutrition Continue to Slow Progress in Carrying Out World Food Objectives" dated Jan. 11, 1980; and (3) a staff study on "Status Report on U.S. Participation in the International Fund for Agricultural Development (IFAD)" dated March 27, 1981 which is particularly addressed to the issue of United States contribution to the first replenishment of a 1.27 billion fund for the continued operation of IFAD.[9]

All of these studies and reports are in varying degrees critical of the accomplishments to date of the efforts to resolve the complex problem

---

*This appraisal by AID was confirmed in a letter from Peter McPherson who served as a Governor of IFAD from 1981–1986. He also described IFAD as the only multilateral financial institution for which AID is principally responsible within the United States government.

of world hunger and malnutrition. But none have proposed canceling the efforts of organizations which have made some progress thus far or to offer a fresh approach and completely new organizational arrangements to do the job. This is not to ignore the criticisms or brush them under the rug in excessive optimism. Improvements in policy formulation, operating procedures and perhaps most of all in renewed determinations of developed and developing countries cooperating together to do a more creative and sustained effort are needed to feed the world's poor!

## Comments on Hannah's Performance

• *Letter from Secretary General of the United Nations Kurt Waldheim to Hannah dated 2 November 1978.* (MSUAHC)

. . . I wish to express my appreciation to you for your devoted service to the United Nations, as Deputy to the Secretary-General of the World Food Conference in 1974 and subsequently as Executive Director of the Council. You assumed heavy and important responsibilities which the General Assembly entrusted to the World Food Council nearly four years ago. Today, as a result of your untiring efforts, the Council is developing into an effective mechanism for the mobilization of the political will of governments and agencies to achieve the goal of the eradication of hunger and malnutrition for all peoples of the world.

I would like, in particular, to thank you for the role you played in assisting me to secure the necessary financial commitments from governments to the new International Fund for Agricultural Development. Your contribution was vital in bringing into being the Fund which is an important source of assistance for increasing food production by the poorest developing countries.

• *Letter from Sayed A. Marei,\* Secretary General of the World Food Conference and World Food Council to the author dated 7 November 1986.*

. . . I was delighted to write on John Hannah. Rather than list, as it were, the activities of John Hannah, I find it more fitting to record the impressions that he left on me during that period. Indeed, this is the more so because in a world conference which is dealing with a subject such as

---

\*Mr. Marei, a distinguished political and civic leader and close personal associate of the late President of Egypt, Mr. Anwar Sadat. President Sadat was assassinated in the presence of Mr. Marei, who himself was shot, but recovered, in the same tragic event.

food, nothing could ever have been accomplished unless actions emanated from the core of one's nature. To talk of food is at once to talk of hunger. And unless one has a feel of what that means, one's actions would be thwarted.

Myself, a man of the third world, I have my appreciation of what all this means. When John Hannah was nominated as my assistant, I must confess I had doubts as to what extent could a man of the advanced or rich world understand, feel, and react to the hunger problem.

This, I felt, without any misgivings on my part as to his reputed academic and professional achievements. In my first meeting with him, the sole purpose I set my mind on was never to test his professional capabilities, but solely to gauge the extent of his appreciation for famine, hunger, undernutrition and poverty in general.

It was indeed a pleasant surprise when it became clear to me from the first meeting with John that I was talking to someone who not only demonstrated a genuine concern for this complex issue, but was also outlining solutions which he felt should be shouldered by the developed world.

Thus we started working together. As time went on, John Hannah's actions only confirmed my favourable initial impressions of him. He felt that the U.N. organizations such as FAO were pursuing theoretical approaches. He wholeheartedly agreed with me that we could follow an action-oriented path which the U.N. institutions are reluctant to follow. He felt that these organizations kept duplicating their research and the result was inertia. He therefore insisted that we do our own research, we interpret our own findings, and be frank in our dialogues.

An issue to which I devoted considerable attention from the very start was the necessity of creating an Agricultural Development Fund. Apart from channeling funds for agricultural development in the third world, I felt that such a Fund would have another impact in terms of drawing attention to the importance of agriculture and thus indirectly influencing the flow of funds from other organizations.

After two years of hard work, our dream for a fund became a reality. It was in this respect that John Hannah played a most constructive role which will be remembered for a long time. The position of the U.S.A. was not favouring the creation of the Fund and was against multilateral aid in general. The amazing thing is that John never wavered about his belief in the Fund and went on persistently emphasizing the need for it, in the face of serious opposition from the U.S.A. His work in this unveiled a trait in his character: an unusual sense of determination. In the end an international Fund was created . . . As such it became the only international financial institution where the developing countries as a group had two-thirds of the voting power. It therefore represented a concrete step in a new international economic order, with nothing matching it to date, and perhaps for a long time to come.

Throughout his work, John depicted a conspicuous modesty and preferred to work steadily and quietly away from the media to which he showed some sort of distaste.

Whenever I asked him to talk to the press about his efforts, he replied: "You are the boss and our job is to help you." Once there was a press conference which I couldn't attend and I asked him to deputize for me. He went to the Conference. Then I met him and found him rather agitated. He said: "I can't deal with these people. They do not want to hear about the hunger of Third World. They are only interested to know if there will be a Fund in which the U.S.A. will participate." He added that someone with my past political experience can deal with them. John recognized the delicate nature of the subject so as not to jeopardize my efforts with the OPEC countries.

John was always honest to himself, honest in his dealings with others.

• *Letter from Sartaj Aziz to the author dated October 30, 1984.* Mr. Aziz served as Deputy Secretary to Hannah at the World Food Conference and Council and is currently the Pakistan Minister of State for Food, Agriculture and Cooperatives.

. . . The second phase of our association began in January, 1975 when Dr. John Hannah was appointed as Executive Director of the World Food Council and I joined the Council Secretariat as Deputy Executive Director. The first year of the council existence was rather difficult because of the wide gap between the expectations of developing countries about the role and mandate of the World Food Council and the perceptions of the developed countries. The political heat generated by the World Food Conference in November 1974 was still in the air when the first meeting of the World Food Council was held in June, 1975. The developing countries adopted a resolution expressing their lack of confidence in the Secretariat of the World Food Council and rumors began to circulate that Dr. Hannah might resign. It was a very trying period for Dr. Hannah because after such a distinguished career, Dr. Hannah did not deserve such a political reception from the developing countries. The manner in which he reacted to this situation is a testimony of his political acumen and maturity . . . Dr. Hannah left in 1978 with a great deal of good-will and admiration from all the members of the World Food Council including the developing countries.

• *Letter from Abelmuhsin M. Al-Sudeary, President of IFAD to the author dated July 24, 1984.*

. . . As regards Dr. Hannah's work methods and leadership qualities, he brought a great deal of experience, which he had gained in various fields. He shared this experience with his colleagues, though he often gave the impression that he was at the same time learning from others. He was a man who dealt with matters swiftly, avoiding bureaucratic delays. As Executive Director of the World Food Council, he adopted a free-wheeling method in directing its affairs and was completely on top of every situation, however difficult.

He was a tireless traveller and, even though he was 74 when he was heading the World Food Council, he made frequent trips to Third World countries.

As Executive Director of the World Food Council, he played a crucial role in the various U.N. preparatory meetings for IFAD and in the complex and difficult negotiations between the two major donor groups. He actively mobilized the support of the U.S. Government for the creation of IFAD. This positive U.S. support in turn helped to convince other industrialized countries of the value of this new initiative.

• *Excerpts from Dale E. Hathaway's "Recollections of the role of John A. Hannah in the World Food Conference and subsequent World Food Council" sent to the author January 27, 1984.* Dr. Hathaway's recollections provided insight into problems of strained relationships with the FAO and the working of the special research staff (which Hannah recruited) to provide a factual basis for a limited number of significant issues for the Conference and Council deliberations, which Hannah supported fully. He also provided information on some of the delicate international political issues which surfaced during the Conference and Council. He closed his reflections with these comments:

> . . . In closing I would say that the World Food Conference and the World Food Council was a significant and positive achievement in John Hannah's distinguished and long career. There was never any question of his extreme dedication and commitment that were involved in that situation. Mr. Hannah in my view had a problem, which was less of a handicap during the period of the World Food Conference than during his tenure as Executive Director of the Council. That handicap was that Mr. Hannah never really came to understand or be willing to participate in the petty politics which are the life blood of the U.N. System and thus could not operate great effectiveness within that system. His judgment was that remaining above and somewhat aloof from the system was as effective as playing at the full time politics which is a usual part of the system.*

---

*See also letter from George J. Klein to the author dated 11 February 1987. George Klein had important professional relations with John Hannah as Chief of the U.N. Relations Division in AID; as Assistant Secretary of IFAD and in other international organizations in Switzerland and Austria. Because it provides insights into the operations of the U.N. system and Hannah's work within the system, extensive excerpts from his letter are provided in Appendix F, pp. 233–239.

## Epilogue

The food situation in the year of Hannah's resignation from the position of Executive Director of the World Food Council was reported by his successor Maurice J. Williams, to the General Assembly of the United Nations on October 28, 1978. Some of the highlights of the Williams report shows, in the following excerpts, some gains but also the persistence of unsolved problems.

> The progress of the past year and a half is significant. Good harvests have contributed to a presently improved world food situation . . . Contributions have nearly met the five hundred thousand ton target of the Emergency Grain Reserve . . . Steps are being taken in the United Nations to improve nutrition levels and there is a growing awareness throughout the world of the need for stepped up action to eliminate hunger and malnutrition.
>
> But much more needs to be done. The primary needs of millions of people and specifically their right to food on a regular basis is far from being met. Future trends of food production and consumption project an increasingly precarious situation in many parts of the world . . . The world imbalance in food production and consumption between developed countries and developing countries continues to worsen . . . Growing trade restrictions limit the ability of the developing countries to earn more foreign exchange for larger food imports . . . Slow progress in negotiating the new international wheat agreement. Consequently, the world still lacks an adequate grain reserve to underpin food security . . . There will be a *continuing need* for the 500,000 ton emergency reserve to provide assistance in emergency situations that do not affect the total international grain system.
>
> Increased food production in the developing countries is universally agreed to be the central part of the solution to the problem of world hunger and poverty, along with improvements in food distribution and actions to ensure that food reaches those who need it most.*

These declarations of "unfinished business" and others which could be assembled do not surprise Hannah or others who are aware of the magnitude of world food and nutritional needs addressed by the World Food Conference/Council and IFAD. But what we don't know too precisely is how many children and adults are better fed, or how basic improvements have been made in farming practices by many poor and illiterate farmers, or how many governments have finally come to a realization that the production of food is basically *their* national and

---

*As demonstrated in the recent food crisis in Ethiopia.

regional problem. These and many other facets of the complexities of food production, preservation and distribution need to be constantly appraised, along with incentives for production, land reform measures, specific projects for landless laborers and other components of the complex.

These problems cannot be solved, as are possibly some even more threatening problems of world peace, which involve relatively *fewer decision makers,* in contrast to *millions of decision makers* involved in food production, distribution and use to achieve the goals of the World Food Conference, Council and IFAD. (Italics added)

The actions to improve agricultural production, nutritional levels and rural life more generally, reported by IFAD, are consistent with their obligations set forth in their charter. The loans made, research undertaken or contracted for, governments of developed countries nudged into more effective attention to agriculture and other constructive measures reported are obviously not enough to solve the persistent global food problems dramatized in Secretary Kissinger's and President Ford's speeches, and other speeches given in the World Food Conference. They weren't satisfactorily solved in the first ten years of the World Food Council and IFAD efforts—a very short time considering the magnitude and complexity of the problems. Nor are they likely to be completely solved in the next fifty or even a hundred years. Children may still go to bed hungry. But it is a start. And Hannah, and his colleagues, lit a candle in the darkness, as Adlai Stevenson said of Eleanor Roosevelt's efforts to achieve world peace. Many children and adults have been the beneficiaries of these efforts and a novel international structure, oriented to the needs and potentialities of small farmers, has been created. It is reasonable to predict that if these policies, organizational arrangements and cooperative endeavors with developing countries do not work out over time, it is quite unlikely that a more potentially effective formula for international cooperation will be created in the foreseeable future.

## Chapter VI

# Other National and State of Michigan Public Service Organizations

John Hannah participates or had participated as a member or Chairman of a number of important off-campus organizations while President of Michigan State University and after he retired from the Presidency. All of them reflect his continuing interest in national and international affairs and in Michigan business and civic activities. They all demonstrate his capacity to work effectively with persons of varying backgrounds and interests. They have brought prestige and satisfactions to him personally and broader contacts with distinguished persons in and outside of academia who became knowledgable supporters of an evolving university. Hannah's relationship to these organizations differed from his relationship to the other organizations previously described, in that he did not serve as the chairman or principal administrative official of all these organizations—but often only as an active member of the committees or boards which were responsible for the policies and operations of the organizations. Accordingly, he was not responsible for the administration, *per se,* of these organizations. Furthermore, they were all relatively smaller in scope, somewhat shorter in duration and all essentially private, non-governmental or quasi governmental organizations. The descriptions which follow are essentially vignettes of a cross-section of the work of these organizations. Unless otherwise noted, background materials for the follow-

ing organizations were provided by the Hannah Collection in the
Michigan State University Archives & Historical Collections.


## Education and World Affairs

Education and World Affairs (EWA) was incorporated as a private,
non-profit educational organization in January 1962. John Hannah was
one of the original incorporators along with Herman Wells, Chancellor
of Indiana University, who was elected Chairman of the Board; Franklin D. Murphy M.D., Chancellor, University of California at Los
Angeles, as Vice Chairman; Douglas M. Knight, President of Duke
University; Robert F. Coheen, President, Princeton University; J. L.
Morrill, former President of the University of Minnesota; Henry
Heald, President of the Ford Foundation; James Perkins, former President of Cornell University, who with William Marvel, were officers of
the Carnegie Corporation. Marvel was chosen as President and Executive Officer. Ralph Smuckler served as Vice President for one year
before being brought back to Michigan State University as Acting Dean
of International Programs.

The purposes of EWA as set forth in the articles of incorporation
were to:

(1) *enhance* the capabilities of the universities, colleges, schools of
the United States and other elements of the educational community of
this country in carrying out their responsibilities and their aims in the
area of education and world affairs, including the advancement of
teaching and research.

(2) *interpret* and advance the interests of the educational community
in world affairs before the councils of the nation, both public and
private and especially to assist in maintaining effective communication
between that community and the government on problems and activities of common concern.

(3) *promote* the investigation and consideration of means by which
United States educational institutions and resources can contribute to
international cooperation in education and to the advancement of
education in other nations.

(4) *encourage* and facilitate communication and contact on the part
of the educational community of this country with all relevant institutions and groups in this and other countries and thus to foster a

widening network of international interchange, of both persons and ideas.

The Board was given authority to conduct research and experiments, hold conferences, prepare, disseminate and publish books, pamphlets, reports and articles and to "support and sponsor through grants and loans (free of interest or other charges) any or all such activities conducted by others including those institutions providing teaching and instruction."

The above powers and authorities gave EWA a sufficient legal basis and flexibility to engage in all of the activities highlighted below. Furthermore, the distinguished members of the Board, who were appointed after incorporation, provided a wealth of experience background to provide policy direction and program resources. The initial grants of six million dollars from the Ford Foundation and $500,000 from the Carnegie Corporation provided sufficient launching funds for the first six years, which were later enhanced from other government and foundation grants.

Hannah and the other university officials, who were incorporators, plus Marvel, continued to serve on the Board after its creation. The Board was later expanded to include Edward S. Mason, Dean of the Littauer School, Harvard University and Vincent M. Barnett, Jr., President of Colgate University. Other distinguished persons who broadened the backgrounds of the Board included Ellsworth Bunker, Ambassador at Large; Sol M. Linowitz, Ambassador to the Organization of American States, David E. Lilienthal, Chairman of the Board, Development and Resources Corporation; Robert C. McNamara, President of the World Bank; Frank McCulloch, Bureau Chief, China and Southeast Asia, Time-Life Foreign News Service. Officers representing organizations, with which EWA had close working relationships, included Frederick Seitz, President of the National Academy of Sciences; Logan Wilson, President of the American Council on Education; T. Keith Glennan, President of Associated Universities Incorporated and Kenneth Holland, President of the Institute of International Education.

The framework for the creation of the EWA and for the major activities undertaken by EWA for the seven years of its existence was provided by the Morrill Committee, whose 1960 report on *The University and World Affairs* published the following principal conclusions:

- In the postwar years American universities, responding to the nation's new involvement in world affairs, have taken on many new and expanded activities. These include new courses on Asia, Africa and the Soviet Union, and United States relations with them; research on economic, political and social development of the newly independent nations; foreign students in large number; and special overseas projects to help build and strengthen educational institutions in other countries.

- The universities' response so far, however, has been largely sporadic and unplanned. To meet the challenge of their potential role in world affairs adequately, they now have an historic opportunity to undertake, individually and in cooperation, a major effort as institutions. They have the responsibility, in the best university tradition, to make a contribution which no other institutions can: to enlarge our horizons as a free society, to help educate the leaders and help create a free international society. These tasks require the sustained participation of the best American university competence and the pioneering of new academic traditions.

Some of the principal activities of EWA, which were conducted within this framework, included consultation services to universities on International Education policy making; studies and reports on International Education activities of U.S. colleges and universities; conferences and seminars; and several significant publications including John Gardner's *AID and the Universities*.

### Hannah's Participation and Contribution

Hannah served as a member of the Board of Trustees from 1962 to 1969 when he resigned to become Administrator of AID. He also served on the Executive Committee for five years and as a member of a Special Review Committee and the Audit Committee. He also served as Chairman of one of the three Board committees which supervised the work of the Overseas Educational Service (OES) which provided personnel recruiting and placement services for American academics to supplement instructional and research staff in foreign universities.

Meetings of the Board were held for the most part on week-ends at quarterly intervals and were attended by Hannah for approximately thirty-two sessions including meetings of the Executive Committee which usually preceded the meetings of the full Board.

The minutes of Board meetings reveal that Hannah's position in the deliberations within the Board and in private consultations with the president were generally focused on relating research and service activities of American universities and other educational institutions to practical ways of extending professional and public understanding of international issues and developments. He was actively involved in securing financial and public support for these activities. One of the far-sighted talks which he made to the trustees, on one of their annual retreats, was on "The University in World Affairs—Its Role in the Next 20 Years."

The minutes of one Board meeting focused on the issue of "the strengths and weaknesses in the United States position in the world today, in general but more especially the picture our country projects of itself through the activities in the realm of education and cultural affairs." In response to comments of one of the Board members at a meeting of the Board, the record shows that:

> Mr. Hannah said that there is a great job of "disturbing the American public that must be done." A part of this disturbance should take the form of making Americans generally understand the complexity of the situations and problems with which we must deal. Only if they are aware of the intricacies of the kinds of operations will they begin to appreciate why our failure rate may appear higher than is justified. Mr. Hannah would like to see EWA put someone to work to determine how we get this element of disturbance generated and then how to assure that it is effectively communicated.

At the same meeting when the Board was discussing the question of security and education, Hannah's perceptive remarks were recorded as follows:

> Hannah confirmed the need for military assistance "to hold the fort" but to approach the problem in more long range and fundamental ways also. A primary attack must be made through education to eliminate illiteracy; secondly, we must assist other countries in their formation of capital, and through these means to help in raising standards. However, we must recognize that education in itself is not enough. A good example of this is the long relationship the United States has had with the Philippines where we have apparently missed the opportunity to impart a sense of social responsibility in our educational efforts. We have somehow neglected to inspire with that missionary spirit with other peoples to serve the best interests of the greatest number in their own countries. Moreover, on a long range basis we must equip our university representatives who are going abroad to understand the country and its people. Through special training and preparation we can thus better equip our people for international service.

Hannah was also helpful to the Board and staff in meetings which were had with Foundation executives and with U.S. government officials with whom he was well acquainted and highly regarded.

**Feedback to Michigan State University**

Although Hannah's interest in EWA was far broader than his Presidency of Michigan State University, his participation in EWA had direct value to the University in several important ways:

• In putting Michigan State University in the forefront, with other American universities, of leadership in expanding involvement in international affairs when the American public was not sufficiently concerned with issues and developments beyond our borders.

• In selecting MSU as one of the leading U.S. universities for inclusion in a series of case studies of the overseas programs of these universities and in the administration of one of the regional conferences on international affairs sponsored by EWA.

• In feedback to the University trustees, administrators and faculty in the evolution of policies and programs of the University in international affairs in the early years under the leadership of Glen Taggart who was appointed as the first Dean of International Studies and Programs of any United States university, and his associate Ralph Smuckler.

## International Fertilizer Development Center
## Muscle Shoals, Alabama (IFDC)

John Hannah was elected as the first Chairman in 1974 and still serves as Chairman (1988) of the Board of Directors. IFDC was incorporated as a private, non-profit, international corporation. The corporation was established on the site of the chemical engineering plant for experimental fertilizers established by the Tennessee Valley Authority (TVA) in 1933 as part of its resource development program, which was focused largely on domestic problems but which had also been involved in technical assistance programs requested by foreign governments.

Hannah brought to the chairmanship of the IFDC a broad experience in agriculture; an abiding faith in the need for and capacity of agricultural research, adapted to the needs of food deficient countries; and specific background experience as Director of the Agency for International Development. He had participated in the national experimental fertilization program of the TVA as the president of a land grant university outside the Tennessee Valley. David Lilienthal, former Chairman of the TVA Board frequently referred to John Hannah as the most interested and cooperative president of a Land Grant University outside of the Valley.

Joining Hannah on the Board of Directors of the IFDC are distinguished professors, ministers of agriculture, and other officials associated with organizations concerned with food production and distribution in Germany, Australia, Norway, Colombia, Nigeria, Indonesia and the Philippines. A Vice President of the World Bank and a Director of the Tennessee Valley Authority also serve ex-officio as well as two officials of the IFDC.

The IFDC program includes research and production of experimental fertilizers as its laboratory at Muscle Shoals, Alabama; extensive national programs in Bangladesh, Indonesia and Mali; technical assistance to many countries in South and Southeast Asia, Africa and Latin America on agricultural fertilizer production adaptation, marketing, socio-economic research and other production problems. It also conducts training programs from 12 days to six weeks duration for foreign nationals at its headquarters in Alabama, and in India, Thailand, Mali, Bangladesh, Columbia, Peoples Republic of China and Mexico for over 250 trainees from 45 developing countries.

The IFDC had revenues of almost ten million dollars in 1984 from grants received from the United States Agency for International Development, International Fund for Agricultural Development, Australian Development Assistance Bureau, International Development Research Center and from the Ford Foundation.

Dr. Donald McCune, Managing Director of IFDC, in 1986 evaluated Hannah's services as Chairman of the Board as follows in a letter to the author dated March 12, 1986.

> Dr. Hannah was IFDC's first Chairman of the Board of Directors. He continues in this position until this time—over 11 years. He is the only Board Member that has served continuously during this period. The fact that he has continuously been elected Chairman, I feel, is an indication of the value that the Board as well as the Management of IFDC places on his contributions.
>
> Having Dr. Hannah as Board Chairman has served as a magnet in attracting other top level people to serve on the Board. These include the Director-General of the OPEC Special Fund, Ministers of Agriculture, Sir John Crawford of Australia, Rectors of universities, a Vice President of the World Bank, *et al.*
>
> His high regard within the U.S. Government, regardless of the party in power, has been extremely valuable as has his influence been within the United Nations, especially the United Nations Development Programme

(UNDP) and the International Fund for Agricultural Development. Other donors, such as Australia and Canada, have contributed greatly to IFDC's funding success.

Dr. Hannah has continuously been able to foresee shifts in emphasis that are needed to keep our programs current and responsive. He has the respect of the IFDC senior staff and they seek his advice and counsel in their programs and activities whenever the opportunity presents itself. . . .

## Winrock International Institute for Agricultural Development (WIIAD)

John Hannah has been a member of the Board of WIIAD since its creation in 1985. WIIAD* was established on July 1, 1985 as a merger of three previously created agricultural development and research institutions founded by the Rockefeller family. These organizations were the Agricultural Development Council (ADC), which grew out of the Council on Economic and Cultural Affairs, which was created by John D. Rockefeller in 1953. ADC was primarily focused on economic training related to agriculture and human welfare in rural Asia. It was once headed by Clifton R. Wharton, who became President of Michigan State University and later as President of the State University of New York. The International Agricultural Development Service (IADS) was founded in 1975 primarily to provide advisory services to developing countries to strengthen their agricultural research and development programs for the purpose of increasing agricultural production and the incomes of rural people.

The Winrock International Livestock Research and Training Program (WILRTC) was also established in 1975 in response to the request of Winthrop Rockefeller that the trustees of his estate in Arkansas establish a training and research institution focused primarily on animal agriculture in the United States and developing countries.

All three organizations had fostered fellowships and other training programs for personnel from Third World countries to increase the competencies of these highly selected individuals to improve food production and living standards for low income people in their countries; to help them build strong agricultural development institutions; and to provide higher standards of research and administration of agricultural programs. All of them had highly qualified headquarters

---

*Shortened to "Winrock International."

and field staff to administer the program and to provide advisory assistance. Factors which were taken into account in supporting the merger of the three organizations included, but were not limited to: (1) changes in the priorities and interests of the major foundations which supported agricultural production and productivity; (2) growing interest in the importance of environment issues and use of natural resources; (3) changes in technical cooperation relationships which recognized the larger number of trained personnel in developing countries which made for more "equal-partner professional, scholarly and scientific exchanges than traditional technical assistance approaches;" and (4) changes in the policies and programs of the Agency for International Development which has provided financial support for non-governmental organizations (NGO's) and private non-profit organizations. There seemed also to have been a need for more innovative and creative methods for achieving better results from the long-time efforts of the Rockefeller family for assisting less developed countries to increase their agricultural productivity, nutrition, and living standards of the rural poor.

John Hannah came to his membership on the Board of Winrock International* after serving for four years on the Board of IADS. As Administrator of the Agency for International Development (AID) from 1969–1973, he was instrumental in developing policies and programs which were supportive of the objectives of Winrock. He also brought to Winrock knowledge of the work of the International Fertilizer Development Center (IFDC), as well as his experiences as Deputy Security General of the World Food Conference and Executive Director of the World Food Council.

But Hannah brought much more to his membership on the Winrock Board than his technical knowledge of agriculture world-wide. He brought almost 30 years of experience in university administration and management of United States federal programs which called for leadership in the formulation of broad policies on complex developmental

---

*The Winrock International Board included only four members who had been members of the IADS Board—John Hannah; Clifford M. Hardin, Stifel Nicolaus & Co. of St. Louis, Missouri; Clayton K. Yeutter, President of the Chicago Mercantile Exchange, Chicago, Illinois; and Robert D. Havener who became the President of Winrock. The other eighteen members includes Norman Borlang, Nobel Prize winner for his achievements in agriculture, Winthrop Rockefeller, key personnel from universities, the Conservation Foundation, Resources for the Future, and other organizations interested in international agriculture and rural development and William M. Dietel, President of the Rockefeller Brothers Fund.

and public policy issues and the capacity to forge working compromises on divisive issues which tend to bog down the effective operations of boards. His colleagues on the single Board, who experienced
the trauma of the process of merging of three agricultural development
boards into one, reflecting on Hannah's work with them, wrote at the
request of the author:

As to merge or not to merge—

. . . There was never any question as to where John stood. At every
opportunity he urged that we get on with the merger. That was the prime
objective. Lesser details could be worked out later. But the three "Rockefeller nurtured" institutions should be merged into the strongest organization possible (a) to do the essential development work of which it would
be capable and (b) as a living, working tribute to the family whose
agricultural philanthropy had made such a difference in the lives of so
many Third World countries.

Also from another Board member on the same question—

. . . John could see clearly and dramatically what Winrock might become.
He was critical, sometimes caustically so, in his views of some of the
individuals involved in the governance of the three Rockefeller related
agencies which were contemplating merger, but that never blinded him to
what might be. Personally, he played a major role in sustaining my own
convictions, and on more than one occasion when I was close to giving
up because of problems and recalcitrant individuals, I was re-energized
by John's vision and commitment. The merger needed to be brought
about, it could be effected, and he expected me to get on with it, and he
insisted he would help me. And he did, often, and in a compelling fashion.
Every one of the directors of the merged institutions, all found, who were
present at meetings at which the merger was under discussion will testify
that at just that moment when we started to falter in our resolve to create
WIIAD or when we seemed to lose our way and were on the verge of a
degenerative discussion of minutiae rater than concentrating our talents
on the main objective, it was John who dragged us back to the vision that
made the merger eminently sensible and desirable.

And from a third—

. . . Among the board members of the IADS, John perceived more acutely
than others the vacuum in leadership, flexible technical expertise which
was resulting from the retrenchment of the Ford Foundation, Rockefeller
Foundation staff posted abroad. He also believed that the experts within
USAID had failed. Therefore, he was an enthusiastic supporter of the
merger and, more than most other trustees, had a grand vision of its
potential importance for international agricultural development. He never

wavered in his enthusiastic support for moving forward with the merger.
. . . He has been an extremely dedicated and effective director. So far as
I can recall, he has never missed a committee meeting which he was
expected to attend, and has given of his personal prestige, time and
money to fundraising activities on behalf of Winrock International. . . .
His optimistic vision of the future is truly remarkable. His belief in what
one individual or one organization can accomplish for an improved human
welfare and destiny is refreshing and invigorating. His belief in education,
in the value of the individual and in the promise of America is complete.
When the theoretical debate in our board meetings begins to deal with
somewhat esoteric minutia, John is the first to say "enough of this, let's
get on with the big issues and let the staff get on with their work." He is
a tower of positive strength in all board deliberations.

The merger of the three organizations has proven to be a wise
decision, joining as it does the combined experience of experts in
several key academic disciplines related to agriculture and field experiences in Asia, Africa, Latin America and the United States. During
the first six months of its existence it had provided funds for 253
fellows from 9 countries and had involved 68 universities in 14 countries to administer the training programs for these fellows. It had
operated over 60 projects in more than 24 countries, some of which
had formerly been initiated by the three merged institutions. During
1985 it received grants for contracts and donations from 53 organizations and individuals including nine national governments, 11 philan-
thropic foundations, eight international organizations and two development banks, along with universities and other development related
agencies. Winrock has a staff of over 200 persons who work in the
headquarters office and in regional offices in Washington, D.C. and
Bangkok, Thailand and 16 field offices in Asia, Africa, South and
Central America and the Caribbean. It had assets of over 40 million
dollars as of December 31, 1985 and an annual operating budget of
over 20 million dollars.


## Select Committee on the Future of Private and Independent
## Higher Educational Institutions in New York State

Hannah was appointed as a member of the above committee in
February 1967 by Governor Nelson A. Rockefeller. The Committee
was chaired by James Bryant Conant, President of Harvard University
and included, besides Hannah, Theodore M. Hesburgh, President of

Notre Dame University and Abram L. Sachar, President of Brandeis University.

The charge to the committee was to advise the Governor and the State Board of Regents on the following critical issues which faced the state of New York at the time.

• How can our vital private and independent institutions for higher education be further encouraged and strengthened in the decade ahead?

• How can these private resources be appropriately related to our expanding public institutions?

• What further specific aid should the State provide to private institutions in the context of existing and potential Federal, State and local financing?

• Can this be done and their full independence maintained?

After reviewing the work of a research staff, the Committee unanimously advised that the following policies be adopted and measures be taken: (1) to provide direct financial assistance to private colleges and universities; (2) to amend the State Constitution to conform to the Federal model of support for four year institutions which have "significant religious affiliation." In reaching this conclusion the committee was convinced that "there is no virtue in testing educational quality by the presence or absence of a religious connection;" (3) that the existing responsibilities of the State Board of Regents be confirmed and that the staff of the State Department of Education be strengthened to provide statewide planning of higher education and to maintain "proper standards of quality in all state-aided institutions;" and (4) that the private institutions and the State Board of Regents take steps to create an information and reporting system which will provide a basis for making statewide educational decisions.

Governor Rockefeller expressed his appreciation to Hannah and the Committee upon completion of the report:

Thank you for the Committee's report you jointly presented to Chancellor Couper and to me last Wednesday. It is my great personal pleasure to express to you formally on behalf of the people of New York State, deep appreciation for a difficult task exceedingly well done. I said to you earlier that the Committee's task would not be easy. You have brought wise and balanced judgment to the great issues at stake, and the unanimous findings of the Committee will be a bench mark for higher education in New York—and across the country, I am certain.

## United Service Organization (USO)

Hannah served in 1962–63 as Chairman of the National Ad-hoc Survey Committee to review the policies and operations of the USO Voluntary Civilian Services for Military Personnel. Hannah's experience with the U.S. Department of Defense and other national organizations was an important factor in his being selected for the chairmanship by President Eisenhower, the Honorary Chairman of USO. The USO had rendered distinguished service to military personnel domestically and internationally during World War II but needed a fresh examination of its potential services in peacetime. Hannah was joined on the committee by 10 other members, from all religious faiths, who had distinguished records as business executives, lawyers, labor leaders or educators. Specifically, the committee was charged: (1) to determine the need for a voluntary civilian program to serve military personnel; (2) to determine the type of organization, if such is needed; (3) to evaluate USO's ability, as presently constituted, to meet such a need; and (4) to suggest how such an organization should be financed.

The ad-hoc committee employed an experienced survey staff headed by Dr. Arnold F. Emech, who conducted a ten month's study of the problems which the committee was charged with examining. The final report, addressed to Harvey S. Firestone, Jr., Chairman of USO, Holger J. Johnson, President of USO, and Robert S. McNamara, Secretary of Defense, included 19 recommendations covering the major items involving the transfer of USO management of operations in the USA from a national organization to local USO boards of directors or community membership associations with responsibility for local financing, but with some national funding for program consultants to give advice and counsel to local organizations upon request. The other recommendations of the committee were all in the context and consistent with the reasoning back of this comprehensive recommendation.

Ray R. Eppert, President of the Burroughs Corporation, wrote Hannah regarding his experiences as a member of the committee.

. . . I think it is an excellent and very important statement to the Defense Department, to United Funds and Community Chests, and to the American people on the essential future role of the USO.

This report should be very significant in the United States because the USO, which is not just a national agency but an international one, is voluntarily relinquishing a domestic territory, thus supporting the vital thesis of "local autonomy and local support of and by local communities.'' The National USO will ask our communities only for the minimum aid necessary to do those things which good citizens want done and which, because of the situs involved, cannot be done on a local community basis.

As a long time advocate of United Funds and local autonomy, I hope that the action of our Committee and the National USO may help to generate similar definitive planning by other national agencies, to the end that the great forward progress of federation and united giving in the United States will be accelerated.

I have served on many committees and I want to emphasize that the privilege of being a member of your USO team has been one of the most satisfying experiences I have ever had. This Committee has been the hardest-headed, the most blunt, the most meticulous, and the most sincere and dedicated group I have been associated with and this can be directly identified with your leadership as *Chairman,* or *referee.* . . .

Congratulations on a tough job very well done!

Some other National organizations in which Hannah served as a committee member were:

- American Management Association 1967–68
- American Institute of Management 1967
- Emergency Committee for Tibetan Refugees 1959–60; 1960–65; 1968
- American National Red Cross 1958–61
- American Public Health Association 1961
- Atlantic Council 1963–66
- Market Research Corporation of America 1958–61
- Overseas Development Council 1968–69
- United Nations Association of the United States 1968–69

## Michigan Advisory Boards and Committees

### Chairman of the Legislative Organization Committee of the Michigan Constitutional Convention—1961–1963

The Michigan Constitutional Convention was convened in 1961 to prepare a new Constitution for the State.* One hundred forty-four

---

*The first Michigan Constitution was ratified in 1835 and came into effect when Congress admitted Michigan to the Union. New constitutions were adopted in 1850 and 1908. An effort to call a convention to revise the Constitution in 1958 failed. A financial crisis in 1959 provided the incentive for another try but it was not until 1961 when a majority of voters called for the convening of another Constitutional Convention. The old issues between cities and rural areas, labor and management, plus issues related to the economic depression faced the delegates in 1961.

persons were elected on partisan ballots as delegates to the convention. Hannah, elected as a Republican, was selected to serve as Chairman of the Committee on Legislative Organization consisting of fourteen Republicans and eight Democrats. The composition of the committee reflected the relative political strength of the two parties and the strongly held positions of both parties with reference to the apportionment of seats in the Senate and House of Representatives. Resolution of this issue was believed to be the most crucial in the preparation of the new Constitution. The conflicting interests of citizens and pressure groups representing the large cities, farmers and farm groups, labor organizations, business and commercial organizations and, to a lesser extent, non partisan groups such as the League of Women Voters and George Romney's (presumably non-partisan) "Citizens for Michigan" organization as well as conventional major differences between Democratic and Republican political parties were represented by the elected delegates. Other committees of the Convention included Public Information, Rights, Suffrage and Elections, Emerging Problems and Education. Hannah also served on the Education Committee.

As the Committee became organized, three identifiable groupings of the delegates became apparent. They were classified as: (1) "Localists" composed of nine Republicans who favored area/location as the principal basis for apportionment; (2) "Middlemen" consisting of five Republicans who favored population and area criteria for Senate seats but only population for House seats and (3) "Populists" consisting of seven Democrats who favored population as the basis for Senate and House seats. These were the principal issues of the debates along with less divisive issues such as size of legislative chambers, district boundary lines and related smaller issues.

The Committee was presented with the maps of the state showing the effects of different plans for apportionment; heard testimony at public meetings from spokesmen for many affected groups such as the Farm Bureau, NAACP, AFL/CIO, National Municipal League, Association of Supervisors, Michigan Citizens Clearing House, League of Women Voters and several others. A number of experts on several aspects of the issues also testified. Dr. Charles Press, a member of the faculty of Political Science of Michigan State University, acted as a Research Consultant.

Hannah, as Chairman, and other members of the Committee, were sent many letters and telegrams which expressed strong views on the issues before the committee. Debate was vigorous and coverage of the deliberations was extensive.

*The Task Facing Hannah.* Observers conceded that the apportionment committee chairman faced the most difficult, politically delicate job in the convention. Many delegates emphasized, as did the press, that the fate of the new constitution might well depend upon the quality of the apportionment article.

Problems before the chairman as the group convened were:

(1) How to encourage the study of factual data and opinions and yet suppress potentially explosive, time-consuming partisanship.

(2) How to help the group work toward bipartisan consensus, or failing that, how to hold the committee together long enough to reach Republican majority decisions.

(3) How to structure the group's approach on the problem . . .*

Hannah was not unfamiliar with this kind of challenge which he had faced in his previous chairmanship of the Civil Rights commission and other assignments which he had undertaken for President Eisenhower as well as during his long tenure as President of Michigan State University.

### Hannah's Methods as Chairman*

The chairman's approach was characterized by the seizing of the leadership initiative in early meetings, and then in firmly holding the group to its task. He established a cordial attitude toward witnesses, giving each spokesman a chance to complete his statement before answering questions from the committee. He urged that the committee hold up debate until all testimony had been heard, and while this norm was ignored by some committeemen, members soon were insisting on the no debate rule as if it were part of a formal convention code. In applying controls over interaction, he skillfully led the committee around argumentative difficulties, acting with a deftness which often left the impression that the combatants themselves voluntarily had changed course.

In the first meetings, the chairman circulated raw data on apportionment, including maps showing districts and their population. Later en-

---

*This appraisal of the job confronting Hannah as well as subsequent observations of Theodore R. Ervin, who served as an official observer of Hannah's performance as Chairman, are recorded in his book *Cross Currents of Influence,* published in 1964 by the Institute for Community Development of the Continuing Education Service of Michigan State University. His comments on "Techniques of Leadership" also follow and are included because they probably characterized Hannah's chairmanship of other committees and commissions.

larged and mounted on the walls of the committee room, the maps served as a constant conditioning factor and were extensively used in illustrating testimony. While stating that it was not his intent to establish any norm of representation, this was the clear drift of the materials he presented and discussed with the committee. In a tone of voice which blended just the right amount of amazement with a touch of indignation, he pointed to the large discrepancies in district populations, both outstate and in multimember metropolitan counties, emphasizing that present apportionment left much to be desired, and appealing to committeemen from both parties. . . .

In the course of the debates which ensued, Hannah apparently used some interesting techniques to keep discussion on an even keel, in a democratic framework, with introductory phrases which he commonly used such as:

- Then if agreeable, it is my understanding that . . .
- Now let's pause for a moment to ask . . .
- Let's just stop on this one . . .
- Let's do it any way the Committee wishes . . .
- If the Committee is agreeable, let's talk about . . .
- Let me interject another thought . . .*

At one point, Ervin reports, Hannah did interject a proposal for Senate apportionment which he had prepared with the "hope that he might hold it for use only if the group became deadlocked," but the Committee members became aware that he had a plan and requested that it be presented. In offering the proposal, the Chairman stated that he would discuss it, and then "this will be the last you'll hear from me." In other words, he promised that he would step out of the role of neutral chairmanship only long enough to put the plan on the table.

Apparently Hannah's methods of fomenting as well as controlling discussion were successful as attested to by the fact that the "records for the first 20 Committee meetings show only 34 absences and 12 of these were accountable to two members, an overall percentage score of over 90%." Furthermore, the chairs for delegates, spectators and newsmen for committee meetings were hard and closely spaced. "Interaction was elbow to elbow. It was no place to dawdle." This setting was broken on one occasion when, at Hannah's invitation, the committee met at a more comfortable and commodious facility at Michigan State University (not unlike the retreat of the Civil Rights Commission

---

*Op. cit, page 84.

to a lake resort in Northern Wisconsin previously referred to). Both of these arrangements apparently facilitated informal discussion and broke down restraining barriers.

The apportionment issue and the proposals of the committee for resolving the issue continued to be debated when the new draft Constitution was submitted to the voters for ratification, but the new Constitution was finally adopted (after a recount of the voters by the Election Commission) in June 1963.

Hannah was not given to formulation of techniques of leadership or discussion methods for chairing meetings, especially those involving highly controversial subjects. He rather operated as an interested, astute, understanding, fair but pragmatic, leader interested in reaching positive and acceptable results as a product of discussion. Even at the risk of appearing didactic, a summary or distillation of observations by a studious observer of this methods for conducting discussions is included in this account as a potentially useful diagnosis of the methods used by a highly successful administrator.

## Techniques of Leadership

Techniques used by the chairman in fulfilling the group leadership norm can be summarized in the following ten points:

1. *Establish rules early.* By establishing procedures as soon as possible, the chairman organized the expectations of committee members and gave them a common basis for operation early in their deliberations.

2. *Provide study materials.* The chairman continuously arranged for staff work so committeemen would share a common factual background on the issue. In late sessions, the committee worked surrounded by large maps of proposed districting plans.

3. *Operate on schedule.* The chairman was able to establish reasonable punctuality by beginning and ending meetings on time. Thus, each committee member was responsible for what he missed by being late, since the chair made it clear that all meetings would start on schedule.

4. *Know the substantive content.* The chairman concentrated on substantive testimony as it was given, sometimes finding discrepancies, or relating the testimony of one witness to that of another. This attitude established a high index of accuracy in the committee.

5. *Summarize alternatives.* The chair would rephrase and restate various positions. This function was particularly marked during the marathon debate on the Senate, in which the chairman repeatedly

emphasized that the majority of the committee would not accept both houses on population.

6. *Clarify data and positions.* The chairman attempted to simplify complex or vague data and to crystalize points of view.

7. *Delay satisfactions.* If the chairman was unable to give immediate approval to a suggestion or a position, he tried to indicate how this might be worked in at a later time. For example, when members started to debate in early committee meetings, the chairman would remind them that there would be adequate time for this later on.

8. *Let every view be heard.* The chairman was meticulously careful about recognizing all committee members and giving equal opportunities to witnesses for all points of view.

9. *Force meetings of polar views.* The chairman often would ask for opinions on questions from a leading Populist and then from a leading Localist, seeking some common denominator. When Populists and Localists were unable to agree, the chairman often would avoid any immediate conclusion based on either of the views.

10. *Speak for the group.* The chairman represented the committee's cause and needs to the convention and the press, attempting to reflect the committee's wishes and reporting back on convention actions which might affect the committee. While the committee did not reach bipartisan agreement, without the firm and judicial leadership of the Chairman, the group might not have stayed together long enough even to explore alternatives. The Chairman channeled the external influences into a decision making system. Had he not done so, the divisions in the group might well have led to prolonged emotional debate and even precluded recommendations.*

## Member of the Board of Directors of the Motor Wheel Corporation

The Motor Wheel Corporation produced wheels and other assemblies for use on automobiles, tractors, railroad cars and aeroplanes and had subsidiaries which produced lawn mowers, stoves, appliances and other commodities.

John Hannah was an active member of its Board of Directors from 1957–1964 while President of Michigan State University. He was elected, periodically, by vote of the stockholders of the Corporation.

---

*Op. cit., page 67

This multi-million dollar corporation, with income for example, of over 57 million dollars in 1959, had its corporate headquarters conveniently located in Lansing, Michigan. Five meetings were scheduled for each of these years which Hannah attended except when conflicting with other meetings, such as the Civil Rights Commission, which he was obliged to attend.

Hannah actively participated in decisions of the Board on a wide range of corporate managerial problems such as: organization and reorganization of divisions, major personnel changes, provisions in labor contracts, acquisition, sale and rental of corporate facilities, bank loans, declaration of dividends and the review and approval of numerous financial reports and other operational documents.

## Federal Reserve Bank—Detroit Branch

Hannah served as Chairman of the Detroit Branch of the Federal Reserve Board from 1955–1961.

The agenda for meetings, the reports of bank operations and the status of the United States economy, distinguished guest speakers such as Gabriel Haugh, Economic Advisor to the President, William Chesney Martin Jr., Chairman of the Federal Reserve System, and others provided Hannah with insights into the role of the Federal Reserve System in the national economy. He also brought some information to the attention of the Dean of Michigan State University Graduate College of Business and other members of the faculty.

At the end of the six years of Hannah's chairmanship of the Board, the Chairman of the Federal Reserve System expressed his appreciation of Hannah's services.

> In keeping with the spirit of the Board's general policy of rotating Federal Reserve directorship, the end of the year will mark the completion of your service as a director of the Detroit Branch of the Federal Reserve Bank of Chicago.
>
> The period during which you have been a director of the Branch has been an important one, and on behalf of the Board I wish to acknowledge the contribution you have made in enabling the Federal Reserve System to carry out its responsibilities. The availability of men such as you to serve as directors has provided a wide background of knowledge, experience, and training which has been of genuine assistance in carrying out the important tasks with which the Federal Reserve System is charged.

## Manufacturers National Bank

Hannah was a member of the Board of Directors of the Manufacturers National Bank of Detroit from 1960 to 1967. Toward the end of his service as a Director of the Bank a general question was raised in the legislature as to possible conflict of interest of directors of banks and other corporations and their personal or institutional connections. Hannah took the initiative in seeking an opinion of the Attorney General of the state on the question. The Attorney General ruled that because Michigan State University had some financial business with the Bank there would be a potential conflict of interest. Hannah promptly resigned as a Director to avoid any criticism of himself or the University.

## Michigan Bell Telephone Company

Hannah served as a member of the Board of Directors of the Michigan Bell Telephone Company from 1959 to 1969. During this decade he attended most of the monthly meetings, usually convened in the late afternoon or weekends, except when he was committed to University business or meetings of the Civil Rights Commission or other national educational or governmental organizations to which he gave priority. Although there was no potential conflict of interest in his service on the Board as far as Michigan law applied, since he owned no stock in any organization doing business with Bell Telephone, he resigned from the Board before he accepted the position as Administrator of the Agency for International Development.

## Sparrow Hospital

Hannah was a member of the Board of Directors of the Sparrow Hospital from 1959 to 1970. The development of the hospital reflected the growth of the city of Lansing and surrounding area and of Michigan State University. Hannah's presence on the Board was helpful in developing collective bargaining agreements with the hospital staff and in other managerial problems which were involved in the Hospital's expansion. The experience on the Board also provided some opportunities to relate some of the developments and problems in the medical field to the creation of the University's new medical colleges and to foster an integration of medical services for the community.

Some other Michigan organizations and committees on which Hannah served:

* Michigan Academy of Sciences, Arts & Letters 1958–59; 1964; 1966–69
* Committee on Michigan's Economic Fugure 1959
* Michigan Agriculture Conference 1964–65
* Advisory Committee for Civil Service Reform—1979
* Committee for Improvement of Management in Government 1965–68
* Governor Romney's Blue Ribbon Committee on Higher Education
* Governor's Commission on the Future of Higher Education in Michigan 1984

Hannah's active association with numerous national and Michigan educational, business, economic development, and civic organizations, principally while President of Michigan State University, provided him with numerous opportunities to associate himself with other leading citizens largely outside of academia. He made a point, however, of relating these contacts, experiences and responsibilities to the needs and opportunities of Michigan State University to make a contribution to these activities and developments as well as to contributing his services as a citizen.

## Epilogue

Hannah had his 85th birthday in 1987. He maintains an office in the "Hannah Center for Research and Development" in which the University Development office is located. He serves informally as an adviser to University officials when his advice is requested, and he and Mrs. Hannah attend various university and community functions. He maintains communications with numerous alumni and others with whom he has interests in University service and world affairs.

He has given up all active membership on boards of organizations except "Winrock," the "International Fertilizer organization" and the "Academy of Educational Development," but continues to be actively interested in what's going on in the world.

As an inveterate agriculturist, he still supervises and, to a degree, actively participates in a large farm in Good Hart in Northern Michigan and a smaller one in Dansville, Michigan where he also maintains a home. He also enjoys fishing at his fishing lodge in Canada.

# Appendices

## Appendix A—*Awards and Honors*

**Awards**

Presidential End Hunger Award 1986—Lifetime Achievement

Medal of Freedom—July 1954 (Highest U.S. award for civilian services)

Award of Distinguished Service in International Agriculture—June 1983 Association of U.S. University Directors of International Agricultural Programs

Michigan Advancement Council Distinguished Service Award—June 1983 (He was the first recipient of this award)

Phi Kappa Phi Distinguished Member Award—May 1979

Award from AID in recognition of 18 years of service and dedication to the Government of the United States—Sept. 1973

Award from AID—July 1969 "In recognition of your interest in agricultural education and participation in the national FFA Leadership & Citizenship Conference"

**Honorary Doctors Degrees**

Thirty honorary Doctors Degrees were awarded to Hannah including the Universities of Michigan, Florida, Maryland, Maine, Nigeria and South Dakota; and Ohio State; Howard, Arizona State and Central, Northern and Western Michigan and Michigan State Universities, and several colleges.

**Honorary Academic & Professional Fraternities**

Phi Beta Kappa and six others

**Appendix B**—*Point 4 Program: Exchange of Correspondence Between President Truman and John Hannah*

THE WHITE HOUSE
Washington

February 14, 1949

My dear Dr. Hannah:

I am most grateful for your thoughtful letter of February fourth, setting forth the skills to be found in our Land-Grant Colleges and Universities which could be utilized in carrying out the fourth point of the Inaugural address.

I appreciate fully that in these institutions is a reservoir of talent and I heartily appreciate your pledge of full cooperation.

In order that your suggestions may be brought to the attention of those who carry out our foreign policy I am forwarding your letter to the Department of State.

Very sincerely yours,

(Signed) Harry Truman

Dr. John A. Hannah,
President
Association of Land-Grant
    Colleges and Universities
Michigan State College
East Lansing, Michigan

February 4, 1949

Hon. Harry S. Truman
President of the United States
Washington, D.C.

Dear President Truman:

This is to offer the full cooperation of the members of the Association of Land-Grant Colleges and Universities in carrying out the fourth point of your Inaugural address, which gave new inspiration to many of us who have long been convinced that such a program is basic to progress toward the stable, democratic, peaceful world which we all want.

One of the greatest contributions America can make to the improvement of living standards, elimination of hunger, and fostering of peace in certain parts of the world is by encouraging education in food production, food handling, food utilization, and better homemaking and family life among rural and urban people. These have been the objectives, the basic philosophy and the outstanding role of the Land-Grant Colleges and Universities in American life since the passage 87 years ago of basic legislation for federal-state cooperation in a national system of "people's colleges" dedicated to the "education of the industrial classes in the several pursuits and professions of life." It is time this basic philosophy and the "know-how" developed in more than fourscore years of operating under it is extended to the rest of the world on a much broader scale than has been the case in the past. Your message will furnish a powerful impetus in that direction.

Some foundation has been laid and some progress made in such a program through the work of the United States Department of Agriculture, the Food and Agriculture Organization of the United Nations, the Economic Cooperation Administration, UNESCO, the Pan-American program, the efforts of other government agencies, and of individuals and groups outside government.

It seems to me, however, that in spite of some encouraging developments, there has been a regrettable failure to include representatives of agriculture, technology, and of education in agriculture and homemaking in the formulation and development of our foreign policy. The trouble areas of the world are primarily agricultural, and their political problems derive primarily from their need to develop a higher standard of living—more and better food, and better clothing and housing for their people. It is this problem which the United States, for all its deficiencies, has solved better than any other major nation. It is in the solution of this problem for other nations that we offer the services of the Land-Grant institutions and their nationwide staffs and experience in the fields of research, teaching, and extension work in agriculture, homemaking, and in the technology of improved industrial production.

In the fields of agriculture and homemaking our institutions are unique, and in engineering technology they include a substantial portion of the educational resources of the nation. They are, of course, by no means limited to these fields, and their cooperation in the entire range of education is available to you.

The stimulus of federal aid and encouragement was in large part responsible for the creation of the nationwide Land-Grant system of higher education to serve the practical and cultural needs of the people. Although these institutions in their resident teaching work are now largely supported by the states, I assure you that they have a deep historical and present sense of their debt to the nation, and a desire to assist the nation in its world efforts as they are now helping the people of this country.

The potential contribution of our institutions in an international program may be indicated by the fact that staff members from the Land-Grant institutions have participated in (and in most instances headed) United States and FAO missions to the Near East, China, the Philippines, Siam, Poland, and various countries of Central and South America, and that the agricultural missions or advisors of the USA and in the occupied areas are largely made up of graduates or staff members on leave from Land-Grant institutions. In this country, the workers engaged in the great task of the improvement of farm and home life, the conservation of natural resources, and in research and teaching in agriculture and homemaking, whether employed by the federal or state governments, are largely graduates or staff members of our institutions. We feel that in our international efforts, we would be in position to make a much larger contribution than has been the case heretofore if given a wider opportunity to participate in the planning and carrying out of programs.

The offer of our full cooperation is not made lightly. It is extended with the unanimous approval of the Executive Committee of the Association of Land-Grant Colleges and Universities after full consideration of all its probable implications. The release of staff members on leave for work abroad or consultation in this country would handicap some institutions in carrying out their domestic responsibilities.

The training of foreign students and consultation with foreign visitors would involve serious demands on crowded facilities and on the time of staff members. But being fully aware that sacrifices are involved in a world program such as you have outlined, I am personally convinced, and our member institutions collectively are convinced, that the stability, welfare and domestic freedom of the world demand the cooperation of all Americans in such a program. We feel that this responsibility is particularly incumbent on us as colleges and universities supported by state and federal funds and carrying on in a long democratic tradition.

My own travels in Europe last summer, and particularly in Germany, lead me to think that bringing the American know-how to bear on the problem of taking the resources of science, technology, and education generally onto the farms, into the factories, and into the homes of peoples abroad is essential to the rehabilitation of the post-war world economy.

As institutions and individuals, and collectively, the Land-Grant institutions and their staff will welcome an opportunity to do their part in realizing the program you have outlined.

Yours sincerely,

President

cc—Dean Acheson—Secretary of State
R. I. Thackrey
J. L. Merrill    Officers of the Association

## Appendix C—*Background Thinking and Research on the Foreign Aid Program*

As indicated earlier in this chapter, the decade of the sixties was a period of deep concern on the part of practitioners and scholars for the basic rationale undergirding technical assistance programs, and of finding more effective ways of translating global concern for the world's poor into programs which would do for the underdeveloped world what the Marshall Plan had done for Europe. Hannah was knowledgable about the ideas and proposals which were being expounded which served as general background for his task as Administrator of AID. But possibly of greater immediate and more detailed concern for the members of his policy staff whom he looked to delve more deeply into this massive material and distill what was most useful for the policies and programs of AID. A brief rundown on a few of these formulations follows:

### Paul G. Hoffman

One of the earliest formulations of concern and policy implications for efforts to assist underdeveloped countries become better fed and improve their living conditions was expressed by Paul G. Hoffman in his *World Without Hunger,* published in 1962 by Harper and Row. Hoffman was an American industrialist and United Nations official who had served as Administrator of the Economic Cooperation Administration (ECA) from October 1950 to September 1951. He contributed early definitions of the plight of almost a billion people in the Third World; was an architect of the United Nation's "Decade of Development—Goals for 1960–70;" projected costs of 440 billion dollars in goods and services which were needed for the ten year program; provided by "soft loans" from the World Bank; identified priority needs of schools, hospitals, communication systems; power and other infrastructure components of development; housing and population control programs and related needs. He advocated multi-national participation in the program with a smaller United States share of the burden and an emphasis on "action" in contrast to more general studies of the problem.

### Max F. Millikan & W. W. Rostow

An early economic analysis and provocative study of international development was written by the above two authors, professors at the

Massachusetts Institute of Technology in 1959. Their "Proposal—Key to Effective Foreign Policy" was published by Harper & Brothers.

**William & Elizabeth Paddock**

Their thoughtfully searching book on mistakes being made in international programs was published in 1973 by the Iowa State University Press under the provocative title of "We Don't Know How."

**Stanley Andrews**

An analysis of what had happened to selected technical assistance projects in nine countries, many of which were maligned by some critical members of the U.S. Congress and others, was made by Stanley Andrews in 1961. Andrews was an interim administrator of the Technical Corporation Administration (TCA) after its first Administrator, Henry Bennett, was killed in an airplane accident while on duty abroad. Andrews later served as a consultant to John Hannah and Glen Taggart, Dean of International Programs at Michigan State University.

**Judith Tendler**

One of the most comprehensive bibliographies of development assistance policies and practices was prepared by Judith Tendler under the title of "Inside Foreign Aid" published by Johns Hopkins University Press in 1975. In this compendium, Tendler cites some 85–90 books and articles plus references to numerous congressional hearings on foreign aid. Included in this comprehensive listing were books and articles by some of the key thinkers such as Nelson Rockefeller, formerly Assistant Secretary of State for Inter-American affairs and later Vice-President, plus many significant commissions and committees on international development.

**Lester B. Pearson Report: Partners in Development**
**Report of the Commission on International Development: 1969**

The "Pearson" Report was a major research undertaken at the request of Robert S. McNamara, President of the World Bank, and was published in August, 1968. Mr. Pearson, a former Prime Minister of Canada, was joined by seven distinguished colleagues from the United Kingdom, Brazil, Federal Republic of Germany, Jamaica,

France, Japan and by C. Douglas Dillion of the United States. The Commission was supported by a staff of fourteen international development experts headed by Edward K. Hamilton plus ten research assistants, including Joseph Stern, Consultant to the Commission (who later served on the staff of AID) and Sartaj Aziz (a Pakistani—then from Princeton), also served later with John Hannah in the World Food Conference and World Food Council.

The staff made a thorough review of the recent history of international cooperation. At three full meetings of the Commission, reports of the research staff supplemented by twenty two consultants, including several who were later involved in the work of AID, officers of the United Nations and other business financial leaders discussed "their experience with development and the part played in it by transfer of resources from other countries." These inputs provided the basis for the Commission's conclusions and recommendations. The final report was timed to be in the hands of the Governors of the World Bank for their annual meeting in 1969 and to be helpful to the United Nations in their preparation for the "Second Development Decade." Briefly stated, the report was timely and comprehensive in its coverage of issues, development needs and possibilities. It elected to refer to countries as "developed" and "developing" (which became commonly adopted terminology) rather than characterizations like "rich," "poor," "advanced," or "backward."

The 400-page report was organized under eleven major chapters covering such critical subjects as:

1. A Question of Will—including discussions of the crisis in AID, Why Aid?, and an outline of a strategy.

2. Two Decades of Development—covering such areas as agriculture, industry, public health, education.

3. The Problems Ahead—covering problems in the areas of politics, population, education, research and development, financial problems of foreign exchange and related financial considerations.

4. Private Foreign Investment—including material on private and corporate investments as "an alternative to AID."

5. Population, Education and Research—were of special interest to Hannah and became priority programs under Hannah.

6. An International Framework for Development—covered discussion of issues and problems of bilateral and multilateral aid, the United Nations, World Bank (including the soft loan department known as IDA) and recommendations for improved international coordination of aid giving organizations.

Some recommendations of particular reference to policies which were adopted by the Nixon administration and implemented by AID under direction of Hannah were:

• Emphasis on research and education to deal more effectively with the global population problem.

• Greater emphasis on international collaboration by AID donors and more effective participation in policy formation and education by leaders of developing countries.

• Reduction or elimination of policies and practices of tying aid by donor countries to procurement of supplies and equipment from those countries.

• Greater emphasis to technical assistance as a component of loans or grants.

• Increase of budgetary commitments for technical assistance to longer periods of time.

### National Planning Association (NPA) report on "A New Conception of U.S. Foreign Aid, March 1969

The NPA is a private planning organization which is headed by a Board of Trustees which is highly representative of leaders of American business, agriculture, labor, public administration, educational and professional organizations. The members have included such leaders of labor as Walter P. Reuther, I. W. Abel and Joseph D. Keenan of the AFL-CIO; of business such as William C. Ford of the Ford Motor Company and R. E. Brooker, President of Montgomery Ward and Co. and J. E. Johnson of Texas Instruments; of academia such as Salomon Barkin of the University of Massachusetts and Luther Gulick, Chairman of the Board of the Institute of Public Administration; Elmo Roper, Dean of the early "pollsters" and others; and several leading attorneys and heads of other organizations. John Miller serves as Executive Secretary of the Board. John Hannah was particularly knowledgeable about Canadian-United States relations about which the NPA produced several important reports.

The breadth of participants in producing the NPA report is indicated as supportive of the recommendations made in the other reports cited and in the abundance of scholarly work mentioned above.

With reference to the changing requirements of the development assistance relationship which characterized both governmental and private programs in the 50's and 60's, the NAP report pointed out that:

This active and directive U.S. approach . . . has become less necessary for most recipient countries . . . in consequences of the development, progress that so far has been achieved. (p. 3) . . . There are today increasing numbers of people and leadership groups of even the remotest and least developed countries who are aware that it is possible for them to accelerate and guide the processes of economic growth and cultural change . . . They understand (however) that if they expect to get financial and technical assistance from abroad, they have to prepare, or obtain help in preparing programs or projects which are relevant to their development goals and meet the donors' minimum standards of utility and efficiency.*

With reference to the political leadership which is necessary and crucial to put the jigsaw of development components together, the NPA report quite bluntly put it this way:

This is a political problem and, while the ability to solve it can be improved by the availability of external assistance, the *will to do so cannot be imported.* (italics supplied) Moreover, an effort to generate the necessary concensus and commitment from outside, particularly by officials of the most powerful nations in the world, tends to exacerbate rather than to lessen the problem (p. 3).

A critical aspect of the understandings of "sociocultural change" and work method of the professional staff of AID, and its predecessors, which Hannah dealt with when he became Administrator of AID, was expressed in the NPA report as follows:

The consequences of this major disparity in understanding the aspects of sociocultural change, as compared with economic growth, can be most clearly seen in that portion of U.S foreign aid effort consisting of technical assistance. In both the country missions and the Washington headquarters . . . a substantial majority of the professional personnel is engaged in initiating, designing, negotiating and staffing such projects, and they tend to be the most active to undertake them. Moreover, lacking acequate knowledge of the non-economic aspects of the development process, they have been prone to excessive enthusiasm for changing fashions in development panaceas. (page 5)

With reference to the interplay and inter relationships of U.S. and multilateral support for development assistance, the NPA report pre-

*This kind of help is being provided by "Winrock" and its predecessor organizations described briefly in Chapter VI. John Hannah is currently a member of the Winrock Board.

sented a candid, but balanced, group of observations and recommendations which Hannah understood and later took action on:

• "Multilateralization" (of support) is not a panacea nor should it be made the sole, or even the major, channel for U.S. foreign aid for some time to come, for reasons of the national interests and responsibilities and the capacity of the U.S. to provide more rapid assistance in some situations and for the helpful assistance which U.S. contributions can make to the more effective performance of multilateral agencies."

• The proclivity of some multi-national organizations to allocate their resources on a "fair share" basis without reference to "substantive criteria" and on an "expedient principle" was sharply criticized . . .

• Development lending by consortia of donors was recommended and be made on "concessionary" terms, involving low preferably nominal interest rates, long-term maturities, and initial grace periods of at least a decade (the formula adopted by International Development Assistance (IDA) organization of the World Bank).

• Supporting assistance to countries to deal with external aggression, natural disasters etc., rather than for development assistance, should continue to be made on a grant (rather than loan) basis for a limited period but be subject to an annual review by the Congress.

Hannah supported these kinds of recommendations and also for more involvement of the Congress in making decisions about countries to be so aided.

• With reference to a problem on which Hannah had long and expert judgment, namely food aid, the NPA recommended that "periodic reexamination of the food aid program be made to make certain that it is not inhibiting farmer initiative (in developing countries) or postponing adoption by recipient governments of modern agricultural development policies."

• Strong support was given to basic and adaptive research on development problems to assure that assistance be better suited to particular conditions in host countries and to minimize projects, the efforts of some have been "transitory." Hannah found it comfortable to act on this recommendation and that of the Peterson task force and the Nixon directives which developed later.

• Aid was recommended for private enterprise development, which was also emphasized by the Peterson task force and Nixon directives and was also compatible to Hannah's conceptions of foreign aid.

• Recommendations for restructuring the U.S. aid effort, in such respects as: (1) "transforming AID from a large institution extensively engaged in overseas operations to a much smaller organization primarily concerned with policy making" and the allocation of funds to be administered by other agencies became a major contribution of Hannah to AID.

In a transmittal letter to the President, the NIPA Task Force stressed that: (1) . . . "many with whom we consulted are deeply troubled by particular aspects of U.S. foreign assistance programs and by the apathy and misunderstanding that seem to surround the issues . . . ;" (2) many outstanding Americans have contributed direction, insight and imagination to these programs in the past and continue to do so;" (3) but the Task Force saw a need for a "time for change, a time for reappraising our programs and designing them for the decade ahead . . . , It is also a time to stake out in most positive terms America's involvement in the way mankind manages its common problems" which in time "may prove to be the most important, and the most rewarding, determinant of America's role in the world."

The Task Force concluded:

• The United States has a profound interest in cooperating with developing countries in their efforts to improve conditions of life in their societies.

• All peoples, rich and poor alike, have common interests in peace, in the eradication of poverty and disease, in a healthful environment and in higher living standards. This country shall not look for gratitude or votes, or any short term foreign policy gains from our participation in international development. Nor should it expect to influence others to adopt U.S. cultural values or institutions . . . Development implies change, political and social as well as economic, and such change, for a time, may be disruptive. What the United States should expect from participation in international development is steady progress toward its long-term goals: the building of self-reliant and healthy societies in developing countries, an expanding world economy from which all will benefit, and improved prospects for world peace.

• United States international development programs should be independent of U.S. military and economic programs that provide assistance for security purposes . . .

• Both types of programs are essential, but each render a different purpose. Confusing them in concept and connecting them in administration detract from the effectiveness of both.

• Military and related economic assistance programs will strengthen military security only to the degree that they help move countries toward greater self-reliance . . .

• The United States should help make development a truly international effort. A new environment exists; other industrial countries are now doing more, international organizations can take on greater responsibilities, trade and private investment are more active elements in development, and most important, the developing countries have gained experience and competence. Recognizing these conditions, the United States should redesign its policies . . .

• United States international development policies should seek to widen the use of private initiative, promote skills and private resources in the developing countries . . . Popular participation and dispersion of the benefits of development among all groups in society are essential to the building of healthy and dynamic nations.

• The Task Force recommended a new focus for U.S. programs, and a new emphasis on multilateral organizations, plus new institutional organizations consisting of: (1) a U.S. International Development Board; (2) a U.S. International Development Institute; (3) on Overseas Investment Corporation; and (4) a U.S. International Development Council.

The basic recommendations of the several reports cited above were reasonably consistent and formed part of the factual judgmental and strategical basis for the Hannah administration of AID.

## Appendix D—*Excerpts from Appropriation Requests for AID—1970–1973*

*FY 1970 Request.* The request basically reflected the amended provisions of the Foreign Assistance Act of 1969 which authorized the AID program to "reflect new priorities and new directions, primarily the increased use of private enterprise in development and the greater focus on technical assistance."

Within this framework the request included the following specific information:

• Data on the "development gap" between the developed and the less developed countries such as: per capita GNP of $2,417 for developed countries as compared with $196 for the less developed countries. Similar disparities were shown regarding percentage of literacy, doctors per 100,000 of the population, life expectancies and other criteria.

The total United States requests for foreign aid represented about 2.3% of the Federal budget or 1.2% of our GNP.

• The major components of the 2.66 billion dollar requests were for: (1) Development Assistance (675.5 million) loan funds which must be used for the purchase of goods or services, many of which were provided by U.S. universities, private organizations and U.S. government departments in the United States*; (2) Technical Assistance—worldwide, Alliance for Progress and multilateral (United Nations and other organizations)—463.1 million. These funds were requested principally for priority programs in agriculture, family planning, education and public administration; (3) Supporting Assistance (515 million) for help in restoring the economies and for political stabilization in seven countries, almost all of which was for Vietnam, Laos, and Thailand, with small amounts to Korea, Nigeria, Dominican Republic, Haiti (malaria eradication program) and regional activities in Africa and East Asia.

Organization changes included those previously cited.

*FY 1971 Appropriation Requests.* The FY 1971 appropriation requests opened with information addressed to the question: "Why does the

---

*The Congressional requirement for purchase of USA goods was not wholly supported by Hannah and many other students and practitioners of development on economic or political grounds. These purchases were mainly for fertilizer, machinery, chemicals etc. and were greatly expanded in FY 1970 over FY 1960.

United States provide Foreign Aid?'' The reasons given were summarized in two reasons: *"simple humanity* and *national self interest"*
(italics supplied). The language for each reason clearly reflected Hannah's priorities as reflected in Hannah's letter to Senator Inouye:

> . . . We persist for two basic reasons. Our self-interest requires it. Our
> ideals compel it. The future of the United States cannot be separated
> from the future of the world. Recognition of this basic truth is essential to
> achievement of a new more stable structure of peace. . . . Our children
> and our grandchildren must live in the same world with the children and
> grandchildren of the peoples of the rest of the world, all continents, all
> races, all creeds. The kind of lives our children and their children after
> them will live, and the kind of world they will live in tomorrow, depends
> on whether we do our part to help today.

Besides data on the ''Development Gap'' etc. and other information
referred to in the FY 1970 appropriation, the 1971 request included
more information on: (1) reducing population growth (in 44 countries,
25 of which have given some support to official family planning
programs and to research; (2) disease control, environmental health
and nutrition in the field of health; and (3) education, which includes
aid to teacher training institutions in which 180,000 students were
enrolled plus AID financed fellowships for advanced technical training
in the United States and other host countries where such facilities are
not available in the developing countries. About one half of the amount
in new funds were requested for Overseas Private Investment Corporation. Not much change was requested in the number of countries
being affected but considerable attention was paid to increasing ''popular participation'' in development and to better coordination of multilateral aid contributions.

*FY 1972 Appropriation Requests.* By the time the 1972 requests for
appropriations were submitted to Congress, President Nixon had formulated his views in the form of a special message to Congress which
had three main objectives: (1) ''to help strengthen the defense capabilities and economies of our friends and allies . . . ;'' (2) ''to assist the
lower income countries in their efforts to achieve economic and social
development . . .'' and (3) ''to provide prompt and effective assistance
to countries struck by natural disasters or the human consequences of
political upheaval. . . .''

Funding of these purposes were reflected in the budget request.

Plagued by the inaction of Congress in clearing out appropriation bills in a timely fashion in previous fiscal years, which created great policy, organizational, personnel and morale problems for the Hannah administration, a total of $3.023 billion authorization was requested for FY 72, 73 and 74 of which only 1.515 billion dollars was requested for FY 1972 program expenditures. Included in the FY 1972 program were almost a billion dollars for development lending, including 141 million dollars for World Bank loans and other international organizations such as the United Nations Development Fund, UNICEF and other UN organizations. Over the three-year period 1,153 million dollars would be provided for the "Food for Peace" program and smaller amounts for the Peace Corps and other programs.

Considerably more details were supplied to the Congress which explained the strategy of providing technical assistance for food production and population control programs, improvement of technical and managerial skills of host country personnel; research and the creation of institutions in developing countries to carry on development programs, after United States aid is reduced.

*FY 1973 Appropriation Requests.* The 1973 appropriation request reflected the major decisions on program priorities and organizational changes which Hannah took on the basis of extensive staff review and recommendations previously described. In brief, these were:

• To give greater focus on a limited number of high priority problems such as food production, human nutrition, population control; health care, and low cost education and humanitarian assistance.

• To focus on projects designed to achieve more equitable income distribution through emphasis on employment creation in small industries and farms, land reforms and other measures.

• To improve organizational arrangements and management procedures to support new program emphases.

• To accelerate the adoption of a more collaborative assistance style to reflect the increased capacity of personnel in aid receiving countries to do the job.

**Appendix E—*Resume' of Secretary Henry Kissinger's Address to the World Food Conference***

The Secretary General of the Conference and other dignitaries laid out a broad agenda in the first plenary session of the Conference for the delegates to consider. The comprehensive and moving address by Henry Kissinger, Secretary of State, in the opening of the second plenary session, however, greatly expanded the scope of interrelated critical issues before the Conference. Kissinger also made a number of significant policy and financial commitments of the United States in the context of expanded participation of other developed countries. He linked these commitments to necessary policy changes and actions by developing countries, thus setting the stage for an expanded collaborative international research and action efforts. With reference to the financing of an expanded global program he deftly identified the need for the participation of oil producing and oil wealthy OPEC nations. Although his remarks were properly put in the context of policies proposed and strongly supported by President Gerald Ford, he quite correctly, under the circumstances, did not mention the role and special competence of the Deputy Director of the Conference but he gave strong emphasis to two areas of major importance in which Hannah was particularly active, in addition to his long and active involvement in agriculture generally. These were the International Agriculture Research Centers which Hannah strongly supported and for which he secured generous financial support while Director of the U.S. Agency for International Development and for the critical international role of modern fertilizers and expanded production as one of the original members of the Board of the International Fertilizer Center, affiliated with the Tennessee Valley Authority located at Muscle Shoals, Alabama.

Other aspects of the interrelated food problem which were highlighted by Secretary of State Kissinger in his comprehensive and emotion charged address included: (1) the projected doubling of world population by the end of the century; (2) the appalling extent of malnutrition; (3) the complexities of distribution of food to the neediest even when supplies are available; (4) the problem of ample reserves (in the order of 60 million tons over current carryover levels) as protection against the vagaries of weather and natural disastes; (5) the need for increased production by food exporters as well as accelerated production by developing countries through the application of modern cultivation techniques, seeds, fertilizers and research findings; (6) the need for more complete and reliable crop reporting procedures; (7) the need for a "coherent investment strategy" for the following major purposes: (a) "to encourage bilateral and international assistance programs to provide the required external resources, (b) to help governments stimulate greater resources for agriculture and (c) to promote the most effective use of new investment by chronic deficit countries.

The above recitation of specific and practical points made by Kissinger do not reflect the philosophical, historical and boldly prophetic and moving tone of his remarks which are reflected to some extent in the following excerpts:

### On the present state of the world

• The world is midway between the end of the second World War and the beginning of the twenty-first century. We are stranded between old conceptions of political conduct and a wholly new environment, between the inadequacy of the nation-state and the emerging imperative of global community . . .

### Necessity for global action

• While poverty and misery still afflict many parts of the globe, over the long run there was universal hope; the period was fairly characterized as a 'revolution of rising expectations.' That time has ended . . .

• We must act now and we must act together to regain control over our shared destiny. Catastrophy when it cannot be foreseen can be blamed on a failure of vision or on forces beyond our control. But the current trend is obvious and the remedy is within our power . . .

### The political challenge

• The political challenge is straightforward. Will the nations of the world cooperate to confront a crisis . . . or will each nation or bloc see its special advantage as a weapon instead of a contribution? . . . Recognition of our condition can disenthrall us from outdated conceptions, from institutional inertia, from sterile values . . .

• No social system, ideology or principle of justice can tolerate a world in which the spiritual and physical potential of hundreds of millions is stunted from elemental hunger or inadequate nutrition. National pride or regional suspicions lose any moral and practical justification if they prevent us from overcoming this scourge . . .

**The promise of our era**

• The profound promise of our era is that for the first time we may have the technical capacity to free mankind from the scourge of hunger. Therefore, today we must proclaim a bold objective—that within a decade no child will go to bed hungry, that no family will fear for its next day's bread, and that no human being's future and capacities will be stunted by malnutrition . . .

• Our responsibility is clear.

• Let the nations gathered here resolve to confront the challenge and not each other.

• Let us agree that the scale and severity of the task requires a collaborative effort unprecedented in history.

• And let us make global cooperation in food a model for our response to other challenges of an interdependent world—energy, inflation, population, protection of our environment.

These and other major points and USA commitments made by Kissinger provided the broadened outline of basic considerations which were developed in the staff papers and which guided the subsequent discussions and debates by the delegates. The resolutions of the conference provided the rationale and the global will for the creation of the World Food Council, directed by Hannah, and its operational arm, the International Food and Agriculture Development Organization (IFAD), which are described in Chapter V.

**Appendix F**—*Letter to the author from George Klein regarding Hannah's work with the World Food Conference/Council and IFAD*

I'm sorry to be a bit behind schedule with these few comments concerning Dr. Hannah's post-AID involvement with the world food problem. As indicated in my last letter, my knowledge in this regard stems from little more than an occasional glimpse into an intensive period of activity, lasting at least four years (1974–1978). You must bear this clearly in mind in considering my responses to your questions regarding Dr. Hannah's qualities, talents, and relationships.

My first contact with him occurred in the summer of 1974, while he was engaged in the preparations for the World Food Conference, so let me start with some observations relating to that period.

One may suppose that the nomination of a distinguished figure such as Dr. John Hannah to the post of Deputy Secretary-General of the World Food Conference was intended to signal the U.S. government's strong interest in the Conference. In fact, as is not infrequently the case in similar circumstances, Washington's initial attitude toward the Conference was anything but one of strong support. A likely explanation for this may be found in the mistrust, if not actual contempt, with which Secretary Kissinger and his associates normally viewed multilateral initiatives, particularly of a global kind involving all of the United Nations. While the United States could not oppose the convening of such a Conference outright, it presumably had little hope that useful results could be achieved. Accordingly, the U.S. government's interest in the Conference at the time almost surely did not go beyond wishing to ensure that no real mischief would come of it and that appearances were preserved.

If the foregoing analysis is correct, Dr. Hannah's appointment no doubt owed more to the State Department's concern with public relations than to any genuine desire on its part for global cooperation on the food problem, which was seen as a complex and sensitive political issue.

Be that as it may, if anyone imagined that they would be getting a good "front man" in Dr. Hannah and nothing more, they couldn't have been more wrong. By the summer of 1974 it must have been as evident to everyone as it had become to me, that Dr. Hannah was playing a dynamic role both in mobilizing external support and resources for the Conference and in ensuring, internally, that the preparations were of a nature and quality as to best ensure the Conference's chances for success.

One of his most crucial contributions—which well illustrates his superb sense of strategy—was to recognize the overriding importance of securing the active participation of the United States Government in the preparatory phases of the Conference as well as in the Conference itself. He lobbied for this tirelessly for many months within both the Executive and legislative branches—charming, persuading or cajoling his many contacts in Washington and effectively conveying to them his conviction that the WFC could provide some helpful answers to the world food problem.

I do not know (but Dr. Hannah does, no doubt) whether or not President Ford's accession to the Presidency that summer and Dr. Hannah's connection to him had any role in creating a more positive U.S. attitude toward the Conference (it certainly was a major factor the following year in connection with IFAD's establishment—but more on that below). But I do remember another event in which Dr. Hannah played a predominant role. I am referring to the U.S. visit of Sayed Marei, Secretary-General of the World Food Conference, during the course of which Mr. Marei was to pay his first call on Secretary Kissinger.

Dr. Hannah took the greatest pains (I recall this distinctly since I worked closely with him on this matter) to assure that Mr. Marei was thoroughly briefed and prepared for his meeting with the Secretary. He "drilled" him on the essentials of the "talking points" and made sure that the point concerning the indispensability of active U.S. support for the Conference would not be lost on Mr. Kissinger. Mr. Marei apparently made a convincing case, and I believe—although I'm not fully certain of the cause-effect relationship—that his meeting with Secretary Kissinger resulted directly in two developments of far-reaching significance: 1) the Secretary's decision to attend the Conference personally; and 2) the appointment of Ambassador Edwin Martin (former Assistant Secretary of State for Latin America) as U.S. Coordinator of preparations for the Conference and working head of the U.S. delegation. The Secretary's decision to go to the Conference gave a terrific lift to its international standing and assured that the necessary internal preparatory work would be carried out by the participating governments in a serious manner. Perhaps more importantly, it was a "decision-forcing event" within the U.S. context, obliging the various concerned departments to focus on the Conference and, with the participation of the private sector and key Congressional actors, to work out a common U.S. position on the various issues. Ambassador Martin's appointment assured that the key coordinating role would be carried out by a person of stature and authority and someone who was highly sympathetic to the aims of the Conference.

I believe that Dr. Hannah's leadership was also important in mobilizing non-governmental support for the Conference, through his appearances before important constituency groups such as agribusiness leaders (I particularly recall his giving the keynote address at a large international convention of agribusiness people in Ottawa or Toronto in the summer of 1974) and his contacts with voluntary agencies and the media.

Dr. Hannah's relationships with Mr. Marei and other members of the WFC secretariat were exceptionally productive. He was a figure of real presence and authority within the secretariat and everyone held him in great esteem.

Sayed Marei, who was one of Egypt's most important political and social figures at the time and much used to instant compliance from everyone, was particularly influenced by Dr. Hannah's charm and placed great reliance on his counsel and political wisdom. I cannot assess their relationship fully but I think it was most fortunate, given Marei's rather breezy approach to things, that Dr. Hannah was able to influence him so strongly. As a result, the entire effort was steered toward much greater realism and a more marked orientation toward practical accomplishment.

Dr. Hannah's relationship with his Soviet counterpart as Deputy Secretary-General, Mr. Roslow, provides another example of his remarkable political vision and sense of strategy. Being keenly aware of the Soviet Union's traditional refusal to engage in international cooperation in the field of agriculture (viz. its refusal to join the FAO, etc.) and recognizing the importance to world food security of bringing this great agricultural trader into the mainstream, he went to exceptional lengths to cultivate a good relationship with his Russian counterpart. He encouraged him to take a positive interest in the preparatory work, made sure that he was kept abreast of things, and worked tenaciously to convince him that his country had everything to gain and nothing to fear from active participation in the Conference. Again, I'm in no position to make a direct cause-effect linkage, but I can't help thinking that without Dr. Hannah's careful "massaging" of the Soviet representative and his determined campaign to keep the Russians "in play," the USSR's role at the Conference might have been far less positive, particularly as regards the creation of the World Food Council.

This same type of purposefulness marked Dr. Hannah's other relationships . . .

I have no first-hand information concerning Dr. Hannah's relationships with people like Henry Kissinger, Kurt Waldheim or President Ford. I believe that he got along quite well with Mr. Waldheim although, like everyone else, he found him a rather elusive character. I had the impression that after using his appointive powers to good purpose (in appointing Marei, Hannah and Sartaj Aziz), Secretary-General Waldheim did not play much of a role in subsequent developments relating to the Conference. He came back into the picture at the follow-on stages, of course, notably by having the good sense to name Dr. Hannah as the first Executive Director of the World Food Council and to entrust him with responsibility for getting the international negotiations concerning the establishment of IFAD off the ground.

Key U.S. officials, such as Ambassador Martin, treated Dr. Hannah with obvious confidence and clearly considered him as a major player. I also know that Dr. Hannah was able to exert a healthy influence on Secretary Butz although, as far as I can recall, he never became a real supporter of the Conference. Dr. Hannah was particularly effective, I thought, with senior government officials from Third World countries, who seemed to trust him implicitly and to see in him the embodiment of American good will and generosity toward their development aspirations.

Since I am trying to adhere to some notions of chronology in writing this, I should make one or two additional remarks regarding Dr. Hannah's immensely valuable role in insuring that the Conference would not merely be a public relations or diplomatic success but also a real success in terms of providing an intellectually and technically sound basis for practical decision-making. To this end, he exerted leadership in organizing, with assistance from the Ford Foundation, an outstanding group of agricultural economists and experts who, working under Dale Hathaway, were able to assure that the voluminous documentation being prepared for the Conference reflected the best of American thought and knowledge . . .

Without Dr. Hannah's leadership the Hathaway group might not have come into being at all, and without his great personal and moral authority the insights and proposals emanating from the Hathaway group—which were often at odds with the more ideological thrust of Aziz's group in Rome—would not have been incorporated into the documentation.

Regarding difficulties that Dr. Hannah may have encountered within the UN arena, the only significant instance of that kind I can recall occurred in the summer of 1975 or 1976. The details of the incident escape me but it concerned criticism—from some political quarter or other—either of Dr. Hannah personally or of something he had done or had failed to do at the World Food Council. Since the critics had some political clout at the UN, Mr. Waldheim—never famous for stoutness of heart—reacted to the affair by issuing a statement in New York which, in effect, disavowed Dr. Hannah. Such cowardice brought down upon the head of the Secretary-General the Churchillian wrath of Daniel Patrick Moynihan, who was then the United States Representative to the United Nations. Ambassador Moynihan caught up with Mr. Waldheim in Geneva, where they were both attending the opening of ECOSOC's summer session, and Dr. Hannah's position was then immediately vindicated.

I recall being quite surprised at such an overt attack on Dr. Hannah since he was known to enjoy a great deal of personal support within the various multilateral organs. He was much admired, for example, by many of the senior New York-based ambassadors who sat on the Economic and Social Council, and I am sure that he had equally cordial relations with all the Ministers on the World Food Council. In light of this, I suspect that any difficulties Dr. Hannah may have had in working within the UN organizational environment were due not to any lack of aptitude on his part for dealing with the UN labyrinth but, rather, to the "turf war" with various vested institutional interests that the WFC's creation had unleashed. Considering FAO's unremitting hostility toward the WFC, and how bitter the conflict between the two agencies became under Dr. Hannah' successor, Maurice Williams, it seems to me that by his ability to stay on speaking terms with FAO's Director-General—without abandoning any of WFC's rightful perogatives—Dr. Hannah showed greater skill in coping with organizational conflicts than might appear at first glance . . .

Of the famous "three pillars" upon which the post-World Food Conference effort to deal with the food problem were to rest, namely greater food security through a system of buffer stocks, etc.; an improved food aid system; and an increased flow of resources for food production in the developing countries; the latter objective was surely the one closest to Dr. Hannah's heart. This is not to say that in his work at the World Food Council he neglected the other "pillars" but, being first, last and always a great builder, Dr. Hannah found the challenge of helping to bring IFAD into being particularly irresistible. His special enthusiasm for IFAD also stemmed from the prospect that IFAD would become a major vehicle for channelling assistance to the hitherto neglected small farmers who, in his view, held the real key to the eventual resolution of the problem of hunger in the developing world.

Dr. Hannah's specific responsibility, as you know, was to organize and chair an initial series of meetings of countries "interested" in IFAD's possible establishment—a process that was to determine whether or not there was enough potential support—both political and financial—to warrant proceeding with the formal steps (negotiation of Articles of Agreement, etc.) required to bring the Fund into being.

Steering that initial process and bringing it to a positive conclusion would have been a daunting task for even a seasoned practitioner of multilateral diplomacy. Let me mention just a few of the many obstacles and difficulties that had to be surmounted:

• relations between the Western countries and the OPEC states, which at the best of times were tense and mistrustful, had become greatly exacerbated by the "oil shock" of 1973 and were still extremely strained in 1975;

• the OPEC countries were almost totally unfamiliar with the concepts and practices of multilateral development cooperation (and had an ingrained preference for bilateral aid relationships);

• a number of influential countries were initially strongly opposed to the very idea that a new multilateral lending institution should be established (the Federal Republic of Germany, for example, refused even to attend the first meeting of "interested countries");

• there was a great deal of scepticism, and even active covert opposition, from some of the existing multilateral development banks and international agencies.

Perhaps most importantly, for many months the conception of the United States regarding the nature and purpose of the new "fund" was so at variance with the ideas of most other potential contributors as to make progress at the discussions virtually impossible. (As you know, the U.S. position at the time was that it should not be required to make actual contributions to IFAD but should be allowed, instead, to "attribute" to IFAD any increase it may make in the level of its bilateral funding of agricultural programs through AID. That approach was not only impractical but so unrealistic politically as to be, literally, laughable).

Dr. Hannah's success in managing and eventually overcoming these and a host of other problems and conflicts was not just a brilliant diplomatic performance but also, in my view, a personal triumph. It was his tenacity, his profound understanding of character, his unerring sense of occasion and timing, his eloquence and persuasiveness, his vision, and his gracious simple manner both in individual contacts and in chairing meetings that, more than any practical or political factor, enabled him to win through to the end.

I well remember a climactic meeting of the group of "interested countries," in the summer of 1975 in Geneva where, but for Dr. Hannah's unique personal qualities, the entire effort could have foundered. The crisis arose when the U.S. delegation was obliged by circumstances—much against its inclination—to reiterate, at a very critical moment, its extremely unpopular and unacceptable position (as described above) regarding the Fund's character. Dr. Hannah had to draw upon all of his authority and on all the trust and affection he had earned over the previous weeks and months to prevent a rupture in the negotiations.

That near catastrophe convinced Dr. Hannah that he would need to intervene personally with President Ford to have the U.S. position reversed. In the event, as you know, Dr. Hannah succeeded not only in that goal but in obtaining from President Ford the pledge of a $200 million U.S. contribution. The President's response fully vindicated Dr. Hannah's faith in the generosity of the American people and in our government's continued readiness to act constructively in addressing the problem of world hunger—a conviction to which Dr. Hannah held unswervingly throughout the entire period.

Dr. Hannah's contributions to IFAD's viability did not end with his enlistment of U.S. support, although that did remove the most important roadblock to the successful conclusion of the preliminary negotiations. At other times when difficulties were encountered, Dr. Hannah again came to the rescue. He was instrumental, for example, in obtaining last-minute increases in the contributions of the Federal Republic of Germany (and also of Japan, I believe) so that the minimum required level of $1 billion could be reached. As late as 1982, he was still helping IFAD by effective lobbying on Capitol Hill for needed appropriations that were being inordinately delayed.

One can only marvel at the impressive record of Dr. Hannah's benefactions and creativity. His accomplishments in the world food area, when added to his long, and brilliant domestic career, clearly make him one of the most successful and distinguished Americans of the century. To me he has always exemplified all that is best in the American character. Knowing him is one of life's real pleasures for me.

## Appendix G—*Hannah's Letter to Secretary Charles Wilson*

Dear Mr. Wilson:

I would like this to be a personal note and not an official one.

Much of the following I recognize as presumptuous on my part, can be classified in the category of the gratuitous, and really none of my business.

It will deal with two general subjects—(1) some commentions and suggestions about the operation of the Defense Department and (2) my future relationships with the Defense Department and your Office.

—I—

I am sure you know without my repeating it here of the great personal admiration and respect that I have for you. That accounts for my willingness to risk incurring your ire by the frankness of this epistel. You put in long hours and devote your time, energy and talent to every problem placed before you. I may be wrong but it appears to me that there is a failure to effectively screen the matters that reach your desk with the result that you must use much of your time and energy on matters that should and could be handled by others, and that more important matters fail to reach your attention as promptly as they should, or not at all.

Some of your Assistant Secretaries find it very difficult to reach you with any regularity and when they do they are often interrupted by others who come into your office with other items calling for your attention. The present relationship with the Assistant Secretaries is not such as to maintain the highest morale or effectiveness on their part.

I would like to suggest that you institute a firm policy of meeting with the Assistant Secretaries at a firmly fixed hour once each week with the understanding that both you and Mr. Anderson attend whenever you are both in Washington and that when you are away he will carry on for you. The staff meetings Mr. Kyes used to hold occasionally on Friday were no substitute for this. I suggest that a distributed agenda in advance be avoided and that the routine be an informal statement from you of any information you think the whole group should have and then a quick report by every Assistant Secretary, limited to those matters of general interest in his area currently under consideration, with particular emphasis on those requiring cooperation or action by others.These meetings should be planned to occupy not more than an hour. Weekly meetings of your Assistants would do several things. They will save your time by covering in one hour per week the personal contact with all nine of your Assistants, which they need. They will serve the purpose of making all of them feel that they know what is going on and are in fact members of a team. They will greatly improve liaison and cooperation between the various offices of the Assistant Secretaries. It should be understood that only under unusual circumstances will a Deputy or Assistant be permitted to represent the Assistant Secretary at these sessions. If the Assistant Secretary is out of town he should not be represented by someone else, as a matter of routine. (Secretary Wilson accepted this suggestion)

You know, from our discussions, of my conviction that our system for handling our legislation leaves much to be desired. I was never convinced that the combination of public relations and legislative liaison was logical, and am not now. The combination results in bringing practical political considerations to bear on decisions that should be made in the Defense Department based only on the national interest, leaving the political compromises to the Congress or elsewhere. The office for legislative liaison, in my view, should not be a policy making office but should be concerned only with securing approval for the legislative program you have decided upon.

An Assistant for Health and Medical has not worked well, as seen in the bogging down of our "medical care for dependents" legislation and in other ways. This responsibility should be an office in Manpower and Personnel, where it can be coordinated with and made a part of the total Manpower and Personnel program, which it is. When and if Dr. Berry leaves, this set-up could be rearranged to give you that post for the legislative assignment if you should decide upon it.

The Assistant Secretary for Installations is in an anomalous and, I should think, an impossible position since there does not seem to be a required clearance by the Services of major policy and specific decisions with reference to planning or implementation of construction projects. I know very little about this except that were I you, I would feel better if all major policies and decisions pertaining to construction, including the letter of contracts for major structures or plans involving large projects were subject to review and veto by the Assistant Secretary for Installations before they were consummated. The Services could always appeal his decisions to you if they were unhappy with his decisions. You will always be subject to criticism for every well-advised decision in this area because of the visibility of construction and because of the public interest in every community in local military or other public construction.

Without belaboring this whole matter of the Assistant Secretaries, their relations with your office and with each other—I would call to your attention that not the least of the reasons why you will have increasing difficulty in attracting men of stature to accept these positions is the fact that the only reward that will cause a good man with important responsibilities and opportunities to leave them and accept a position in government is the assurance that his responsibility in government is really significant and that he will have an opportunity for some recognition for the fact that he has such responsibility. To be one of nine Assistant Secretaries of Defense provides no such recognition, now. The situation is totally unlike industrial employment where the Assistant is paid in dollars and future opportunity. Here the job entails substantially less income than the man gives up to accept the position, and almost no recognition by the public or within the government, and they lead to nothing in future opportunities. All of this can be overcome by an internal "esprit" within the Defense Department, by the creation of a situation where the Assistants feel that they are, in fact, members of a team with a great responsibility, that they know of and participate in the significant decisions that can affect so profoundly the future of our country and the welfare of their families.

The next item is a little unfair to my successor, since he will have to live with the consequences. I am satisfied that a large portion of the energy expended in the Pentagon and in the Washington area, excluding the purely military operations such as the military bases, the air fields, Naval Gun Factory, Bethesda, Walter Reed, etc. is routine "busy work" that could be eliminated—without any loss to the effectiveness of the defense of the country. I refer to the use of both military and civilian personnel. The degree of wasted effort or no effort is not uniform. I feel that it approaches 25% of the total in the over-all of our headquarters and supervisory operations. I am satisfied that everything that needs to be done can be done effectively by a further reduction in our personnel that should be applied to military as well as civilians and possibly the heaviest reduction should be accomplished among those in uniform. I think no harm would be done if you were to direct an arbitrary reduction in force of 10% for the Pentagon and Washington area, excepting the active military installations, to be accomplished in the three months, September, October and November, with these cuts made in anticipation of a possible further reduction of 10% in the next three months of December, January and February. The decision on the second reduction to await the result of the first. It should be made clear that this is not due to a lessening of the total responsibility but is to be accomplished through elimination of unnecessary work, through better utilization of personnel, and reductions in duplication. The full 10% of men in uniform should be assigned by the Services to important military duties elsewhere, since all of the Services are pleading for more men for important military jobs. This 10% reduction could, in my opinion, also be applied to all headquarters organizations everywhere, including those overseas.

—II—

I appreciate your recent letter appointing me on a consulting basis as an Assistant to the Secretary of Defense effective with the resignation from my present responsibility.

When I leave my present assignment next Saturday, in fairness to my successor, I feel that the break with all Manpower and Personnel matters should be clean cut. A predecessor looking over the shoulder is a great handicap to a man on a new job. I will, of course, be glad to be available for advice, counsel, or comment—but only upon his request and then only to him or to you.

A rearrangement of the offices of the Permanent Joint Board on Defense is in progress and, with your approval, I shall maintain a desk there for use when here. If my work with the Board is to be effective I think I should spend a day or two each month here and keep reasonably well informed on developments that have to do with continental defense. I think it is particularly important that I know of the progress of the joint planning and operations between the two countries as carried on by the Services and that I know as much as possible about the accomplishments in Research and Development in the field of early warning, for the land lines and seaward extensions, and progress in anti-air warfare and other areas with continental defense implications. I think it would be helpful if you would advise the Services and Research and Development of your approval of this proposal (Secretary Wilson approved this request)

I should also like to be authorized to visit our Project 572 (Western Electric Early Warning Arctic) in Alaska and Northwest Canada in the near future, and at some time, our installations in Greenland and Iceland with as much freedom as can be arranged to visit other areas in Greenland. I assume that there will be no objection to such travel in the United States or Canada as is desirable with the Permanent Joint Board on Defense. I should like a blanket travel authorization, with the understanding if at any time you think it is being abused it is to be revoked.

Because of the continuing project in Okinawa in which Michigan State College is involved, if at some time in the next year some VIP is making a trip to that area with room in the plane for a non-paying passenger, I would welcome an opportunity to again visit that area. It is about a year since I was last there and I spent only about an hour at the University on that occasion.

If in the years ahead there are occasions when you would like me to act for you in an "eyes and ears" capacity to gather information or impressions for you on assignments that will not take too much time away from Michigan, possibly I can be of use to you in such a capacity.

In conclusion, Michigan State College, which claims you as an Honorary Alumnus, will be celebrating its Centennial next year beginning on February 12, 1955. There are a series of events planned that I think will be of real significance as we commemorate not only the Centennial of our institution but the Centennial of agricultural education and the whole philosophy of turning higher education to the solutions of the problems of living people. I am serving advance warning that I may want to call upon you for help to get participation by the President. The key event of the year is to be a great state-wide convocation in the early fall which is planned about the participation of the President. President Theodore Roosevelt played the same role in the fifty year celebration. (The President, regretfully, was not able to accept Hannah's invitation)

I shall return to Michigan feeling that in spite of our failure to achieve some things we hoped for, it has been a fine experience—made so largely by the opportunity to work with and for you.

Sincerely,

John A. Hannah

# Notes

## Preface

1. An account of the first hundred years of MSU (the Centennial year) is provided by Dr. Madison Kuhn in his *Michigan State—The First Hundred Years*, Michigan State University Press, 1955.

A more recent volume which focuses on the Hannah years 1935–1969 has been written by Dr. Paul Dressell under the title of *College to University*, Michigan State University Publications, East Lansing, Michigan, 1987.

2. John Hannah's responses to questions put to him by two of his close colleagues are recorded in his *A Memoir*, Michigan State University Press, East Lansing, Michigan 1980. The contents of the volume include questions and Hannah's responses on: (1) the early years, (2) the development of the University, (3) University administration, (4) intercollegiate athletics, and (5) campus activities—which included references to the University's involvement in International Programs.

## Chapter I—Defense Department

1. Background material and quotations, unless otherwise noted, were provided from original documents and letters in the files in the Archives and Historical Collections of Michigan State University. All quotations are from these letters and documents.

2. In William Bragg Jr.'s *Eisenhower, the President's Crucial Years 1951–60*, Prentice Hall, 1981, he wrote: ". . . Eisenhower tested his adviser's convictions. He didn't like yes-men; he wanted to know what a man really thought, off guard. The organization did not always exude sweet harmony." Jim Haggarty's diary for 1954 would sparkle with sudden rage, often his, often Ike's; when John Hannah unilaterally released a secret document on military manpower, he made the President "sore as the dickens," (page 67.) Note:

245

Hannah did not remember the incident and indicated that if it happened it had no serious consequences as Eisenhower appointed him to head two major programs, namely Chairman of the U.S. Section of the Permanent Joint Canadian-American Defense Board and the U.S. Civil Rights Commission. He had warm personal relations with Wilson before his appointment to the Defense Department and after.

3. Nicols, Lee, *Breakthrough on the Color Front*, (VIII) Random House, New York 1954.

4. Ibid. page VIII

5. Ibid. page 11

6. Dwight D. Eisenhower Presidential Library

## Chapter II—Joint Canadian-United States Defense Board

1. Background and quoted material provided by Michigan State University Archives and Historical Collections unless otherwise noted.

## Chapter III—Civil Rights Commission

*General*

1. Most of the background information for this chapter, during the twelve year tenure of John A. Hannah as Chairman of the Civil Rights Commission was provided by the approximately 50 linear feet of primary source material in the Hannah Collection located in the Michigan State University Archives and Historical Collections (MSUAHC). The material included correspondence between Hannah and his fellow Commissioners and staff; with four Presidents; members of the Congress and with high placed persons in the government and outside; minutes of meetings of the Commission, draft final reports of the Commission; statistical reports on voting rights violations and on other programs of the Commission; resumes of hearings; press clippings and other informative material.

All quotations, unless otherwise noted, are from the MSUAHC Collection.

Published Commission reports were also examined as were House and Senate reports on hearings in the Michigan State University documents collection.

The following books were also especially informative and helpful in the writing of this chapter.

• Foster Rhea Dulles' scholarly book on *"The Civil Rights Commission: 1957–1965"* published by the Michigan State University Press, East Lansing, 1968.

Dr. Dulles, a Professor of History at Ohio State University, had prior access to the publications and other materials of the Civil Rights Commission and to the personal files and papers of Dr. John A. Hannah related to the Commission. Although the author leaned heavily on Dr. Dulles' book and the materials in the MSUAHC for background on the work of the Commission, Chapter III emphasizes the role, method of work, relationships and motivations of John Hannah as Chairman of the Commission for all of the years covered by Dr. Dulles plus four additional years not covered by Professor Dulles. It is, thus, not a resume or recapitulation of the work of Dulles or others but a focused treatment of the style and indispensable contributions of Hannah in steering a "fragile" ship through the muddy and turbulent waters of racial conflict and dissension tempered only by the mandates of the Constitution, civil rights laws and support of numerous persons of good will, for more equitable treatment of the Negroes and other minority groups.

• The comprehensive focus on the Kennedy brothers, John F. & Robert Kennedy and Coretta and Martin Luther King Jr. by Harris Wofford in his *Of Kennedy and Kings: Making Sense of the Sixties* (Farrar, Straus & Girouy, New York, 1980) was very helpful particularly in illuminating what was going on in the White House. The Appendix—*Precursor and Conscience: The Commission on Civil Rights*, is not an ordinary appendix, but very important material which the editors (so Wofford told me) did not see as consistent with the major thrusts of the comprehensive treatment of the Kennedys and their times in history. A legal assistant to Commissioner Hesburgh and later as Assistant to President Kennedy for civil rights and chairperson of the White House task force on civil rights, as well as his long established interest in civil rights as a student of Ghandi, Wofford's views were particularly illuminating.

• Arthur M. Schlesinger Jr.—*A Thousand Days: John F. Kennedy in the White House*, Houghton Mifflin Co., Boston, and Theodore C. Sorensen, *Kennedy*, Harper and Row, New York 1965, both provided insights in their separate treatments of President Kennedy's inner feelings, convictions, vacillations, and ultimate strong executive and legislative support for an aggressive and comprehensive program in civil rights. Their historical accounts are consistent with the records of conversations which Hannah had with the President on several occasions during his tenure as President and up to his tragic death. One quote from Sorensen regarding Kennedy's basic motivation regarding civil rights is almost an "echo" or restatement of Hannah's views expressed on several occasions in speeches and writings before Kennedy was elected as President. The quotation follows:

. . . His assumption of the powers of the Presidency accelerated the change in his outlook (from a more conservative, politically calculated view of civil rights) . . . Racial discrimination was divisive and wasteful . . . It was an historic challenge, a dangerous and unpopular controversy, the nation's most critical domestic problem . . . Above all, he was motivated by a deep sense of justice and fair play.s 'I do not say that all men are equal in their ability, their character or their motivation,' he declared more than once, but 'I say they should be equal in their chance to develop their character, their motivation and their ability!' . . . His instinctive inability to be bound by artificial and arbitrary distinctions had in 1953 caused him to pay little attention to the Negro as a Negro. In 1963 (six years after Hannah assumed the chairmanship of the Civil Rights Commission) it caused him to pay little attention

248 NOTES

to those unwilling to accept his basic commitment to fair play. Simple justice required this program, he would tell Congress in concluding his Civil Rights Message of June 19, 1963, not merely for reasons of economic efficiency, world diplomacy and domestic tranquility, but above all because *it is right,* (italics supplied), page 530.

Sorenson further commented (in his Chapter XVIII—*The Fight For Equal Rights*) on Kennedy's positive voting record on civil rights and on his support of appointment of Negroes to major positions while Senator. He continued his policy of appointments of Negroes to a Federal judgeship and to a cabinet position while President. He had numerous and important consultations with Martin Luther King and other Negro leaders from 1961–63. Furthermore, he used his Presidential powers to issue several Executive Orders to further civil rights. The highly emotional challenges to civil rights by such persons as Governor George Wallace, "Bull Connor" *et al.* also persuaded him to greater personal involvement in civil rights issues.

Another important source of information on Kennedy's involvement in civil rights is Section II of Kenneth W. Thompson's *Portraits of American Presidents: The Kennedy Presidency*, published by University Press of America, Inc. Lanham, Md. 1985. This volume provides memories and insights of Nicholas de Katzenbach, Bruce Marshall, John Seigenthal (all close associates of the Kennedy brothers) on the relationships and complex political issues and choices confronting the President. Further comments on these many points would, however, have greatly expanded the chapter and possibly diffused the focus on John Hannah's role and contribution to civil rights while Chairman of the Civil Rights Commission.

The letters to the author from Commissioners and others closely associated in the work of the Commission, provided rich and sometimes poignant comments on Hannah's leadership, relationships and method of work in the Commission. All quotations, from these sources, unless otherwise noted, are from the MSUAHC.

2. The testimony of Hannah before two meetings of the Senate Judiciary Committee; two meetings of the House Judiciary Committee; and seven meetings of the House Appropriations Committee between February 24th, 1959 and April 16th, 1968.

3. Wofford op. cit. (page 466) in Note No. 1.

4. From the transcript of a tape addressed to the author by Father Ted Hesburgh while sailing down the Danube River on July 30, 1985.

5. Hesburgh, op. cit.

6. Abridged 1959 Report of the Civil Rights Commission *With Liberty and Justice For All*, U.S. Government Printing Office, Washington, D.C., 1959 (The abridged report contains all of the background material supporting the recommendations and exceptions taken by some of the Commissioners.)

7. Ibid, page 6

8. Ibid, page 16

9.  Ibid, page 14
10. Ibid, page 15
11. Ibid, page 10
12. Ibid, page 22
13. Ibid, page 91
14. Ibid, page 92
15. Ibid, page 94
16. Ibid, page 96
17. Ibid, page 96
18. Ibid, page 98
19. Ibid, page 104
20. Ibid, page 104
21. Ibid, page 140
22. Ibid, page 180
23. Ibid, page 184
24. Ibid, page 184
25. Ibid, page 85
26. Ibid, page 186
27. Ibid, page 194
28. Ibid, page 201
29. *1961 Report of the Civil Rights Commission*—U.S. Government Printing Office, Washington, D.C. 1961—Vol. 1—Voting; Vol. 2—Education; Vol. 3—Employment; Vol. 4—Housing; Vol. 5—Justice.

*Education*

30. Ibid, page 1
31. Ibid, pages 182 and 183
32. Ibid, page 184

*Employment*

33. Ibid, pages 161–163

*Housing*

34. Ibid, pages 150–153
35. 1963 Report of the Civil Rights Commission *Challenge & Response*, U.S. Government Printing Office, Washington, D.C. 1963

*Voting Rights*

36. Ibid, page 28
37. Ibid, page 30

*Education*

38. Ibid, page 69

*Employment*

39. Ibid, page 91

*Justice*

40. Ibid, page 124

*Health Services*

41. Ibid, page 143

*Negroes in the Armed Services*

42. Ibid, pages 215–217
43. *Freedom to Be Free*—United States Government Printing Office, Washington, D.C., 246 pages

## Chapter IV—Agency for International Development

1. Most of the extensive (15–20 linear feet of reports, operational memoranda and other file materials) which provided background for this chapter was assembled for the author by the Library staff of the Agency for International Development at the request of M. Peter McPherson, Hannah's successor as Administrator of AID. The material was primarily focused on the years of Hannah's administration of AID.
2. Hannah Collection MSUAHC.
3. The Pearson Report, *Partners in Development*, was initially published in 1969 by Praeger Publishers, New York. It went through four printings.
4. *A New Conception of U.S. Foreign Aid*—A Joint Statement by the NPA Joint Committee on U.S. Foreign Aid, the NPA Board of Trustees, and the NPA Committees on Agriculture, Business, Labor and International Policy, NPA Special Report No. 64, Washington, D.C., March 1969.
5. Hannah Collection MSUAHC.
6. *U.S. Foreign Assistance in the 1970's: A New Approach*. Report to the President from the Task Force on International Development: Superintendent of Documents, U.S. Government Printing Office.
7. "New Directions in Foreign Aid"—President Nixon's message to Congress, May 28, 1969.
8. "Foreign Assistance for the Seventies"—President Nixon's Second Message to the Congress. Sept. 15, 1970, U.S. AID Library.

## Chapter V—World Food Conference and Council

1. Most of the background material and excerpts from these materials were provided by the voluminous files on the WFC, Council and IFAD in the Michigan State University Archives and Historical Collections (MSUAHC).

Among these was a relatively brief, but comprehensive account of the Conference, published by the United Nations as a *Report of the World Food Conference*, after the 16th plenary meeting of the Conference, under UN publication reference E/Conf. 65/20.

2. Grant, James Dickinson, "The International Fund for Agricultural Development: A Case Study in Global Cooperation," 1976. (MSUAHC)

3. From Annual Reports of the United States participation in the United Nations. House Document 360, Gerald R. Ford Library, Ann Arbor, Michigan.

4. From the official record of the White House meeting on April 21, 1975 in the files of the Gerald Ford Library, Ann Arbor, Michigan.

5. Grant, op. cit., page 66.

6. Grant, op. cit., page 76.

7. Annual Reports of the International Fund for Agricultural Development 1985—107 Viadel Sacrifico, Rome, Italy.

8. AID Evaluation Special Study No. 21: Program Review of the International Fund for Agricultural Development (IFAD) published by the Agency for International Development, January 1985.

9. Report by the Comptroller of the United States on *World Hunger and Malnutrition Continue Slow Progress in Carrying out World Food Conference Objectives*, United States General Accounting Office, January 11, 1980. Also "Status Report on U.S. Participation in the International Fund for Agricultural Development," General Accounting Office, March 27, 1981.

# Index